The Wedding of the Lamb

The Wedding of the Lamb

A Historical Approach to the Book of Revelation

JAMES L. PAPANDREA

PICKWICK *Publications* · Eugene, Oregon

THE WEDDING OF THE LAMB
A Historical Approach to the Book of Revelation

In accordance with c. 827, permission to publish is granted on July 30, 2010 by Very Reverend John F. Canary, Vicar General of the Archdiocese of Chicago. Permission to publish is an official declaration of ecclesiastical authority that the material is free from doctrinal and moral error. No legal responsibility is assumed by the grant of this permission.

All scripture quotations are the author's own translation.

Pickwick Publications
An Imprint of Wipf and Stock Publishers
199 W. 8th Ave., Suite 3
Eugene, OR 97401

www.wipfandstock.com

ISBN 13: 978-1-60899-806-7

Cataloging-in-Publication data:

Papandrea, James Leonard.

The wedding of the Lamb : a historical approach to the book of Revelation / James Leonard Papandrea.

x + 258 p. ; 23 cm. Includes bibliographical references.

ISBN 13: 978-1-60899-806-7

1. Bible. N.T. Revelation—Criticism, interpretation, etc. I. Title.

BS2825 P21 2011

Manufactured in the U.S.A.

The church historian T. R. Glover, commenting on the observable fact that the Church outlives every empire that persecutes her, is said to have written:

> *There would come a day when men*
> *would name their dogs Nero,*
> *and their sons Peter and Paul.*

This book is therefore dedicated to all the martyrs, past and present, who worship and share the faith at the risk of their own lives, and who choose to give up their lives rather than their faith. They are the great cloud of witnesses who have preserved and passed the faith on to us, who intercede for us, and who inspire us.

Midnight Light

It was the 18th of July, back in 64
The familiar humid air that night breathed a smoke it never had before
And as the spark turned to flame, we felt the blame
The hot wind blew and carried along the cries of our pain

And he watched his city burn, in his mind he slowly turned
The plans that he had made for his golden estate
Shine, midnight light, from the ground to the sky
Cry, innocent eyes, from our hearts to the universal mind

From the circus to the bay flaming crosses lit the way
And the children of the light never saw the light of day
So the spectacle went on, but we never lost the truth
Today's blood feeds tomorrow's grass, but you to us and God to you

Burn in our hearts as the smoke rises higher
Burn in our spirits like a wild immortal fire
Burn into our minds this image, burn it deep
Burn into our lives the one thing we would die to keep

—Jim L. Papandrea/Remember Rome

Contents

Preface: The Method of This Study

THE READER WILL QUICKLY discover that the interpretation presented in this book does not fit neatly into any of the existing categories of dispensationalism or millennialism. By calling it a *historical* approach to the book of Revelation, I intend to convey two things. First, I do not plan to explore every interpretive option that contemporary scholarship has to offer. This book is not a commentary, and while it does present an interpretation of every verse in Revelation, it is not written as a verse-by-verse commentary, and it is not intended to replace the many fine commentaries that already exist. Rather than go over ground that has been covered again and again, I intend to focus on the way the book of Revelation has historically been interpreted, looking primarily at early Christian sources, in order to offer what I argue is an interpretation that is as close as possible to the way the majority of early Christians would have understood it. Wherever it is appropriate, I have included footnotes that cover alternative interpretations of specific passages.

The second thing I wish to convey by the title is that this book is a departure from popular end-times fiction and other treatments that assume that most of the events depicted in the book of Revelation are still to be realized in the future. On the contrary, I intend to show that the majority of the imagery in Revelation is meant to describe events in the past. This approach takes seriously the history of the Roman Empire and the Church's place in it as a major influence on the writing of Revelation. Therefore, whenever possible, I will choose an interpretation of a given passage that relates to an event in history, rather than some event in the future.

That being said, I do not reject out of hand the possibility that God might give someone a vision of things to come, and in fact this interpretation assumes that there is an element of predictive prophecy in the book of Revelation and in the related preaching of Jesus. However, in the end, the interpretation presented here is meant as an attempt to capture the understanding of the author of Revelation, and to clarify the way the original audience would have heard its message. It is up to the reader to decide whether to adopt it as his or her own interpretation.

I begin by clarifying the genre of literature we are dealing with. As an example of apocalyptic prophecy, the majority of early Christians would have understood Revelation using various types of non-literal interpretation. Which type of non-literal interpretation (allegory, typology, etc.) would have been used is not a matter of concern, since early Christians would not have had our contemporary categories in mind. Once we have defined the genre, we have to interpret the individual symbols in the text, using the Old Testament as a reference point. After I have explained each of the symbolic images in the text of Revelation, we can use this information to reconstruct a chronology of the text. With Revelation 1:9 as the hermeneutical key, I then categorize the images as relating to events in the past, present, and future relative to the author. These images can then be compared to historical events and placed into a timeline. Finally, in Appendix A, the entire text of Revelation is recast, translating the images into their historical counterparts, resulting in "The Book of Revelation in Plain English."

Before we move on, a note about the capitalization of "Church." When the word refers to the universal Church, it is capitalized. When it refers to a local congregation, or the Christians in a particular place, it is not capitalized.

I do not claim to have exhausted the topic of the interpretation of the book of Revelation, only to have entered into it, and I offer this study as food for thought, coming from a place of convergence of New Testament interpretation and the history of the Roman/early Christian period.

Signs of the Times?

INTRODUCTION

DOES THE BOOK OF Revelation contain secrets that will help its readers survive the chaos of the end of the world? Is it an encrypted roadmap to the future? If one were to believe the popular media phenomenon of end-times fiction, such as the *Left Behind* series and its predecessors, *A Thief in the Night* and *The Late Great Planet Earth*, one might think so. But as this book will demonstrate, the setting of Revelation is more to be found in the past than in the future.

It has always been tempting to try to read the book of Revelation with the Bible in one hand and a newspaper in the other, as if the text will illuminate or even predict current and future events. However, as we will see, this exercise is misguided. The book of Revelation is better understood when one reads with the Bible in one hand and a text of Roman history in the other. Too often, the history of Christianity (and the theology that comes out of that history) is taught without enough attention paid to the history of the Roman Empire. Imagine trying to write a biography of Abraham Lincoln without mentioning the Civil War. One would get an incomplete picture of Lincoln's presidency, to say the least. It is the same with the history of Christianity. One cannot study the early Church without seriously examining the role it played in the drama that was the Roman Empire. The two are interdependent, and documents like the book of Revelation would not exist without the conflict between Church and empire.

This present book is not a commentary on Revelation, nor is it an attempt to have the last word on the subject. This is a beginning, a new framework for future discussion and interpretation. In a sense, it is an attempt to free the book of Revelation from the need to find parallels in the modern world. This can be done by seeing it through the eyes of its original audience and by examining the connection between the Roman Empire and the early Church.

The Bible is not a code to be cracked or a puzzle to be solved. In fact, the very name of the book of Revelation refers to that which is *revealed*, not that which is hidden. If the meaning of Revelation were a hidden secret, it would by its very nature belong to the realm of the occult, not to sacred Scripture. To be sure, the book of Revelation is highly symbolic, and it requires careful interpretation to find the meaning for contemporary readers, but it is not as though God has intentionally made it difficult to understand. The truth is, for its original audience it was not difficult to understand, and if it is difficult for us, that is because we forget that it was not written for us. Those who try to interpret the book of Revelation as if it contains secret messages for Christians in our time are missing the point. The book was written in language that would be relatively clear to its original audience but obscure to readers outside the Church, should it fall into their hands. This is because the book is the product of a persecuted Church, and it predicts the end of the empire persecuting its readers.

I have seen a bumper sticker that exclaims, "The Bible says it, I believe it, that settles it!" While I respect the sentiment behind this statement, it simply is not correct. The matter is not settled when one knows what the Bible says. What the Bible says is one thing—what it *means* is another thing. In this distinction between what the Bible says and what it means is the challenging, but very rewarding, task of interpretation. The book of Revelation is a perfect example to demonstrate the difference between what the Bible says and what it means. Revelation says that the unfaithful and oppressive government is Babylon (Revelation 18). That's what it says. But what does it mean? Does it refer the ancient city of Babylon, capital of the nation that conquered Judea in the sixth century BCE and destroyed the Jewish temple? No, it refers Rome, capital of the current oppressive empire that destroyed the second temple in 70 CE.

Contemporary confusion over the book of Revelation derives from various sources. It comes from misunderstanding the nature of apocalyptic prophecy, from studying the text of Scripture without also studying the historical context of the Roman Empire, and from irresponsible interpretations in popular books and films about the "end times." In fact, the current craze of end-times fiction, and the schools of interpretation that have fueled it, only overcomplicate the matter with a need to fit the square peg of current events into the round hole of early Christian apocalyptic literature.

When one reads the book of Revelation in light of the history of the Roman Empire, one finds that we are not headed for a renewal of the worldwide persecution of Christianity. Of course, we must acknowledge that even today there are still places in the world where Christians are discriminated against, and even persecuted. But the future systematic persecution of Christianity, in which a remnant of Christians must fight a war against the powers of the world, simply is not found in the text. While a correct reading of the book of Revelation rejects the popular attempt to interpret most of the text as a prediction of near future events, it does acknowledge an element of future prediction, as we will see. But we must not make the mistake of assuming that everything that was in the author's future is also in our future. Over nineteen hundred years of history have elapsed between the time that Revelation was written and the present day. As we will see, many of the events that the author of Revelation saw in his future already came to pass in the early centuries of the Church.

AN OLD TESTAMENT BOOK IN THE NEW TESTAMENT

The first thing to remember when reading the book of Revelation is that the Bible read by Jesus and the apostles was (for the most part) what Christians today refer to as the Old Testament. And while the writer of the book of Revelation probably knew most of our New Testament, there was as yet no standardized collection of specifically Christian scripture. In addition, even though the message of Revelation was given as a vision, we cannot imagine the seer writing down exactly what he saw while he was seeing it. Therefore, when the author of Revelation needed images to describe visions of things that defied human language, he would naturally turn to his Bible, our Old Testament. When the author needed metaphors to speak of things other Christians would understand while keeping any potential non-Christian readers in the dark, again he drew from the Old Testament. Even the very genre of literature that the book of Revelation emulates, apocalyptic prophecy, originally comes from the Old Testament. When we keep this in mind, it will help us interpret the metaphors and images of Revelation. Even more important, it keeps us focused on the bigger picture, which is the very purpose of this type of literature.

The Old Testament, while it contains history, was not primarily written to record historical events. It was written to describe the relationship between God and humanity, encourage (or discourage) certain behavior in humans, and to show how God is a saving God in spite of human disobedience. The prime example of this is the Exodus, in which God's people are released from slavery by divine intervention. The Exodus is first and foremost a lesson about salvation. So reading the Old Testament requires a certain amount of reading between the lines, to get behind the narrative to the moral or theological lesson that is being taught. An even better example of this is the binding of Isaac (Genesis 22). Abraham is tested when God commands him to sacrifice his son Isaac. Abraham is ready to obey, but God stops him at the last minute and provides a substitute sacrifice. The theological lesson in this passage is that Abraham's God does not require human sacrifice (as practiced by Abraham's neighbors). Also, Abraham sets an example as one who trusts God to the extreme. He has faith that God can keep his promises even without the child of promise, Isaac. And of course, for Christians the story foreshadows the substitutionary sacrifice of Jesus Christ. Therefore, the point of the passage is not in the narrative of the story but in its significance for understanding the nature and activity of God. This is important for the study of Revelation because the book of Revelation also was not written to record a sequence of historical events. It was written to show Christian believers a light at the end of the tunnel of oppression and persecution. Revelation is a book of theology, a book about salvation, not a history book written ahead of time.[1]

Another key to understanding Revelation is Jesus' apocalyptic teaching. It is assumed that the writer of Revelation knew Jesus' teaching well and would understand what was revealed to him in light of Jesus' words in the Gospels. Therefore, any interpretation of Revelation must compliment the apocalyptic preaching of Jesus. The vision of Revelation is presented as a message that comes directly from Jesus, and placing it side by side with Jesus' words in the Gospels can help us interpret it. As we look at Jesus' teaching on the Kingdom of God (or Kingdom of Heaven), we will see that there are striking parallels with the book of Revelation. For now, it is enough to say that Jesus promised he would

1. Beasley-Murray, *Revelation*, 51.

bring the full *revelation* of the Kingdom at his return, just as he brought the seed of the Kingdom with his first advent. Ultimately, that is what the book of Revelation is about: the *revealing* of the Kingdom of God.

During his ministry, Jesus said the Kingdom was already present *among* his followers (Luke 17:21).[2] This could also be translated, ". . . for the Kingdom of God is *within* you." With Jesus' first advent, the Kingdom is *within* us, within individuals and within the Church, but hidden like the mustard seed buried in the earth (Luke 13:18–19). The return of Christ, which is the climax of the book of Revelation, is that event of divine intervention that brings the Kingdom in its fully revealed sense, like the full-grown mustard plant. Now, the Kingdom is within us; at that time we will be within the Kingdom. Now, the Kingdom is the reign of God on earth, planted like a seed; at that time the Kingdom will be the Realm of God, like a full-grown plant, in which the people of God will "nest" for eternity.

One additional point about Jesus' apocalyptic teaching must be made at this time. When the disciples asked Jesus if his resurrection was the revelation of the Kingdom, his answer implied that it was not (Acts 1:6–7). Jesus said to them, "It is not for you to know the times or seasons that the Father has established by his own authority." Before his death, Jesus had said that even he didn't know ". . . that day and hour" (Matthew 24:36). Therefore, we are misguided if we assume that we can use the book of Revelation to decode the signs of the times and see the future coming. Can we know something Jesus did not? If we want to understand the book of Revelation, we need to understand it for its intended purpose and in its historical context. We must also understand Revelation within its literary genre, apocalyptic prophecy.

THE GENRE OF APOCALYPTIC LITERATURE

The book of Revelation, as apocalyptic literature, is a subgenre of what we loosely call prophecy.[3] Before we enter into the discussion of apocalyptic literature specifically, we must address prophecy in general and rescue it from some popular misconceptions. The primary purpose of prophecy is not the prediction of future events. While there is an ele-

---

2. In this passage, Jesus is actually speaking to the Pharisees, so within the context of this gospel, "among you" is a better translation than "within you."

3. Beasley-Murray, *Revelation*, 14.

ment of prediction in biblical prophecy, the main purpose of prophecy is to be the voice of God in the world. For example, someone who predicts the scores of sporting events is not a prophet, even if the predictions come true, because they are not speaking for God. Their predictions are based on probability and chance. But Dr. Martin Luther King Jr. could be considered a modern prophet, because even though he did not *predict* the future, he had a dream of what the future could be, and he challenged everyone—from those in power to those who had not yet been empowered—to work to make that dream a reality. Therefore, the prophetic voice is one that places expectations on its hearers, presumably expectations that are in line with the will of God. It is interesting to notice that in the earliest recorded lists of spiritual gifts or "offices" in the Christian Church, that of "prophet" is among them (see, for example 1 Corinthians 12:10; 14:3–5; and Ephesians 4:11–12). In the second and third centuries, the apostles came to be seen as the prophets of the Church, and the office of prophet came to be part of the preaching role of the clergy, however at the time that the book of Revelation was written, it was understood that there was still room for prophecy in the Church.[4]

The most familiar prophets are those found in the Old Testament of the Bible. While there is an important understanding within Christianity that the prophets of the Old Testament predicted the coming of Jesus, their primary mission was not to predict the advent of the Messiah, it was to give the people of their own time hope and encouragement, while challenging those who oppressed and exploited the powerless. In other words, the prophets were called to be the voice of God in a world that had often either relegated God to a minor role in society, or forgotten about God altogether, or worse, begun to worship other gods. Simply put, a prophet is one who is called to speak for God. Often that meant speaking a message that the people (let alone their leaders) did not want to hear. Many prophets were mistreated because their messages

---

4. The reason that "prophet" ceases to be a distinct office within the Church is that, as the Church hierarchy develops, anyone with the title "prophet" can claim to speak for God, and therefore influence believers without the sanction of the hierarchy of the Church. This became an issue with the controversy over the Montanists, a charismatic movement within the Church in the second and third centuries. The Church suppressed the role and title of "prophet" in favor of the preaching of house-church leaders for the sake of theological uniformity of the message and ecclesiastical unity from one area to another. By the time of Justin's first apology (145 CE), the presider, or "president," preached to the congregated believers, not one who held an office of "prophet." See Justin Martyr, *First Apology* 67.

were seen as subversive. In truth, God's message is often subversive of the established order in the world, especially if the established order is oppressive. Jesus himself took on a prophetic role when he criticized the religious leaders of first-century Jerusalem (Matthew 22:18). Prophecy is by its very nature revolutionary because it intentionally "afflicts the comfortable in order to comfort the afflicted." It is not so much "head in the clouds" as it is "finger in your face."

Prophecy pushes those in power to open their eyes to the needs of the people, especially the poor and oppressed. It can often be a critique of the powers of the time and a call to move beyond the comfort of the few to the kind of justice that God expects of believers. For example, the prophet Amos preached against the oppression of the poor by the wealthy during the reign of King Jeroboam II of Israel. He also criticized the people for their idolatry. His prediction was a warning that if the people did not turn back to God, they would lose their nation (see Amos 7:11). The loss of the land symbolizes a separation from God because the land was the land of God's promise, and the land of God's presence. It was therefore seen as the place where God is. In the end, though, God (speaking through Amos) promised that the people would be restored to the land and to their God (Amos 9:11–15).

A similar example is Micah, who even criticized the "professional prophets" for telling the king what he wanted to hear. Micah's message for the southern kingdom of Judah included a warning similar to Amos'. Also like Amos, Micah's message contains an element of hope, including the famous prediction of a Messiah born in Bethlehem (Micah 5:2). In short, the prophets were protesters, railing against the abuse of power, proclaiming the downfall of those who abused their power, and preaching messages of hope for those who were powerless.

When we think of prophecy in terms of the prediction of future events, we can consider it in two parts. The first is warning. If a prophet predicts the future, it is never just prediction for its own sake or so that the prophet can show off. The prediction supports the message and sometimes comes in the form of a warning. A perfect example is the prophet Jonah. He brought a message that the people of Nineveh did not want to hear, and with that message came the warning: if you do not repent, God will destroy your city (Jonah 3:4). Jonah was disappointed and even a little angry with God that the warning did not come true (Jonah 3:10—4:1). The people repented and God did not destroy their city. But this does not make Jonah a false prophet. It simply shows that prophecy is not the same thing as the fatalistic oracles of Greek mythology. It is not the case that trying to prevent a prophet's prediction from coming true will actually make it come to pass (as happened to poor old Oedipus). Prophecy is a living message in which the people of God participate. As we have seen with Jonah, if the people repent, the prediction need not come true in order for it still to have been an authentic prophetic word from God.

The second part of prophetic prediction is promise. The foundation of this promise is God's faithfulness in upholding the covenant, remembered most often in the Exodus. Christians believe that the culmination of all the Old Testament promises is the coming of Jesus as the Christ, the Messiah whose advent institutes a new covenant, one based on forgiveness (Jeremiah 31:31–34). It is important to note that prophecy is at its core a message of hope. Certainly the prophets' preaching includes admonitions and critiques of those in power, but in the end the message of prophecy is that God will uphold the covenant relationship with the people, even when they are unfaithful. Though there may be exile, there will be restoration. Though there is separation for a time, there will be reconciliation. The message of predictive prophecy is not to tell the people what will happen in the future, but to give the people encouragement and direction in the present. That might mean there is a warning about consequences, or a promise of liberation, but the point of any words about the future is always grounded in the present. The prophetic message always includes a "therefore . . ." that is intended for the people of the time, an expectation or directive that requires action, and a message of encouragement that gives hope. The book of Revelation is also primarily a message of hope for its original audience. This means that as we read the book of Revelation from almost two thousand years after it was written, we must admit that it was not originally written for us. That is not to say that there isn't a message for us in the book of Revelation. As inspired Scripture, it is timeless and will always be "valuable for teaching, for refutation, for correction, and for training in righteousness" (2 Timothy 3:16). However, before we can find meaning for our time and situation in this document, we must first attempt to determine the intended meaning of the author and how it might have been understood by the original audience.

As we read the book of Revelation, it will be helpful to keep in mind these two parts of predictive prophecy—warning and promise—as well as the primary role of prophecy as preaching that calls God's people to justice and carries a message of hope for the oppressed. Prophecy is good news and bad news. Often we hear the bad news first: the people have sinned and turned away from God, and if they continue in sin they risk separation from God. But then comes the good news: God will restore the people and vindicate those who have been unjustly treated. This brings us to our discussion of apocalyptic literature as a specific type of prophecy.

When the warnings and promises of prophecy move beyond this world to the threshold of the next and include the vindication of God's people on a cosmic scale, we have moved into the realm of apocalyptic prophecy.[5] The term *apocalypse* means "that which is revealed," therefore apocalyptic prophecy has to do with warnings and promises that will be revealed in the future. Strictly speaking, this does not necessarily mean the "end of the world." It refers to cataclysmic events in the future, which may or may not signal the end of an age, but do imply a turning point in human history. When it does refer to the end times it is called *eschatological*, referring to the *eschaton*, or the end. However, not all apocalyptic prophecy is eschatological, as we will see when we examine Jesus' apocalyptic preaching in the Gospels. Therefore, apocalyptic prophecy is a subset of prophecy in general, and eschatological prophecy is a subset of apocalyptic. Bearing this distinction in mind, we will find that the book of Revelation is a book of prophecy, with a significant amount of apocalyptic prophecy, yet only a small amount of eschatology.

Apocalyptic literature frequently includes prophetic visions, and the book of Revelation is no exception. The visions include glimpses into the Realm of God, or what we popularly call "Heaven." These visions are outside of the continuum of time, and it would be a mistake to ask whether these heavenly scenes are taking place in the past, in the present, or in the future. They simply are. For example, when Daniel says, ". . . in the night visions I saw someone like a Son of Man coming from the clouds of heaven . . ." (Daniel 7:13), the question is not, "When does this happen?," but, "What does it mean?" On the surface, the present tense of the verb "coming" might imply that it is happening at the time of the vision. However, in verse 14 the past tense, "was given," (or in some translations,

5. Rist, "Apocalypticism," 1:158.

"received") would imply something that has occurred and is completed. The truth is that in these apocalyptic visions we cannot look to the tense of the verbs or even to the context to determine a timeline of events. It is the same with the book of Revelation. Even phrases such as "then I saw …" do not imply a chronological sequence of events, but at most only the order in which the elements of the vision were observed.

Imagine watching a slideshow from someone else's vacation. Now imagine that the slides are arranged according to topic—all the dinners are together, all the afternoons at the beach are together, and all the visits with relatives are together, so that you are not seeing the events in the order in which they happened. You might see one slide after another, but that does not imply that the event in the second slide happened right after the event in the first. In the same way, the book of Revelation is not a linear narrative. We must be careful not to assume that something that is described in chapter 12, for example, takes place after something that is described in chapter 11, just because the event in chapter 12 turns up later in the text. In this example, parts of chapter 11 refer to the destruction of Jerusalem, and chapter 12 includes a reference to the birth of Christ, which historically happened some seventy-five years earlier. While it is true that the book of Revelation refers to events in John's past, present, and future, we would be mistaken to assume that the events are recorded in chronological order or that the line between what has happened and what will happen is easily drawn at the end of a chapter. One must always keep in mind that the chapter and verse divisions were not placed in the text by the original author.

We will look at specific examples of apocalyptic prophecy below, as we explore how they help us interpret some of the images in the book of Revelation. For now it is interesting to note that the book of Revelation, at the end of the New Testament, is in fact the end of a long trajectory, or evolution, of the theology of salvation.[6] Salvation in the early documents of the Old Testament is primarily about rescue from danger.[7] A prayer for salvation is often a prayer for God to protect one from one's enemies (cf. Deuteronomy 33:29). For example, Psalm 7 is attributed to David, one of many passages in which the believer cries out to God for rescue. The psalm begins, "Oh Lord my God, I take refuge in you. Rescue me! Save me from those who pursue me, or they will tear out my heart like a

---

6. Richardson, "Salvation," 4:174.

7. Ibid., 4:176. See also Hasel, *Old Testament Theology*, 141.

lion . . ." (Psalm 7:1–3; see also 68:19–22). Salvation, to the early Hebrew, meant rescue and vindication.[8]

This is evident in the plot against Jesus. Most of his enemies seem to have believed that a Messiah should be one who rescues the people from their oppressors by military force and vindicates the oppressed by defeating their enemies (with God's help of course). The problem for Jesus was that those who wanted him to be that kind of Messiah were disappointed that he was not, and those who did not want him to be that kind of Messiah were afraid that he might be (cf. John 18:14). Both groups were probably represented in the crowd that yelled, "Crucify Him!," and both groups were still thinking of salvation in terms of an earthly rescue and vindication.

As time went on, later Old Testament documents began to broaden and spiritualize the definition of salvation.[9] After all, the return from exile was a salvation of sorts, and yet it did not establish an eternal Davidic kingdom (as promised in 2 Samuel 7:16). Later prophets would push the definition of salvation into the far distant "Day of the Lord," then Jesus would redefine what the Messiah was to be in light of Isaiah 53, and finally the early Christian writers would develop a Christian *soteriology* based on the events of the crucifixion and resurrection.[10] Eventually, the concept of salvation came to have a spiritual meaning rather than an earthly, time-bound meaning. By the time of the book of Revetlation, salvation is all about the afterlife. The book of Revelation is the culmination of this evolution of the concept of salvation. What the believer hopes to be saved from is no longer physical death at the hands of earthly enemies, but spiritual death, or eternal separation from God caused by sin.

As we will see, the book of Revelation was written in the context of persecution. The followers of Jesus were in danger, and the very admission of being a Christian was, at certain times and places, a crime punishable by death. And yet, Revelation does not promise rescue from persecution. It does promise a kind of vindication, but it is a cosmic vindication, and the one who is vindicated is really Jesus, the Crucified One. The book is a message of hope and encouragement to the Christian community living in the midst of persecution. It does not promise that they will not die at the hands of the Romans (in fact, it is well known that

8. Richardson, "Salvation," 4:171.

9. Ibid., 4:170.

10. Hasel, *Old Testament Theology*, 166. See also Richardson, "Salvation," 4:168.

some Christians were literally mauled by lions), instead it is a message that tells them that even if they die, they are still saved. Not from physical death, but from the ultimate death, which is separation from God. They may not, in fact, be rescued from persecution and execution, but they will be preserved for eternal life with God and with Jesus, their Savior. This message is meant to give them hope, to encourage them to persevere in their faith, to help them resist the temptation to denounce the faith to save their lives, and to keep them unified during the persecution.

Old Testament apocalyptic prophecy had a similar function. During times when the Hebrew people were conquered and occupied, colonized, taken into exile, enslaved and oppressed, apocalyptic preaching served as a message of hope, encouragement, and unity.[11] Often it predicted the downfall of the oppressors, as the book of Revelation does. But, like the earlier apocalyptic literature, Revelation is not primarily a message for people who were not born yet when it was written. It was a message for those who were right in the middle of the persecution and suffering, to give them hope and show them the bigger picture of eternity.

SUMMARY

As the end of the New Testament, and the end of the canon of Scripture, the book of Revelation actually brings us full circle. The Bible begins with creation, and it ends with the re-creation of a new heaven and a new earth. The New Jerusalem is an image of reconciled creation and the glorified Church, as the new covenant fulfills and completes the old. It actually is preferable to speak of the entire span of salvation history as one covenant, rather than as a series of covenants or "dispensations." The new covenant is only necessary to fulfill the old covenant, because the people of God could not keep the conditions of the original. It is only by the mercy of God that a solution is offered in the new covenant. As Jeremiah promised, the new covenant would be one in which God would forgive the people for their unfaithfulness (Jeremiah 31:31–34). The people will be reconciled to God, and what is wrong will be made right. The book of Revelation is about the fulfillment of that covenant, and the revealing, or *revelation,* of the Kingdom of God. The new heaven and new earth are a return to the intended paradise described in Genesis, but inasmuch as the entire cosmos is reconciled to God, the realm of the Kingdom must

11. Richardson, "Salvation," 4:169.

be thought of not as a paradise on earth, but as the heavenly place of resurrection.

As we begin to develop a new framework for studying the book of Revelation, it will help us in the task of interpretation if we keep the following assumptions in mind:

- One cannot understand Revelation apart from its historical context within the Roman Empire and during a time of persecution.

- Revelation was not originally written for us. To find what relevance it has for our time, we must remember that it was written to be understood by first-century Christians who knew the Old Testament.

- The key to understanding the images and symbols in Revelation is found in the Old Testament apocalyptic literature.

- Revelation does not describe current events, and it will not tell us when the Second Coming of Christ will take place.

- Revelation is prophecy, and as such it is primarily a message of critique of the government in power at the time it was written, and of hope for those who are oppressed by it.

- Revelation is apocalyptic, and as such it contains visions and other symbolic imagery that cannot be interpreted as a linear sequence of events.

- The interpretation of Revelation can be illuminated by the apocalyptic teaching of Jesus in the Gospels.

- When Revelation seems to predict events that are in the author's future, it is helpful to separate warning from promise. Warnings may or may not come true, and may apply only in limited ways to anyone other than those in the time of the original audience.

- Predicted events in the author's future may have already come to pass in our past, in the more than nineteen hundred years of history since the book of Revelation was written.

- Chapter and verse divisions were added to the text long after its composition and may actually get in the way of interpretation.

Ultimately, Revelation is a book about the hope of salvation and eternal life in the *revealing* of the Kingdom of God.

2

The Historical Background of the Book of Revelation

INTRODUCTION

THE HISTORICAL CONTEXT OF the book of Revelation was a time of persecution, when Christians in some parts of the Roman Empire lived in fear that they would be required to compromise their faith by participating in idolatrous sacrifices. Failure to do so could result in arrest, torture, or execution. Sometimes this persecution was spurred on by their Jewish or pagan neighbors, or even family members, who sold them out to the Roman officials (Matthew 10:21).[1] Not only was this the historical situation of the times in which Revelation was written, the persecution itself created the occasion for the writing of the book. The author found himself banished to an island, exiled as a punishment for preaching the gospel.

Our study of the historical background of Revelation begins with questions of the authorship and the date of Revelation: who wrote it, and when was it written? However, when we explore these questions, we quickly find a kind of chicken-and-egg problem. Whichever question we answer first will limit the possibilities for the other question. Whatever date we assign to the writing of Revelation will influence our discussion of who could have written it, and vice versa. Therefore, we will begin

---

1. Cf. Acts 17:5. The term "pagan" is used somewhat anachronistically to refer to adherents of any of the many Greco-Roman mythologies and cults of the Roman Empire. The term would later come into use to refer to the *pagani*, the country folk who would cling to the old religions when the majority of the population of the cities was Christian. While it may have carried a derogatory tone at that time, modern convention allows the use of the term with no value judgments attached. When used in this book, it simply means someone who was not a Christian or a Jewish believer.

with the internal evidence. We will begin with what the author himself tells us.

The author calls himself John (Revelation 1:1, 4, 9, 22:8). He says he shares with his readers a certain "tribulation" (Rev 1:9). He further tells his readers that he is on the island of Patmos (a small island off the coast of what is now Turkey), and he says he is there because of the proclamation of the gospel (Rev 1:9). With these as our starting points, we will explore the historical setting of the writing of Revelation, beginning with its authorship.

THE AUTHOR

At the cross, Jesus entrusted his mother Mary to his beloved disciple, John (John 19:25–27). The Gospel tells us that from that time on John took Mary into his home. According to a long-standing tradition, after the resurrection and ascension of Jesus, when the disciples carried the gospel to different parts of the empire, John and Mary settled in Ephesus, an important coastal city in Asia Minor (modern Turkey).[2] This puts John the disciple in exactly the right place to have been exiled to the island of Patmos. But was the John who wrote Revelation the same John as the disciple of Jesus? The majority of early Christian writers believed that it was.

Among the earliest extant references to the authorship of Revelation in Christian literature is in Justin Martyr's *Dialogue with Trypho* (written about 145 CE). In the *Dialogue*, Justin says that the book of Revelation is by John, "one of the apostles of Christ."[3] As we will see when we discuss the date of the writing, it is reasonable to assume that Justin's *Dialogue* was written within the lifetime of people who knew for certain who wrote Revelation and perhaps were even among the original audience: members of the seven churches mentioned in the text.

Irenaeus, the bishop of Lyons, writing about 185 CE, also assumed that the author of Revelation was John the disciple of Jesus.[4] Irenaeus

---

2. Eusebius of Caesarea, *Ecclesiastical History* 3.20.8–9. See also Irenaeus of Lyons, *Against Heresies* 3.3.

3. Justin Martyr, *Dialogue with Trypho* 81. See also Eusebius of Caesarea, *Ecclesiastical History* 4.18. But see Papias 4-8. Although he is in the minority among early writers, Papias seems to have believed that the author of Revelation was John the Elder.

4. Irenaeus of Lyons, *Against Heresies* 3.3; 4.20; 4.30; 5.26. Irenaeus also believed that John the disciple wrote the Fourth Gospel and the letters of 1 and 2 John. See Irenaeus of Lyons, *Against Hereies* 3.11, 16; 5.18.

writes with only two degrees of separation from John himself, since Irenaeus was a student of the martyr Polycarp, who had known John.[5] Tertullian (writing in North Africa at the turn of the third century)[6] and Hippolytus (writing in Rome around 225 CE)[7] as well as Origen (writing in Alexandria before the middle of the third century) also assumed that the author of Revelation was the disciple John.[8]

It is true that a few later writers began to doubt the disciple's authorship, primarily Dionysius, bishop of Alexandria, and a few who followed him. Dionysius argued against apostolic authorship because he was uncomfortable with the way some were interpreting Revelation.[9] Specifically, some of the early theologians interpreted the so-called millennium as a literal one-thousand year reign of Christ on earth, though the majority of the Church understood that the text was symbolic, and should be interpreted allegorically.[10] By arguing against John's author-

---

5. Eusebius of Caesarea, *Ecclesiastical History* 5.20. For the martyrdom of Polycarp, see 4.15.

6. Tertullian, *Against Marcion* 3.14.3.

7. Hippolytus, *On Christ and Antichrist* 36, 50.

8. Eusebius of Caesarea, *Ecclesiastical History* 6.25.

9. Ibid., 7.24–25. Cf. also 3.39. Dionysius' refusal to accept the apostolic authorship of Revelation is made suspect by the fact that his own teacher, Origen, accepted it. See Eusebius of Caesarea, *Ecclesiastical History* 6.25, 29. Thus, if he truly believed that John the disciple did not write Revelation, he did not get that from his teacher.

10. Literal (dispensationalist/millennialist) interpretation of Revelation seems to begin with Papias of Hierapolis, who interpreted the six days of creation in Genesis as six thousand years of human history (from 2 Pet. 3:8): four thousand years from creation to Christ, two thousand years from Christ to the millennium, with the millennium itself as a seventh thousand years, a millennial "Sabbath." See the *Epistle of Barnabas* 15. Early millennialism may have been a reaction against Docetics, who considered creation contemptible. The literal interpretation of an earthly reign of Christ may have been seen as a way to reinforce the goodness of creation in Genesis. In other words, if God created the material universe good, then why would it go away? This interpretation may also have been a reaction against the belief of some philosophers that the world would end in a final conflagration that would be followed by an eternal cycle of renewal and destruction. Following Papias' interpretation were such important writers as Justin Martyr (*Dialogue with Trypho* 80), Irenaeus of Lyons (*Against Heresies* 5.28, 5.35), Tertullian, and Hippolytus, though Justin would admit that not everyone in the Church interpreted Revelation the way he did. In fact, it seems that the majority did not. See Eusebius of Caesarea, *Ecclesiastical History* 3.36–39. Eusebius of Caesarea would later speak for the mainstream Church by saying that the interpretation of Papias and Irenaeus was a misinterpretation. See Photius, *Letter to Aquileias*. The heretic Apollinarius was also said to have interpreted Revelation literally, which Jerome criticized as a "Jewish" (i.e., literal) interpretation. Jerome blamed the beginning of the millennialist interpretation

ship, he was attempting to discredit the document enough to prevent it
from being included in the New Testament canon. In the end, though,
the book of Revelation was included, and its inclusion assumes apostolic
authorship.[11]

Contemporary arguments against the disciple's authorship are
primarily based on perceived differences between Revelation and the
Gospel According to John. Assuming that the Gospel was written by the
apostle John, some have argued that the same writer could not have written Revelation, since the grammar and style of the Greek text appears
to be very different. Those who argue against apostolic authorship also
point out that the author of Revelation does not claim to be an eyewitness of the ministry of Jesus (as the Gospel writer does), and does not
refer to himself as the brother of James or the son of Zebedee.[12]

When one looks closely at the Greek text of Revelation compared to
the Fourth Gospel, there is no denying the differences in writing style and
vocabulary. However, arguments from style are, in and of themselves, not
conclusive for determining authorship, because they can be explained by
the passage of time from one writing to the next, and by a difference of
literary genre. In the case of the Gospel of John compared to Revelation,
the difference in genre couldn't be more pronounced, the former being
primarily narrative and theological, while the later is apocalyptic prophecy with a much heavier use of Old Testament imagery and symbolism.
This difference alone would be enough to explain the change in style and
vocabulary, especially when one remembers that the earliest witnesses

on John the Elder, another John who was possibly a student of John the apostle, whom
Jerome believed to have written the letters of 2 and 3 John. See Jerome, *Illustrious Men*
18. Eventually an Egyptian bishop and composer of hymns named Nepos wrote a book
called *Refutation of the Allegorists*, in which he criticized the mainstream (allegorical)
interpretation of Revelation in favor of a literal interpretation. It was this document that
provoked Dionysius of Alexandria to conclude that the book of Revelation was dangerous, since it was too difficult for the average Chrisian to interpret. Dionysius himself
admitted that he did not know what the book of Revelation meant, but he knew that it
was not meant to be taken literally. Thus, in a treatise called *On the Promises*, he argued
against apostolic authorship of Revelation in the hope that if he could convince enough
people the book would then be excluded from the New Testament canon. One wonders
if there is a connection between the strict rigorist morality of Hippolytus and Tertullian
and the literal interpretation of Revelation. The Montanists apparently interpreted the
millennium literally as well, which may have been part of the reason their movement
was attractive to Tertullian.

11. Ellis, "Pseudonymity and Canonicity," 212–24.

12. Mounce, *Book of Revelation*, 28.

assumed apostolic authorship, and those who first argued against it were motivated by a desire to discredit the document. The truth is, we do not need to discredit or discard the book of Revelation to rescue it from poor interpretation. Such is the purpose of this present book.

There are also many similarities between the Gospel of John and the book of Revelation.[13] Theologically speaking, the two documents are very compatible, and there is no reason to believe that the author who wrote the *Logos* Christology of the Gospel could not also have written the *Lamb* Christology of Revelation. In the end, if one could prove that the differences between Revelation and the Fourth Gospel were so great as to make common authorship an impossibility, the tradition of authorship of Revelation is strong enough to place it in priority over the Fourth Gospel for the claim of apostolic authorship.[14] In other words, if one were convinced that the same John could not have written both the Gospel of John and Revelation, this would be more of an argument against the disciple's authorship of the Fourth Gospel than of Revelation.[15]

If there was any chance of confusion over the authorship, it would beg the question of why the author did not take greater care to identify himself, as Paul does in several of his letters.[16] In truth, the fact that the

13. Ibid., 30–31. See also Beale, *Revelation*, 35.

14. Most early Christian writers also believed that John the disciple wrote the Fourth Gospel, however there seems to have been more debate over the authorship of the Gospel than over the authorship of Revelation. In general, there was a consensus in the early Church that John the disciple of Jesus wrote the Gospel attributed to him, as well as Revelation and the letter of 1 John. However, many believed that another John, possibly a student of the apostle who is referred to as John the Elder, wrote the letters of 2 and 3 John. See Eusebius of Caesarea, *Ecclesiastical History* 6.25.

15. Beasely-Murray, *Revelation*, 34–36.

16. Mounce, *Book of Revelation*, 26. Some have argued that there were two Johns active in Asia Minor. This assumes one would be John the apostle, and the other a lesser-known John, perhaps identified by the title "The Elder," as in the epistles 2 and 3 John. Even if this were true, it would not detract from the case stated here that the author of Revelation did not need any more specific identification, and therefore confidence is high that our author is John the apostle. In truth, the notion that there were two Johns probably comes from confusion over two possible locations for the tomb of John. Two competing pilgrim sites could have given rise to speculation about a second early church leader also named John. Some have argued that fear of reprisal may have led the author of Revelation to obscure his identity, but if that were the case, why mention a name at all? Furthermore, to ascribe pseudonymous authorship to John would still beg the question of which John was meant, unless there was only one possible answer—and since the original audience would know if the author was not John the apostle, pseudonymity would only serve to compromise the credibility of the text.

author does not establish his identity more precisely could point to a greater confidence in apostolic authorship. The lack of any particulars of the author's identity (e.g., that he was an eyewitness of the Gospel events) probably means that he assumed all of his readers knew exactly who he was. Both his identity and his authority would have been well established, especially in the area of the seven churches. There is no evidence to suggest that the tradition of John the apostle in Ephesus is unreliable, and as an apostle he would have functioned as the bishop for the churches in the area. He writes the letters to the seven churches with authority, and while the message originates with the Lord, the effect of the document is that of an episcopal letter to the churches of western Asia Minor.

The evidence from the early Church points to the apostle John, the son of Zebedee and the brother of James, as the author of this book. The burden is on contemporary skepticism to prove that John the disciple could not have been the author, which it has not been able to do. In the end, those closest to the original audience all assume Johannine authorship. Therefore, for the purposes of our study we will proceed on the assumption that John the disciple of Jesus was the author of the book of Revelation. However, even if it could be shown that that author was not the apostle, it would not significantly change the interpretation presented here.

THE DATE AND THE SETTING

John acknowledges what his readers already know: that they are in the midst of a time of "tribulation," and that he is suffering exile for preaching the gospel. The Greek word translated "tribulation" (sometimes translated "distress") is the same word the author uses in Revelation 7:14 (the "great tribulation"), and the same word that is usually translated "persecution" in Acts 11:19. It clearly refers to suffering and oppression at the hands of authorities outside the Christian community.

Persecution against the new Church was a consistent danger for the first three centuries of its existence, but at the start the persecution came primarily from the Christians' closest brothers and sisters, that is, from within the synagogue.[17] Christianity started as a messianic sect within Judaism and only became a separate religion over time. Part of the reason for the separation was the feeling on the part of non-Christian Jews that they could no longer coexist with those who sang and prayed to a crucified man.

As conflict between Christians and non-Christians within Judaism escalated, the Roman government began to take notice. Sometime around the year 52 CE, the emperor Claudius (who reigned 41–54 CE) expelled all Jews from the city of Rome because they were "making disturbances at the instigation of Chrestus."[18] This "Chrestus" is clearly a reference to Jesus, with an attempt to Latinize the title "Christ" as a name. The "disturbances" were probably conflicts within the synagogue between Christian Jews and non-Christian Jews, over the person of Christ (not at the instigation of Christ, as if he were there). At the time, the Roman government did not yet see the two groups as separate religions and understood the conflict as an internal fight within Judaism. Ironically, as long as Christianity was considered part of the Jewish religion, it was safe from Roman persecution because Judaism was a protected religion. Once the Roman government perceived that Christianity was a separate religion, it was suspect, in large part because it was new.[19]

Romans generally took a "the more, the merrier" view of worship. When it came to religion, their advice would have been to hedge your bets by worshipping as many gods as possible. As long as one did not practice human sacrifice, one was generally free to worship all the gods one wanted, provided that the traditional gods who were thought to

---

17. Stephen's martyrdom is recorded in Acts 6–8; John's brother James' martyrdom in Acts 12. The Jewish historian Josephus recorded the martyrdom of the other James, who was a close relative of Jesus and the leader of the church in Jerusalem, in his *Antiquities of the Jews* 20.9.1. See also Eusebius of Caesarea, *Ecclesiastical History* 2.23. Note that some details of the accounts of Josephus and Eusebius of Caesarea may have been reworked by Christians at a later date, and any pro-Christian sympathies exhibited by non-Christians in the narrative are to be treated as suspect.

18. Suetonius, *Life of Claudius* 25.4. The expulsion of Jews from Rome included Christian Jews, of course, and this is the reason that Aquila and Priscilla were in Corinth at the time the apostle Paul arrived there. See Acts 18:1–3.

19. In the ancient world, unlike our own technology-driven age, newer was not considered better. Older was always better, the tradition more to be trusted than the innovation. Therefore any new religion or cult would be suspect in the eyes of the government because it was an unknown—officials would worry that it was a political movement rather than (or in addition to) a devotional or philosophical movement.

protect Rome were included. Eventually, the Romans would figure out that Christians, like Jews, worshipped a God who expected an exclusive relationship. Worshipping the God of Abraham, Isaac, Jacob, and Jesus meant you could not worship any other gods. The Jews got away with this because their religion was an ancient one, and the Romans usually knew better than to try to take away a conquered people's religion.[20] But Christianity was new, and it was not the religion of a particular historic nation or people; it was open to anyone, which meant that it spread across the empire. Roman officials began to reason that if Christians refused to support the state religion, they might also refuse to support the state. Added to this suspicion were rumors that began to circulate which charged that Christians were cannibals and practiced incest.[21] As the small house-church groups of Christian believers gradually separated themselves from the synagogue, and as more and more Gentiles joined their churches, Christianity began to be seen as a separate, new religion. And when Christians did not participate in regular civic cult events, their pagan neighbors often became suspicious of them, increasing their chances of being singled out for their non-participation in the Roman state religion.[22]

In July of the year 64 CE, a fire broke out in the city of Rome, leveling a significant portion of the city (centered in the area where the Colosseum now stands). At the time, many Romans believed that the emperor Nero (reigned 54–68 CE) had actually set the blaze, because he

---

20. The Romans generally allowed people in the provinces to keep their traditional religious practices. While this was in keeping with the Roman attitude toward religion, it also served to guard against rebellion. Judaism was no exception, with Roman officials even making concessions for the Jewish law against images (Exodus 20:4–5) by using special standards for the legions stationed in Judea, and by allowing the Jews to mint their own coins without the image of the emperor. This was the reason for the money changers in the temple courtyard (Matthew 21:12–13). Before the destruction of the temple in Jerusalem, Jews were allowed to pay a tax to the temple treasury rather than to the imperial state treasury, but an offering to the temple had to be made with the coins that did not have the emperor's image on them. Notwithstanding these concessions to Jewish sensibilities, the Romans did not want Judaism to spread, and so the emperor Domitian and others did institute laws against conversion to Judaism.

21. The early apologists often wrote to try to correct rumors of anti-social behavior in the Church. A misunderstanding of the Eucharist led to charges of cannibalism (cf. John 6:22–69), and hearing husbands and wives call each other brothers and sisters in the Lord led to charges of incest (cf. 1 Thessalonians 5:26). See Justin Martyr, *First Apology* 65.

22. Beale, *Book of Revelation*, 15.

had plans to build a new palace for himself in the area destroyed by the fire.[23] To deflect the blame from himself, Nero chose for his scapegoat the new religion that was coming into its own. The Christians were charged with setting the fire, so that simply admitting belief in Christ made one guilty of arson.[24] Nero's persecution was limited to Christians within the city of Rome, and it was relatively temporary, but it set a precedent that made the Christian Church vulnerable to charges of anti-social behavior and sedition. According to tradition, both Paul and Peter were martyred in Rome during Nero's reign.[25] Paul was beheaded (a quick death because of his status as a Roman citizen), and Peter was crucified in Nero's circus, the site now occupied by the Vatican and the great basilica that bears the saint's name.

While Nero's persecution and the events leading up to it are important for understanding later developments, the persecution of Nero was too limited to be the historical setting for the book of Revelation, mainly because it was carried out only in the city of Rome. Under Nero, Christians were executed on the charge of arson, not simply because they were Christians. The book of Acts gives no evidence that there were any laws specifically against Christianity at the time it was written.[26] In fact, as we have seen, Christianity was only just becoming recognized as a separate religion, and would not be fully separate from Judaism until after 70 CE and the destruction of the temple in Jerusalem. Indirectly, the law protected Christians as long as they appeared to be part of Judaism. The situation that brought about the writing of the book of Revelation would only come after another thirty years of growing suspicion.

The consensus of the early Church tradition, along with most contemporary commentators, is that the persecution described in the book of Revelation took place under the emperor Domitian (reigned 81–96 CE).[27] This would have been within the lifetime of the apostle John, and in fact Clement of Alexandria, Irenaeus of Lyons, and the Christian historian and bishop Eusebius of Caesarea all tell us that John outlived

---

23. Stevenson, *New Eusebius*, 2.

24. Tacitus, *Annals* 15.38–44. The event is also mentioned by Suetonius, *Life of Nero* 16.2.

25. Eusebius of Caesarea, *Ecclesiastical History* 2.22–25.

26. Barnes, "Legislation against the Christians," 32–33. The Acts of the Apostles was probably written around 62 CE.

27. Irenaeus of Lyons, *Against Heresies* 5.30.3.

Domitian, living into the reign of the emperor Trajan (reigned 98–117 CE).[28] Eusebius relates what Irenaeus recorded, that John functioned as the bishop (i.e., "overseer") of the churches in Asia Minor, that he was banished to the island of Patmos during the reign of Domitian, and that when Domitian died, his successor Nerva (reigned 96–98 CE) released all the political exiles, and John returned to Ephesus.[29]

According to the Roman historian Cassius Dio, Domitian authorized the execution or exile of those accused of "atheism."[30] The charge was based on the observation that Christians worshipped only one God, which did not seem like enough to the Romans, especially since the Christians did not pray to the gods who were thought to protect the empire, nor did they worship the deified emperors. Christians tended not to participate in the public amusements offered by the city, because these made death a sport and often included rituals that would be considered idolatry. The more the Christians opted out of participation in the Roman cult in its many forms, the more suspicious their neighbors became, because these religious observances were understood to be the very things that held Roman society together. Christianity came to be seen as something inherently un-Roman, and Christians became susceptible to accusation by their neighbors. When accused, Christians were sometimes banished to island exiles, including the famous case of Flavia Domitilla, Domitian's own niece, who died in exile on the island of Pontia (also called Ponza or Pandateria) in 96 CE.[31] Land she owned was used for the catacombs in Rome that now bear her name.

---

28. Clement of Alexandria, *Who Is the Rich Man that Shall be Saved?* 42. Eusebius of Caesarea, *Ecclesiastical History* 3.23.1–4. See also Irenaeus of Lyons, *Against Heresies* 2.22; 3.3. It is interesting to note that in paintings depicting the disciples of Jesus, John is almost always pictured as a youth. This may be based on an early tradition of John as the youngest of the apostles, or it may have been to support the notion that John had to be young in the time of Jesus' ministry in order to still be alive to write Revelation. In any case, if John were between 15 and 20 years old during Jesus' ministry, that would make him between 80 and 85 at the time Revelation was written, which is quite possible, even in the first century. Note that the Roman dole assumed recipients up to 80 years old. See Eusebius of Caesarea, *Ecclesiastical History* 7.21.

29. Irenaeus of Lyons, *Against Heresies* 2.22.5; 3.4.4; 5.30.3. Quoted in Eusebius of Caesarea, *Ecclesiastical History* 3.17–18; 3.20.8–9; 3.23.1–4. See also Tertullian, *Apology* 5.4; and Jerome, *Illustrious Men* 9. The island of Patmos is also mentioned by Pliny the Elder in *Natural History* 4.12.69–70.

30. Cassius Dio, *Roman History* 67.14; 68.1. See also Eusebius of Caesarea, *Ecclesiastical History* 3.18.4; 3.23; 4.15.

31. Eusebius of Caesarea, *Ecclesiastical History* 3.18. Domitilla may have been the

While the persecution of Domitian was far from universal, Roman officials in the larger cities across the empire would have followed his lead in prosecuting Christians. Evidence suggests that there was a statue of Domitian erected in Ephesus, where the apostle John was living.[32] The presence of a statue of Domitian in Ephesus would imply that loyalty to the emperor was a high priority for the Roman officials there. The demands of emperor worship were increasing over time, to the point that a refusal to participate in the imperial cult could be taken as an act of treason. Julius Caesar and the first emperor, Augustus, had been declared gods after their deaths, and with each new emperor the claims for divinity increased. Tiberius anticipated his posthumous deification by taking for himself the title *dominus* ("lord"). The use of divine titles by the emperors escalated to the point that Domitian expected to be called *dominus et deus* ("lord and god").[33] Domitian was even considered by some to be a kind of reincarnation of Nero, and the connection between the two enemies of the Church was not lost on the early Christian writers.[34]

While there is little concrete evidence of laws specifically against Christianity at this time, the precedent set by Nero combined with the charge of "atheism" would have been enough to put Christians in danger, especially if they lived in larger cities where the Roman officials resided. There was a law on the books since 16 CE that made the practice of magic or prophecy a capital offence.[35] It is conceivable that Christian leaders could be condemned under this law, especially if they were said to perform miraculous healings and to prophesy (cf. 1 Corinthians 12:9–10). There also appears to have been an imperial edict by the time of the emperor Trajan (reigned 98–117 CE) that forbade the meeting of secret societies, and it is understandable that Christian worship, since it was held at dawn on Sundays, could have been perceived by outsiders as a secret society.[36]

niece of the Emperor. Other sources say she was the wife of the Emperor's cousin, Flavius Clemens.

32. Price, *Rituals and Power*, 197–98. See also Beale, *Book of Revelation*, 12–16; and Cassius Dio, *Roman History* 68.1.

33. Suetonius, *Life of Domitian* 13.

34. Juvenal, in *Satires* 4.37–38, refers to Domitian as a "bald Nero." There is also a possible allusion to Domitian as another Nero in Martial, *Epigrams* 11.33. Cf. Eusebius of Caesarea, *Ecclesiastical History* 4.26.9.

35. Sherwin-White, "Early Persecutions," 211–12.

36. Pliny the Younger, *Epistle* 10.96.7.

By the time of Trajan's reign, simply admitting to being a Christian was enough to condemn someone. In an answer to a letter written to ask advice on how to handle Christians, Trajan wrote (in about 112 CE) that they should not be sought out, but if any were accused and admitted their "guilt," they were to be executed. However, they could escape death by denying their faith and worshipping before statues of the emperor and various gods of Rome.[37] The demand of pagan sacrifice as a test of devotion to the gods had already been used against Jews in Antioch in 67 CE.[38] Now it was becoming a test of loyalty to the emperor. The correspondence with Trajan shows that persecution against Christians had been growing, and while it was far from empire-wide, Christian evangelists and church leaders would be most vulnerable, especially if they lived in an area where their activities would be visible to enthusiastic Roman officials.

The book of Revelation was written during this time of increasing suspicion toward the Church, and the sporadic but growing persecution that resulted. This makes it very likely that the tradition that John wrote Revelation during the reign of Domitian is reliable. However, though Domitian ruled from 81 CE, he does not seem to have actively endorsed persecution until about 95 CE.[39] Within about a year or so after that, he was dead, and his successor temporarily reversed the trend. Therefore, we can say with a high degree of confidence that the book of Revelation was written in or about the year 95 CE. John found himself at a point in the trajectory of persecution that began with Nero and escalated to the Great Persecution of the early fourth century. Indeed, part of John's prophetic message in the book of Revelation is that things may seem bad now, but it is going to get worse before it gets better.

SUMMARY

- The majority of evidence suggests that the book of Revelation was written by the apostle John, one and the same as the

---

37. Ibid, 10.96–97 (to Trajan, with Trajan's reply).

38. Josephus, *Jewish Wars* 7.3.3.46, 50, 51.

39. This was due in large part to the fact that during the early years of his reign, Domitian was too busy with military pursuits. Cary and Scullard, *History of Rome*, 409–12, 420–24.

beloved disciple of Jesus, the son of Zebedee and brother of James.

- John wrote Revelation in or about the year 95 CE.

- Revelation was written during a time of persecution of the Church by the Roman government. The emperor at the time was Domitian, who was considered by some to be another Nero.

By the time of Domitian, simply associating with Christians was enough to bring suspicion of disloyalty to Rome. If accused and brought before the Roman officials, a Christian could be forced to choose between denying the faith and martyrdom.

3

The Biblical Background of the Book of Revelation

The Sources and Interpretation of the Apocalyptic Images in Revelation

INTRODUCTION

THE FACT THAT THE book of Revelation is an example of apocalyptic prophecy means that it is in many ways a book of images. The images function on two levels, the first of which is description. Most of the book is a quasi-narrative account of a vision, or series of visions, that the apostle John had on the island of Patmos.[1] In these visions, John must have seen things that would defy written language. Whether he was seeing into the realm of heaven, or witnessing events in his future that he could not completely understand, he found himself with the difficult task of describing what he had seen within the limits of human linguistic expression. Therefore, he turned to images that he knew from other visionary writings to describe those things that could not be described in literal terms.

The other function of the imagery is to ensure the security of John's readers. Because the document was written during a time of persecu-

---

1. The authorship of Revelation has been discussed in the last chapter. It is my conclusion that the book of Revelation was written by John the apostle. While the majority of early Church witnesses support this assumption (in fact Eusebius of Caesarea says, "those who have seen John face to face testify . . ." Eusebius of Caesarea, *Ecclesiastical History*, 5.8.5–6), it must be admitted that contemporary scholars are not unanimous on the question. What is universally agreed is that the author of Revelation knew the Old Testament well, and used it extensively in the writing of his text. For our purposes, we will proceed on the assumption that the author of Revelation was indeed the Beloved Disciple, however a different conclusion about the authorship of the document would not significantly change the interpretation that follows.

tion, it would be important to conceal the literal meaning from those outside the community, in case it should fall into the wrong hands. John was in exile for preaching the gospel, and he would not want his readers to be endangered by what he would write to them. Therefore, when writing about elements in the vision that may have been clear to him, but that may have included events and characters too near and dear to the hearts of the Romans, John wrapped these events and characters in symbolic imagery. His readers would know how to unwrap the package, but anyone outside the Judeo-Christian world would not. The visionary and apocalyptic nature of the book of Revelation, combined with the historical setting of persecution, meant that John could not say everything he may have wanted to in plain language. So to convey the message the best way he could, while keeping his readers out of trouble, he writes in images.

Although we are not members of his original audience, we can understand the images that John used because for the most part they come from his Bible—our Old Testament. John borrows images primarily from the apocalyptic sections of Daniel, Ezekiel, and Zechariah, as well as Isaiah and other prophets. In this chapter, we will look at the images used in Revelation and unwrap the meaning of each one. By determining the meaning of the symbols, we will then be able to interpret their function in the text. It is important to point out at the beginning, however, that while John borrows images from books such as Daniel and Ezekiel, the interpretation of those images will not necessarily be the same as they would be in the Old Testament. For example, Daniel used certain symbolic imagery to describe the tribulation of his time as well as his prophetic visions, and John used some of the same symbols in the writing of Revelation, but he used them to describe different events in his own time and in his own vision. It cannot be overstated that while John may have borrowed images from Daniel and the other prophets, the images in Revelation do not necessarily mean the same things, or point to the same realities, as they do in Daniel and Ezekiel. Many interpretations of Revelation rely too heavily on particular interpretations of Daniel. But it is my conviction that once we understand the symbolism of the images from the Old Testament, the book of Revelation can be interpreted on its own terms, and in its own context.

This chapter will survey all the important images in Revelation, and outline how their symbolic meanings are used in the book of Revelation.

We will begin with numbers as symbols and then move on to the other images.

NUMBERS

Numbers in the Bible almost always have a significance beyond their numerical value. In fact, it is not an exaggeration to say that any mathematical value a number might have is secondary to the symbolic meaning of the number itself. In the ancient world, numbers were written with combinations of letters. Most people are familiar with Roman numerals, but in Hebrew and Greek the numbers were written with the same letters used to write words. If words have a symbolic meaning beyond the sounds they make, then numbers were also understood to have a symbolic, and almost mystical, meaning.

What follows is a list of the numbers used in the book of Revelation and their symbolic meanings. The interpretation of numbers is based on their use in a wide variety of ancient literature, including Jewish and early Christian apocalyptic. Some of this writing was more or less contemporary with the book of Revelation, and illuminates the type of mystical importance given to numbers at this time.[2]

ONE-HALF—In Revelation 8:1, there is silence for half an hour. This is not meant to imply that if you were there, and you looked at your watch, exactly thirty minutes would have gone by during the silence. It simply means there was a short pause, or cadence; the calm before the storm. One-half does not necessarily mean exactly fifty percent, it simply means a small amount, or in this case, a short time. One must also remember that any reference to time in the heavenly realm cannot be understood as we would think of time, since time itself is part of creation (Genesis 1:14), and therefore the concept of time in eternity is at least a paradox if not an oxymoron.

ONE-THIRD—Like one-half, one-third represents a certain part or amount of something greater and is not meant to imply exactly one-third of something. But unlike one-half, one-third implies a portioning out or dividing of something (see 2 Samuel 18:2; 2 Kings 11:5–6; and

---

2. Other apocalyptic writings of the late first and early second centuries include the *Apocalypse of Baruch*, the *Apocalypse of Abraham*, the *Assumption of Moses*, as well as the books of 2 Esdras, 2 Baruch, and Enoch (especially the Similitudes, chs. 37–71 and 82–90).

Ezekiel 5:2). The point is that it is an intentionally divided portion, and this implies divine providence. Since the denominator is three, we can assume that the portion is perfect, in the sense that it is equitably or justly divided. In Zechariah 13:8–9, the prophet speaks of a time when the land will be divided. Two thirds will perish, but one-third will be saved. The remnant of one-third of the people will suffer, but will be purified through the suffering (as if by fire), and in the end they will be God's faithful people. In this case, one-third is not meant to represent a literal number, it simply points to a remnant, a remainder that is less than the number of those who were lost. Most were lost, but a divinely appointed portion remained.

In Revelation, the first four trumpets bring the destruction of one-third of the land,[3] the trees, the grass, the sea, the creatures in the sea, the ships on the sea, the rivers, the springs, the sun, the moon, and the stars (Rev 8:7–12). The result of this is that there is darkness for one-third of the time. Eventually, one-third of the people are killed (Rev 9:15).[4] The dragon's tail sweeps away one-third of the stars (Rev 12:4). When Babylon falls, it is divided into thirds (Rev 16:19). In these passages, we are meant to understand that God is at work, "portioning out" justice. The fact that only one-third perish also speaks of God's mercy, in that two thirds are spared. More are spared than destroyed, and so God's mercy is greater than his anger.

ONE-FOURTH—The number one-fourth is used once, in Revelation 6:8. It has a similar meaning to that of one-third, but it refers to the earth, which is represented by the number four (see below, under Four). Therefore, a divinely appointed portion of the earth would have to be one-fourth, and the four parts ("corners") of the earth together represent the whole world.

---

3. The Greek word here is actually the word "earth," however it means the land, as opposed to the sea, which is mentioned in parallel in the next verse. It does not imply that one-third of the planet earth will be destroyed.

4. Though this is often translated "a third of mankind," we are not meant to assume that the death of one-third of all humanity is predicted here. The implications of the vision of Revelation are in many ways limited to "the land," (i.e., the land of promise, Israel) and the known world of the Roman Empire. This verse is probably a parallel to Revelation 11:13, which describes the fall of Jerusalem in 70 CE. On the other hand, the plague of the fourteenth century did kill about one-third of Europe's population.

THREE—Three is the number of perfection. Think of an equilateral triangle with three equal sides and three equal angles. Or think about the appeal of music in three-quarter time, such as a waltz or a Celtic folk song. There is something in the human brain that connects with groupings of three, and when music is played in three, it just "fits." It seems that the concept of three as a perfect number is hardwired into the human mind by the Creator.

Theologically speaking, God is perfect, and God is Trinity—one God in three persons. The number three is prominent in the Bible, often signifying God's perfect providence. Noah had three sons, Jonah came out of the belly of the fish on the third day (cf. Matthew 12:38–41), the magi brought three gifts, and Jesus rose on the third day (cf. also 2 Corinthians 12:2).

In the book of Revelation there two sets of three spiritual beings mentioned: three angels (Rev 14:6–13) and three demons (Rev 16:13). The three angels act as heralds of divine judgment, and each brings a warning: 1) worship only God; 2) Babylon will fall (foreshadowed in the prophetic present, "Babylon is fallen"); and 3) don't worship the beast. The three demons of Revelation are described as unclean spirits like frogs (reminiscent of the second plague of Egypt in Exodus 8:1–15), and the unclean spirits come from the mouths of the dragon, the beast, and the false prophet, respectively. This indicates an identification of the unclean spirits with the blasphemous claims of the "unholy trinity" of the dragon, the beast, and the false prophet (see below, under Mouth).

Finally, the heavenly Jerusalem has three gates on each side (Rev 21:13). Since the New Jerusalem is perfect and eternal, this is represented by the perfect number of gates on each of the four sides (see below, under Four). The total number of gates is twelve, which corresponds to the number of tribes in Israel and the number of disciples of Jesus (Rev 21:12–14, see below, under Twelve and Twenty-Four).

THREE AND ONE-HALF—This is the number seven divided in half. Since seven is the number of completion (see below, under Seven), half of seven implies that something is incomplete. In Revelation 11:9–11, the bodies of the two witnesses lay in the streets of Jerusalem for three and a half days before they are raised. The number symbolizes anticipation. The situation as it was could not stand. The bodies of God's faithful martyrs could not lie in the street forever, so there is an anticipation that something is going to happen to resolve the situation. The number three and one-half denotes that something is only half done, or that God's people are waiting for God to finish what was started. The number also symbolically connects the death of the two witnesses with the events of the Jewish-Roman war, which actually lasted about three and a half years (Rev 11:3).

When used as a number of years, this number may be one exception to our rule against looking for a numerical value, and may have both a symbolic and a literal meaning. In Revelation, the woman hides from the dragon for three and a half years (Rev 12:14) and the beast is active for three and a half years (Rev 13:5). These time frames are further defined as forty-two months or twelve hundred sixty-two days. There is reason to believe that John's mention of the activity of the beast refers to an actual duration of time (i.e., the war with Rome, 66–70 CE) though the number of days would only be approximate (see below, under Forty-two).[5]

The concept of three and a half years of tribulation originally comes from the prophet Daniel, who described a time of oppression at the hands of the enemies of God (Daniel 7:25, 12:7–10). The historical context of the prophet Daniel is the exile of inhabitants of Jerusalem who are forced to live under the rule of Babylon. John certainly knows this reference, and relates it to the rule of *his* Babylon, the Roman Empire. John may also have had in mind the tradition that a famine during Elijah's time lasted three and a half years (1 Kings 17:1—18:2, cf. Luke 4:25 and James 5:17). The point is that John uses this number to remind his readers that the enemies of God are still at work: Herod chased the Holy Family into Egypt (the woman pursued by the dragon, see below, under Dragon and Woman) and the Roman Empire waged war against the holy city of Jerusalem (the activity of the Beast, see below, under Beast). John wants to show a relationship between these more recent events and the events of the fall of Jerusalem in 586 BCE, to tell his readers that the same forces of evil are at work in the Romans and their client kings, the Herodians. The actual length of time of these events is not as important as the connection John is making with the tribulation in Israel's past.

FOUR—The number four symbolizes wholeness. This is different from the number seven, in the sense that four refers to spatial or physical

5. Clement of Alexandria, *Stromateis* 1.21.

wholeness, or geometrical symmetry. It is used to talk about the four corners of the earth, meaning the whole earth (for example, see Isaiah 11:12 and Ezekiel 7:2). In Revelation, there are four angels who stand at the four corners of the earth and release the four winds (Rev 7:1–3; 9:14–15). There are also four "living beings" surrounding the throne of God (Rev 4:6–8). The fact that they are full of eyes on all sides is a reference to the omniscience of God, so that God can see the four corners of the earth (the whole earth) at one time. Finally, the heavenly Jerusalem is a perfect square, with four sides that face in the four directions of the compass (Rev 21:13, 16).

FIVE—In John's vision, locusts sting for five months, an event that is described as the first "woe" (Rev 9:3–12). Five is a number that seems to refer to the physical existence of humans. Whereas three and seven are "spiritual" numbers, five is the number of the flesh. The obvious connections of the number five to the flesh are the five senses, and the fact that there are five fingers on each hand (used for counting) and five toes on each foot.[6] When used in Revelation, five becomes a number symbolic of human suffering. The fact that the locusts sting for five months has something to do with the pain they cause to human flesh. Even more importantly, five months is also about the length of time that the Roman army laid siege to the city of Jerusalem before destroying it in 70 CE. The actual siege was four months and three weeks,[7] but John has combined the symbolic number of physical suffering with the approximate length of the siege of Jerusalem in the image of the locusts (see below, under Locusts).

SIX (666)—The number six is generally understood as the number of sin and evil. It is one less than seven, and since seven is considered perfect, six misses the mark and falls short. This is the very definition of sin (cf. Romans 3:23). Therefore six represents imperfection and that which is flawed. The repetition of the number is an intensification, so that if six is evil, then 666 (three sixes) is "perfect" evil. Just as Jesus is the King of kings (the ultimate King) and the Lord of lords (the ultimate Lord; Rev 19:16), and just as the Old Testament book Song of Solomon is some-

---

6. Hopper, *Medieval Number Symbolism* 9, 86.

7. According to Josephus, the siege lasted from Passover (14th of Nissan) of 70 CE to the 8th of Elul. The duration was four months and three weeks. Josephus, *Jewish Wars* 6.10.1.

times called Song of Songs (the greatest of songs) and the Ark of the Covenant was placed in the Holy of Holies (the most holy place), the number 666 represents the worst evil, the extreme opposite of God (cf. also Matthew 18:21–22).[8]

John tells his readers that the number 666 is the name of the man to whom the symbol of the number refers (Rev 13:17–18). Many attempts have been made to add up the letters of various names or combinations of names to get 666, including the emperor Nero and even some twentieth-century figures such as Adolph Hitler. The truth is, many names can be made to fit, but none fit perfectly.[9] One name fits best, however. The most likely solution to the problem seems to be the emperor Domitian,[10] who was the emperor during John's own time and was regarded by some as another Nero. Domitian's full imperial title, when written with Greek letters and abbreviated as it would have appeared on coins circulating at the time John wrote Revelation, does add up to 666.[11] The identification of the number with the current emperor would have been relatively clear to John's original audience, because he was perceived as the immediate danger, the one who sent John into exile and threatened the safety of those in the Church.[12] There is an urgency to John's message that emphasizes the present tense. John is sending his audience a warning that applies to them in their situation, it is not only for future generations of Christians. That warning is: Do not worship the emperor or his gods, no matter how much the government may try to coerce you. If you do, you will face judgment, but the corresponding promise is that if you resist

---

8. This is not to imply an equal opposite, as if evil and good "compliment" each other. Judeo-Christian religion does not believe in a "yin-yang" type of balance of good and evil; rather the book of Revelation exists to assert the conviction that God is infinitely more powerful than his opposite, and good will finally win over evil.

9. Irenaeus of Lyons, *Against Heresies* 5.30.1–3. Some ancient manuscripts list the number as 616, rather than 666, however Irenaeus of Lyons makes it clear that the correct number is in fact 666. Note that Irenaeus of Lyons connected the number 666 to the dimensions of the statue of Nebuchadnezzar in Daniel 3:1 (sixty cubits by six cubits). See Irenaeus of Lyons, *Against Heresies* 5.29.2.

10. Mounce, *Book of Revelation*, 263–65.

11. Ibid, 265.

12. Beasley-Murray, *Revelation*, 219. The second most likely solution would be Nero, and there is some evidence that early Christian writers assumed Nero was the answer. See Mounce, *Book of Revelation*, 265–66. However, concealing the name of someone who was already dead (and universally hated) would not be necessary.

idolatry, even if you should be martyred, you will be rewarded in the Kingdom of God (Rev 15:2).

We have to remember that John did not intend to create a puzzle for his readers, but to convey this warning. It would not make sense for him to put the warning in terms that his audience could not readily understand. This realization makes the identification of the number with the emperor Domitian even more convincing, since his readers would have had coins in their possession with letters that added up to 666.

We know that the number, which represents a man's name, is also the mark of the beast, without which no one can buy or sell during the time of persecution, but which would constitute idolatry and apostasy for Christians who accept it (Rev 13:16–17). This "mark" is not to be understood literally, as if each person was to be branded or tattooed with the emperor's name, but it is to be understood as the emperor's "stamp of approval," whether that comes from the emperor himself, or from one of his officers, or even from one of his successors (see below, under Seal/Mark).

The number six appears one other time in the book of Revelation. In verse 4:8, the four "living beings" each have six wings. This comes from a vision Isaiah had, in which he saw heavenly beings with six wings (Isaiah 6:1–4). Though the number six appears here, it is probably better understood as three pairs of wings, a reference to their perfect ability to be anywhere and everywhere—in other words, the wings represent God's omnipresence.

SEVEN—Seven is another number of perfection. It differs from three in the sense that here perfection means something more like completion or fulfillment. On the seventh day, God rested because the creation of the world was complete (Genesis 2:1–3). In a way, the events of Revelation are a recapitulation of Genesis; the world is re-created, resulting in a new heaven and earth. This is why the plagues and natural disasters, which are the labor pains of the birth of re-creation, come in sevens. It doesn't mean these things are perfect, in the sense of being good, but it means they are complete in number, and they are a fulfillment of God's perfect plan.

The book of Revelation begins with letters to seven churches. These are the main church groups in the area where John is "overseer," or bishop. That there happen to be seven churches probably also means that they represent all the churches of the world, and perhaps even that each one represents a type of church. The point is that the message is not for these churches only, but for all churches everywhere. The seven churches are represented by seven lampstands (Rev 1:11–12; 1:20—2:1; 11:4; cf. also Matthew 5:15–16; see below, under Lampstand) and seven stars (Rev 1:16; 1:20—2:1; 3:1; see below, under Stars).

At the throne of God is the Lamb, who has seven horns (complete power—he is omnipotent; see below, under Horns) and seven eyes (complete sight—he is omniscient). Also at the throne of God is the sevenfold Spirit of God (Rev 1:4; the Greek literally says "seven Spirits of God," meaning complete presence, therefore the Spirit is omnipresent, and also omniscient; cf. Rev 4:5; 5:6). Therefore, John's Trinity is comprised of the One on the throne (the Father), the Lamb (the Son), and the Spirit of God. The Son and the Spirit are described as sharing the divine attributes of the Father. Interestingly, the seven eyes of the Lamb (his omniscience) are identified with the sevenfold Spirit, "sent out into all the earth" (omnipresence; Rev 5:6; cf. John 15:26; 16:13–15). This implies that omniscience and omnipresence go hand in hand, and one could not exist without the other.

When it comes to the unveiling of God's judgment and the revealing of the Kingdom, the events are described as the opening of seven seals (Rev 5:1; see below, under Seal/Mark), the herald of seven trumpets (Rev 8:2f; 10:7; 11:15; see below, under Trumpet), the secret announcements of seven thunders (Rev 10:3–4), and the pouring out of seven bowls (Rev 15:7; 16:1f; 21:9; see below, under Bowl). The red dragon has seven heads with seven laurel-wreath crowns (Rev 12:3; see below, under Crown, Dragon, and Head), and the beast has seven heads (Rev 13:1; see below, under Babylon, Beast, and Head). Finally, in the destruction of Jerusalem, seven thousand people are killed (Rev 11:13). As we will see, one of the meanings of one thousand is simply a multitude, so the death toll is described as seven multitudes. While it would certainly be a tragic loss of life, the number seven tells us that there is something complete about it.

Ten—This may be another exception to the rule of numbers as symbols. The number ten does not seem to have any great symbolic significance in Hebrew or Greek thought. Here we may be looking for an actual numerical value of ten, because we are told that the ten horns of the dragon

(Rev 12:3) and the beast (Rev 13:1) are ten kings (that is, Roman emperors). John tells us that the ten horns represent ten kings in his future (Rev 17:12), and in fact there were ten emperors who were seen as having persecuted the Church between the time of Domitian and the Great Persecution of the early fourth century (see below, under Babylon).[13]

In the letter to the church of Smyrna, John tells the Christians there that they will go through "tribulation" for ten days (Rev 2:10–11). This clearly refers to persecution, possibly instigated by members of the local synagogue who are antagonistic toward the church (Rev 2:9). The length of time comes from Daniel 1:12–14, where the loyalty of Daniel and his associates is tested for ten days. In the persecution of Christians, it was often a perceived lack of loyalty to the emperor that was at issue (cf. John 19:12). The one who has "ears to hear" should look for the deeper meaning and make the connection to the ten-day test in Daniel. The message is to be ready to face a test of loyalty, being forced to choose between God and Caesar.

TWELVE—The number twelve is a reference to the twelve sons of Jacob, who was called Israel, and the twelve tribes of Israel that were descended from those twelve sons. Early Christian writers understood the Church as the new "chosen people," and the twelve apostles became the New Testament version of the Old Testament patriarchs (cf. Acts 1:15–26). In the walls of the heavenly Jerusalem, there are twelve gates made of pearl (the "pearly gates"; Rev 21:21), guarded by twelve angels. The gates are inscribed with the names of the twelve tribes of Israel. There are also twelve rows of foundation stones, each one named after one of the twelve apostles (Rev 21:12–14; cf. Exodus 28:9–12). Therefore, the heavenly Jerusalem is symbolically entered through the legacy of the Old Testament patriarchs, and its foundation is built on the witness of the twelve disciples of Jesus.[14]

13. It must be acknowledged that it is not always clear whether the emperors were personally involved in persecution. Governors in the provinces had some flexibility to carry out or ignore an emperor's orders, and could in fact continue the policies of a previous emperor after he was dead. Thus the designation of "persecuting emperors" is not meant to imply that we necessarily always know the personal attitudes of the emperors during a time of persecution, simply that from the perspective of the Church there was the danger of persecution in at least some parts of the empire during the reign in question.

14. John doesn't say whether Judas' name is there or the name of Judas' replacement, Matthias (Acts 1:15–26), or in fact whether he saw his own name, but of course that

The woman's crown contains twelve stars (Rev 12:1). The twelve stars are also a reference to the twelve patriarchs, since they function as the "kings" of the twelve tribes (see below, under Stars). Her crown is the symbol of her royal status as a descendant of the house of David, and also as the mother of the King of kings (see below, under Woman).

John sees that 144,000 of the people of Israel were marked with the seal of God, designating them as servants of God (Rev 7:4–8; see below, under One Hundred Forty-Four, and Seal/Mark). This refers to a remnant of Israel and is reminiscent of both the Exodus (the marking of the doors with lamb's blood; Exodus 12:1–20) and the return of a remnant of Judah from exile. There are twelve tribes, and twelve thousand from each tribe are marked with the seal of God. This is not meant to be understood as a literal count. As already noted, the number one thousand signifies a large number—a multitude—so twelve thousand is twelve multitudes. One hundred and forty-four thousand is simply twelve multitudes times twelve tribes.

Finally, in the heavenly city, the tree of life produces fruit twelve times per year, or once each month. The number twelve in this verse may only be significant as the number of months in a year. The point here is that there is no time when the fruit of the tree is not in season. The tree bears fruit for healing all year round.

TWENTY-FOUR—The number twenty-four is simply twelve times two, the number of the patriarchs of the twelve tribes and the number of the apostles of Jesus added together. Thus, the twenty-four "elders" worshipping at the throne are the patriarchs and the apostles (Rev 4:4–11; 11:16–17; cf. Hebrews 12:1–2).[15]

FORTY-TWO—This is the number of months in three and a half years (see above, under Three and one-half). It is a clear reference to the time of tribulation in Daniel 7:25 and 12:7. However, the use of the three-and-a-half-year time frame is more than a symbolic reference to past oppres-

---

is not the point. The number twelve is what is significant, that there must be twelve apostles because there were twelve patriarchs.

15. One might wonder how there can be twelve apostles worshipping in heaven when one of them is witnessing the scene from a distance. But this is not really a problem, since John is looking into eternity and in the context of the vision, we can assume that he must be seeing himself among the elders. The fact that the author of Revelation sees all twelve apostles in heaven is not, therefore, an argument against John's authorship.

sion. John says that the beast was allowed to act for forty-two months (Rev 13:5), and that the Gentiles would trample the holy city for forty-two months (Rev 11:2–3). These two passages refer to the same event, the first-century war with Rome that ended with the siege of Jerusalem and the destruction of the temple in 70 CE. This would be a painful memory in the mind of any Judean, having taken place just twenty-five years before the writing of Revelation. In fact, the war with the Romans was about three and a half years long, from the beginning of the war in 66 CE to the fall of Jerusalem in 70 CE.[16]

John also tells his readers that the woman will flee from the dragon and go into the desert for twelve hundred sixty days (Rev 12:6) or three and a half years (Rev 12:14). This is a flashback to the time when Mary (the Woman), Joseph, and the infant Jesus fled from Herod and went into Egypt. The period of time that the Holy Family was in exile matches the length of the war with Rome in order to connect the "tribulation" of Jesus with Roman oppression, and by implication with the persecution of Christians (cf. Rev 12:17 and Matthew 25:40). It is entirely possible that three and a half years was the actual length of the Holy Family's exile (a fact lost to history, but something John might have known), however the point is that all these circumstances were brought about by the same spirit of evil that is symbolized by the dragon (see below, under Dragon). The connection is made even stronger when one remembers that to persecute Christians is to persecute Christ himself (Acts 9:4).

ONE HUNDRED FORTY-FOUR—When we look at Revelation 7:4–8, we can see that the number one hundred forty-four is really just twelve twelves. One hundred forty-four thousand is one hundred forty-four multitudes, and refers to the number of the final remnant from the people of Israel, twelve multitudes from each of the twelve tribes (see above, under Twelve). This remnant is further described in 14:1–5, where they sing a new song only they could learn. They are marked with the name of the Lamb (Jesus) and of his Father on their foreheads (see below, under Seal/Mark). They follow the Lamb and have remained pure. They are described as unblemished; specifically they are not deceitful. When John says they are "chaste," he makes a point to say that they have not "defiled" themselves with women, implying that the 144,000 are all celibate men. However, this does not mean that a relationship with a woman defiles

---

16. Clement of Alexandria, *Stromateis* 1.21.

a man. To interpret this too literally would imply that even marriage is somehow unholy. Therefore, it seems best to interpret the virginity and spotless purity of the 144,000 in a spiritual sense, meaning that they have remained faithful to God (cf. Rev 3:4), since idolatry in the Old Testament was often described as a spiritual form of adultery (cf. Hosea 1:1–2).

In Revelation 14:4, John says that the 144,000 are "purchased from humanity as firstfruits (dedicated) to God and to the Lamb." The concept of firstfruits signifies something like a down payment or first installment on something owed. In the Old Testament it is an offering of dedication (Exodus 23:16; cf. also Romans 8:23). This implies that the 144,000 are representatives of humanity, like the firstborn of a family or the head of a household. Since the head of a household (normally a man) would stand for the whole household, we must assume that these 144,000 men from the tribes of Israel are simply representatives of the faithful remnant of Israel, and not the whole remnant, as if there were a limit on the number of people who could be saved. In a way, they also represent a new remnant of all humanity who have accepted and followed Jesus. The fact that these are the only ones who could learn the new song may refer to an understanding that the final remnant of Israel is made up of those descendants of the twelve tribes who accepted the new covenant (Jeremiah 31:31–34) and its Messiah, Jesus. Since they have the name of the Lamb on their foreheads, and they follow the Lamb, it is clear that the 144,000 represent those descendants of Israel who are also Christian.

Finally, an angel measures the wall around the New Jerusalem and finds it to be one hundred forty-four cubits high (Rev 21:17). Here again, one hundred forty-four is twelve times twelve, which further solidifies the symbolism of the twelve patriarchs and the twelve apostles as the foundations of the faith.

ONE THOUSAND—When used as a number of people, one thousand refers to a "multitude." It is not an infinite or uncountable number, but it is a lot, and more than one would normally expect to count. When multiplied by another symbolic number, it can be read as that many multitudes. Twelve multitudes from each tribe make up the remnant of the people of Israel (Rev 7:4–8). Seven multitudes are killed in Jerusalem (Rev 11:13).

When applied to a length of time, one thousand years simply means a very long time (cf. Psalm 90:4 and 2 Peter 3:8). The so-called "millennium" is described as one thousand years when Satan is bound and Christ reigns (Rev 20:1–6; see below, under Millennium). We are not looking for exactly one thousand years here, but rather a very long time that is characterized as the reign of Christ.

NUMBERS GREATER THAN ONE THOUSAND—The cubical measurements of the heavenly Jerusalem are said to be twelve thousand "stadia" (Rev 21:16). Some Bible translations attempt to convert this dimension to a unit of measurement we might use, such as "fifteen hundred miles" (or in the case of 21:17, "seventy-two yards"), but this is a mistake, because it loses the symbolic numbers and completely misses the point. Here we have another multiple of twelve, emphasizing that the foundation of the heavenly city rests on the witness of the twelve apostles (Rev 21:14).

The number of heavenly cavalry that bring the three plagues of fire, smoke, and sulfur is sometimes translated "two hundred million" (Rev 9:16). However the Greek here literally says, "two myriads of myriads," meaning something like "thousands upon thousands" (cf. Psalm 68:17–18 and Daniel 7:10). Numbers greater than one thousand generally bring us into the realm of the infinite. The number of the plague-carrying cavalry, though John says he "heard their number," is simply meant to signify an uncountable number.

As we have seen, most numbers have a symbolic meaning apart from their numerical value. In "The Book of Revelation in Plain English" (Appendix A), we will "translate" these numbers into their theological meaning, so that in many cases the number itself will disappear, but will influence the interpretation appropriately. Now we turn our attention to the cast of characters in this apocalyptic zoo we call the book of Revelation.

SYMBOLS AND IMAGES FROM THE OLD TESTAMENT AND EARLY CHRISTIAN LITERATURE

What follows is a survey of all significant symbolic images that appear in the book of Revelation (and a couple that do not!). Each is defined as to its symbolic meaning and its use in Revelation. As I have noted above, the reader must keep in mind that even though John has borrowed these images from other sources (primarily the Old Testament books of Daniel, Ezekiel, and Zechariah), for the most part John uses them to describe different events than his apocalyptic predecessors, and therefore we do not need to interpret them the way we would interpret the same images in the Old Testament. In other words, we do not have to restrict the meaning of symbols in Revelation to match their meaning in Daniel or Ezekiel, and we do not need to incorporate a particular interpretation of Daniel into our interpretation of Revelation.

ANTICHRIST—The term "antichrist" does not appear in the book of Revelation. The word does, however, appear in the Johannine letters (1 John 2:18–22; 4:1–3; 2 John 7). In this context, anyone who denies that Jesus is the Christ and that he has come in the flesh is an antichrist, or operates in the spirit of antichrist. The author of these letters, who may very well be the same John that wrote Revelation (at least in the case of 1 John), says that many antichrists have already come, and (depending on how one interprets 1 John 2:18) at least one more is coming.[17] Most attempts to harmonize this with the book of Revelation will assume that the antichrist is John's "false prophet" (Rev 16:13; 19:20; 20:10; see below, under False Prophet). But this is far from certain. It is more likely the case that the coming antichrist of the Johannine epistle refers to an emperor, and therefore is closer in meaning to the image of the beast in Revelation 13, and the references to "many antichrists" are parallel to the "false teachers" in other New Testament letters (for example, 2 Peter 2:1).[18] Strictly speaking, though, there is no mention of an "antichrist" in the book of Revelation.

ALPHA AND OMEGA—The concept of God as first and last, the beginning and the end of all things, comes from two references in Isaiah (Isaiah 41:4; 44:6; cf. also Exodus 3:13–14). The early Church transferred this designation to Jesus, using the first and last letters of the Greek alphabet: alpha (A) and omega (Ω). In Revelation, both God the Father

17. Some early Christians did associate the antichrist of the Johannine letters with a future Antichrist. See, for example, Irenaeus of Lyons, *Against Heresies* 5.25.1; 5.28.1; and Hippolytus, *On Christ and Antichrist*.

18. In the later letters of the New Testament, the "antichrists" and "false teachers" refer to the early Docetics, sometimes called proto-Gnostics, who did not believe that "Jesus Christ has come in the flesh" (1 John 4:1–3). Note that the author says that "they went out from us," meaning that they had been part of the Christian community (1 John 2:19). In general the Docetics believed that Jesus' physical body was only an illusion, and that the divine *Logos* never really "became flesh" (John 1:14).

and Jesus are referred to as first and last. God the Father is called "the one who is and the one who was and the one who is coming" (Rev 1:4; cf. Exodus 3:14), "the Alpha and the Omega . . . the Almighty" (Rev 1:8), and "the Alpha and the Omega, the beginning and the end" (Rev 21:6). Jesus calls himself "the first and the last" (Rev 1:17; cf. 2:8) and "the Alpha and the Omega, the first and the last, the beginning and the end" (Rev 22:13). Clearly these titles are equivalent, and make the point of Christ's divinity and eternality, as well as his equality with the Father. Jesus, as the eternal divine Word, is co-creator with God the Father (the beginning of all things; cf. John 1:1–3), and Jesus is the agent of the consummation of all things at the end.

ARMAGEDDON—This is a Greek transliteration of the Hebrew place name Har Megiddo, or "Megiddo Hill." It is near the place where the idolatrous queen Jezebel met her death, in the region of Jezreel (2 Kings 9:27–37).[19] Jezebel had convinced her husband, King Ahab, along with many of his subjects, to turn away from God to the worship of idols and the immoral practices of foreign cults (see below, under Jezebel). In Revelation, the place where the great Old Testament idolatress died becomes the place of the great battle between good and evil (Rev 16:16; 19:17–21). This "Battle of Megiddo Hill" is the final defeat of evil, but we should keep in mind that this is a spiritual battle and is not meant to signify an actual war on earth. The word "Armageddon" only occurs once in Revelation, in 16:16, and we should not make too much of the term.

The references to Gog and Magog in Revelation 20:7–9 and the invitation to the birds to eat the flesh of soldiers in 19:17–18 are a link to a decisive victory over the enemies of God in Ezekiel 38–39. The oppressors of God's people would be punished by God because they blasphemed God's name (Ezekiel 39:7). This judgment would be accompanied by a great earthquake with fire and sulfur falling from the sky, signifying divine intervention in the battle (Ezekiel 38:19–22). Mountains would be thrown down and walls would fall, which means that the proud fortified cities of those who oppress God's people would be destroyed. The point is that it is not a human army that defeats the enemy of God—it is God himself who intervenes to defeat evil. And this is precisely John's point in Revelation. Evil will finally be defeated only by divine intervention.

---

19. Megiddo is also the site of several decisive Old Testament battles, and is mentioned in Judges 1:27; 5:19; 2 Kings 23:29; 2 Chronicles 35:22; and Zechariah 12:11.

BABYLON—There is no doubt that "Babylon" is used by John to represent Rome (cf. 1 Peter 5:13). In Revelation 17, Babylon is also referred to as the "great whore," who sits on seven hills (Rev 17:9). Rome has traditionally been known as a city of seven hills, so even the Romans would have understood this reference. In the Old Testament, Babylon was the capital of the empire that captured Jerusalem and destroyed Solomon's temple in 586 BCE (2 Kings 25; cf. 1 Chronicles 9:1 and Psalm 137). Babylon, therefore, represents an oppressive conquering nation that conquered Judea, sacked Jerusalem, and destroyed the temple. The Babylonians then drove the people out of the land into exile. During John's time, Rome was the oppressive conquering empire that had colonized Judea, sacked Jerusalem, and destroyed the rebuilt temple in 70 CE. The Romans would eventually expel all Jews from Jerusalem forty years after Revelation was written, turning Jerusalem into a pagan city.

In Revelation, "Babylon" can stand for the Roman Empire as a whole, or for the city of Rome. Rome, as a city and as an empire, had spread its permissive morality and polytheistic religion to all the nations in its sphere of influence. But more importantly, it had oppressed the people of God, and for these reasons it must fall (Rev 14:8; 18:1–24; cf. Isaiah 21:9 and Jeremiah 51:7–12). Of course the Roman Empire did fall, mainly because it spread itself too far and wide, and could not maintain its own size or keep its far-reaching borders secure, especially when its emperors were focused on maintaining their own power and wealth. The city of Rome was actually "divided" when the emperor Constantine moved the imperial court to his new city of Constantinople but left the senate behind in Rome. The city finally fell to barbarians in 410 CE, an event that the Romans would have thought could never happen to the "great city" (Rev 16:19).

The emperors of Rome are symbolized as "heads" or "horns" (see below, under Head and Horn). In Revelation 17:9–14, we find out that there are five before John's time, one during John's time, one to come who will reign only a short while, and one more who is headed for destruction. After that, there will be ten more. These heads and horns are not meant to be understood as all the Roman emperors, only as the ones who "wage war against the Lamb." In other words, they are the emperors who persecute the Church. This may also include emperors who allowed persecution during their reigns without personally endorsing it, since the Christians in the provinces would hardly know the difference. If one begins with the first emperor to persecute Christians, Nero (reigned 54–68 CE), there are actually six emperors up until the time of Domitian. After Nero, Galba reigned for about a year (68–69 CE), then there were two emperors to come and go within the next year, Otho and Vitellius. Even if we assume that the early Christians would count all of the emperors between Nero and Domitian as persecutors, it is possible that Vitellius's reign was so short that it was either overlooked or it was assumed that he was not in office long enough to persecute the Church.[20] Therefore, if we count Nero as number one, Galba as number two, and Otho as number three, number four would be Vespasian, who led the war against the Jews but left the war in 69 CE to become emperor. Number five would be Vespasian's son Titus, who gave the order to destroy the temple in 70 CE, and who became emperor in 79 CE. The year Titus became emperor, Mt. Vesuvius erupted, destroying the cities of Pompeii and Herculaneum, an event some said was divine payback for Titus's destruction of the temple.

The emperor who lived at the time of John's vision is, of course, Domitian, who reigned from 81 to 96 CE. The seventh emperor is Nerva, and though he released Domitian's exiles, he is not considered a friend of the Church, and his reign was in fact a relatively short one (96–98 CE)/[21] The eighth emperor is described as "the beast who was, but is no longer; he is one of the seven, and also the eighth" (Rev 17:11; see below, under Beast). This is a reference to a belief that Nero's spirit would return in a future emperor. In Domitian's ruthlessness, Christians and non-Christians alike saw a revival of the already proverbial cruelty of Nero. Therefore, the eighth "head" must represent the spirit of Nero that was present in Domitian, and would also return in future revivals of persecution (see below, under Beast). This is John's way of saying that the spirit of Nero (the first persecuting emperor) is alive and well in the present, and will continue into the future with Domitian's successors. John's point would be to emphasize that any emperor who persecutes the Church will be punished by God; he is "headed for destruction" (Rev 17:11).

---

20. Some ancient writers do not count Vitellius as an emperor. See Eusebius of Caesarea, *Ecclesiastical History* 3.5.

21. On the release of exiles after the death of Domitian, see Victorinus of Pettau, *Commentary on the Apocalypse* 10.11. Victorinus, a bishop in what is now Austria, was martyred during the Great Persecution of Diocletian, probably in about 303–4 CE.

The ten emperors to come are best interpreted as the emperors who persecuted the Church from after the time of Revelation until the Great Persecution in the early fourth century, after which the persecution of Christianity ended. After Nerva, the emperors who persecuted or endorsed persecution during their reigns were Trajan[22] (reigned 98–117 CE), Marcus Aurelius[23] (reigned 161–80 CE), Septimius Severus[24] (reigned 193–211 CE), Caracalla[25] (reigned 211–17 CE), Elagabalus (reigned 218–22 CE), Maximinus Thrax[26] (reigned 235–38 CE), Decius, who initiated the first systematic, empire-wide persecution of Christians (reigned 249–51 CE), Valerian (reigned 253–60 CE), Diocletian, who began the Great Persecution at the insistence of his son-in-law (reigned 284–305 CE), and Galerius, the son-in-law (reigned 305–11 CE). We have here ten emperors who would be future persecutors after John's time, and while there may be some debate as to whether all of these emperors were

22. In about 112 CE, Trajan had ordered that his provincial governors should not search out the Christians, but if any should be accused and brought before the local Roman authorities, they should be given the chance to deny the faith and make a sacrifice. If they refused, he ordered that they should be punished, which could mean execution, or possibly a sentence of hard labor in the mines. Pliny, *Epistle* 10.97 (Trajan's reply to Pliny).

23. Marcus Aurelius issued an edict in about 167 CE that required sacrifices in cases where loyalty to the emperor was in question. Possibly based on Trajan's precedent, this associated participation in the imperial cult with loyalty to the state. On the other hand, Tertullian argued that Marcus Aurelius was not anti-Christian. Tertullian, *To Scapula* 4.6. For a (probably inauthentic) attempt to make Marcus Aurelius out to be a friend of the Church, see the letter in Eusebius of Caesarea, *Ecclesiastical History* 4.13.1–7.

24. In about the year 202 CE, Septimius Severus issued an edict against conversion to Christianity. See the Historia Augusta, *Life of Septimius Severus* 17.1. Church leaders and teachers were especially targeted for their evangelization efforts, and were persecuted along with their new converts. This was the occasion for the imprisonment and eventual execution of the famous martyrs Perpetua and Felicitas. See *The Passion of Perpetua and Felicitas*. After the edict of Severus, Christians could be rounded up by Roman soldiers, especially when they could raid a catechetical school and arrest a whole class of converts along with their teacher.

25. In 212 CE, Caracalla made all inhabitants of the empire Roman citizens. This was probably done for purposes of taxation, but it had the added effect that all who lived within the boundaries of the empire were expected to participate in the imperial cult. To celebrate their new citizenship, all provincials were required to go to the temples to sacrifice.

26. According to Eusebius of Caesarea, Maximinus Thrax persecuted the Church because his predecessor had tolerated Christianity. Maximinus ordered that Church leaders should be sought out and put to death. Eusebius of Caesarea, *Ecclesiastical History* 6.28.

personally and actively involved in persecuting the Christian Church, persecution did take place during their reigns, and they are considered by early Christian writers to be enemies of the faith.

BEAST—We first encounter a "beast" in Revelation 11:7, when the beast that comes up from the abyss kills the two witnesses. Coming up from the abyss symbolizes that the beast comes from Satan, but not in a spatial sense. We should not imagine the beast literally coming up from hell. The concept of hell as "below" originally comes from a pre-Christian understanding of the "underworld" and is not to be taken literally. The image should be interpreted in terms of authority (cf. Rev 13:2). The beast is not Satan, but is following Satan and acts on his authority.

In Revelation 13, a beast comes from the sea. As the sea is a place of danger and mystery, this beast is one and the same as the beast that comes from the abyss in chapter 11.[27] The beast has seven heads with blasphemous names, which symbolize the divine titles of emperors who demand that they be worshipped.[28] One head was mortally wounded but has recovered. This is another reference to the emperor Nero, who was assassinated in 68 CE but whose spirit has returned in the person of the then-current emperor, Domitian (Rev 13:3; see also 17:8–13). The beast also has ten horns with ten laurel-wreath crowns (such as the Roman emperors wore). We are told that the ten horns of the beast represent ten future kings, or emperors (Rev 12:3; 13:1–9; 17:12; see above, under Babylon). Therefore the beast represents the Roman imperial rule in general, with the heads and horns representing individual rulers. In 17:1–6, Rome is the great whore who is drunk on the blood of the martyrs and rides the beast, which means that the empire that murders Christians is driven to do so by the emperors, who demand that they be worshipped as gods.

The beast is described as scarlet (meaning bloodthirsty; Rev 17:3), looking something like a leopard, with feet like a bear and a mouth like a lion.[29] Descriptions of the beast in terms of these animals comes from Daniel 7:1–12 (cf. Ezekiel 10:14), and would certainly bring to mind

---

27. Court, *Myth and History*, 99.

28. Ibid., 126.

29. Eusebius of Caesarea understood Paul's reference to the lion in 2 Timothy 4:17 as a reference to Nero. Eusebius of Caesarea, *Ecclesiastical History* 2.22.

Daniel's description of the beasts in his dream.[30] Lions and bears were known to be dangerous predators (1 Samuel 17:37; Proverbs 28:15; Lamentations 3:10; cf. Daniel 7:5 and 1 Peter 5:8). In Daniel's vision, there are four separate beasts that represent four empires: Babylonia, Media, Persia, and Greece. But in John's Revelation, it is one beast that represents the Roman Empire, or more precisely the Roman imperial office. The rule of Rome is a danger to the people of God: it is strong (like a lion, with its teeth), fierce (like a bear, with its claws), and swift to attack (like a leopard). The beast follows the dragon, and the world unknowingly worships the dragon by worshipping the beast (Rev 13:3–4). In other words, those who participate in the imperial cult are actually worshipping Satan. The beast speaks blasphemies against God and makes war on God's people (Rev 13:5–7). The beast, with the dragon and the false prophet, form an unholy trinity of evil resistance to God.[31]

Another beast rises up out of the earth with all of the authority of the first beast (Rev 13:11–12). Coming up out of the earth is a symbol of coming back from the dead. This beast represents a revival of persecution by the emperors, with a renewed emphasis on emperor worship. There would be times under certain emperors when the persecution would subside, and Christians could exist peacefully with their pagan neighbors. But widespread persecution would be revived in the middle of the third century, and again at the beginning of the fourth century, each time more systematic and more brutal than before. Here John is telling his audience that when the persecution seems over, it will come back after a time, so they should not get too comfortable, or too trusting of the imperial state. Therefore, the description of a "second" beast is not really a different beast, but the revival of the "beastliness" of the emperors who will persecute the Church.

In addition to this, the beast that rises up from the earth also represents a revival of the traditional Roman religion, which took place under the emperor Decius in the mid-third century. Decius required all people (including Christians) to sacrifice to the gods as part of his plan to bring back enthusiasm for the traditional Roman cult. Therefore, the beast from the earth also represents the Roman religious system, which was linked to the government by pagan priesthoods. Some of these priest-

---

30. Moyise, *Old Testament in the Book of Revelation*, 52–53. See also Fekkes, *Isaiah and Prophetic Traditions*, 85.

31. Court, *Myth and History*, 123.

hoods were part of the job descriptions of many government offices. In this way, the Roman religious system supported the worship of emperors, because it was the pagan priests who declared the emperors to be gods.

This beast that comes up from the earth is described as having two horns, like a lamb, but speaking like a dragon (from Daniel 8:3, where the two horns represent two threatening empires, Media and Persia). In other words, this beast is a false lamb, imitating the Lamb of God by desiring worship, but speaking on behalf of Satan. The reference to fire in Revelation 13:13 may be a reference to Nero and the fire of 64 CE, again pointing to the idea that present and future emperors who persecute the Church are like Nero come back from the dead. The beast causes those who refuse the sacrifices to be killed, and requires those who submit to emperor worship to carry a sign of loyalty on them in order to buy and sell (Rev 13:15–18; see above, under Six, and below, under Seal/Mark). This is exactly what the later emperors did. The sign was not literally a mark on the hand or forehead, but was a document, called a *libellus*, certifying that a person had made the required pagan sacrifices. The emperor Decius, in 250 CE, issued an edict requiring everyone in the empire to make a pagan sacrifice and acquire a *libellus*. At the time, Decius' edict was interpreted by some in the Church as a fulfillment of the warnings of Revelation.[32] However, the message of Revelation is that anyone who makes the sacrifices will face judgment (14:9–12).

Therefore, on one level, the image of the beast represents the Roman imperial office in general, and we should not try to make too much of the fact that there appear to be two beasts in chapter 13. If there is a particular identification with the revived beast as a second beast, it could be a reference to the emperors Nero and Domitian, or to the emperors Diocletian and Galerius, who were actually co-rulers (two horns) during the Great Persecution that began in 303 CE. Note, however, that in chapter 19 only one beast is mentioned. The beast there represents both beasts of chapter 13 together, the whole institution of the Roman imperial state, including those individual emperors who persecuted the Church and who will face God's judgment. On another level, the "second" beast is related to the false prophet mentioned later in Revelation, and in that context it represents the Roman religious system (see below, under False Prophet), which operated on the authority of the emperors,

---

32. Cyprian of Carthage, *On the Lapsed* 10. See also Eusebius of Caesarea, *Ecclesiastical History* 6.7, 41.

and the two horns represent the two-pronged attack against the Church: pagan religion and imperial government.

Bowl—The angels who pour out the bowls containing God's wrath are said to come from the heavenly temple (Rev 15:5–8), and it is the earthly sanctuary that gives us the image of the bowl. Exodus 25:29 and 37:16 describe the golden bowls that were used to pour out offerings to God (see also Numbers 4:7; 1 Chronicles 28:17; and Zechariah 14:20). The seven priestly angels are given seven bowls of God's judgment to pour out, which are seven plagues (Rev 15:1—16:12). These judgments would remind the reader of the plagues of Egypt during the time of Moses (Exodus 7–11), but here there are seven, and even though that is numerically fewer than the ten plagues of Egypt, it is more complete—more final—because there are seven of them. The first bowl delivers sores on those who worshipped the beast, like the sixth plague of Egypt (Exodus 9:8–12). The second and third bowls turn water to blood, like the first plague of Egypt (Exodus 7:14–24). The fourth and fifth bowls are the two extremes of a burning sun and a darkened sun over the kingdom of the beast, like the ninth plague of Egypt (Exodus 10:21–29). The sixth bowl is poured out and the Euphrates dries up, opening the way for the kings of the east to invade. This is a reversal of the crossing of the Red Sea (Exodus 14). In fact, it was the invading barbarians from the east and the threat of invasion from the Persian Empire that contributed to the downfall of Rome.

With the seventh bowl, the heavenly voice declares, "It is accomplished," or more appropriately, "It is complete" (Rev 16:17). Babylon falls in an earthquake and hailstorm (like the seventh plague of Egypt; Exodus 9:13–35). Here it is clear that "Babylon" refers not just to the city of Rome, but to the whole empire, since John tells us that the "cities of the nations" fell (Rev 16:19).

In a very different image, in John's vision of heavenly worship, the twenty-four elders hold golden bowls filled with incense, "which are the prayers of the holy ones" (Rev 5:8). The prayers of God's people are described in the Old Testament as being like the smoke of incense rising up to God (Psalm 141:2). The saints in heaven are intercessors, presenting the prayers of the people to God as an offering (Rev 8:3–5; cf. Hebrews 12:1).

The key to connecting the different symbols of the bowl (judgment and prayers) is found in Revelation 6:9–11. The prayers of the holy ones which are carried in golden bowls (Rev 5:8) are prayers for relief from the suffering of persecution. In Revelation 6:9–10, even those already martyred ask the question of the psalmist, "How long, oh Lord . . . ?" (Psalms 6:3–4 and 13:1–3). John's readers would have this prayer constantly on their lips. How long would it be before God judges the persecutors? They are told to be patient and wait a little while longer (Rev 6:11). The answer to the bowls full of the prayers of holy ones and martyrs comes from the bowls of God's judgment, poured out as plagues on the persecutors.

BRIDE—In Revelation, the bride is the Church, or more specifically, the Christians who will be united with Christ at his return, and live with him in the Realm of God (Rev 19:7–8; 21:9; 22:17). The concept of the Church as the bride of Christ is based on Jesus' own teaching in the parables of the wedding banquet and the ten bridesmaids (Matthew 22:1–14; 25:1–13). Jesus clearly understood himself to be the groom in this analogy, and John the Baptist considered himself the best man (Matthew 9:14–15; John 3:29). The concept was then picked up by the apostle Paul in the Letter to the Ephesians 5:25–32. There he draws a parallel between the marriage of a husband and wife, and the relationship of Christ to the Church.

CREATURES—In John's vision of heavenly worship, he describes four "living creatures," or more accurately, "living beings" (Rev 4:6–8). The pattern for these heavenly beings comes from the Old Testament images of cherubs (Ezekiel chapters 1 and 10) and seraphs (Isaiah chapter 6). Such creatures were understood to be guardians of temples in the ancient world (cf. Genesis 3:24; 1 Samuel 4:4; 2 Samuel 6:2; 2 Kings 19:15), and in Revelation they inhabit the heavenly temple of God. In Ezekiel, the cherubs are described as moving wherever the Spirit moves, and the sound of their wings is like the voice of God. It is therefore clear that these heavenly beings are images that describe attributes of God, and the presence of these beings represent the very presence and the glory of God himself.[33] Ezekiel's cherubs have four faces, while John's living

33. The fact that they are described as "creatures" in many Bibles does not present a problem for their interpretation as attributes of God. The Greek text does not include a word for "creatures," and literally means something like "living things," or even "living ones." This is why it seems best to translate the single Greek word as "living

beings are four in number, with one "face" each. The fact that there are four of these beings relates to the spatial wholeness of the earth (the four directions of the compass; see above, under Four), meaning that God's reign covers the whole earth. They are covered with eyes, which represent God's omniscience, and they have three pair of wings each, which represent God's omnipresence (see above, under Six).[34]

Though the living beings of Revelation are described in animal terms, they are not related to the beasts of Daniel 7. The living beings of Revelation surround the throne of God and give him honor and glory, therefore the interpretation of their animal attributes will differ from those of the beast, even though some of the same animals are used in their descriptions. The first creature is like a lion, which symbolizes the royal sovereignty of God, as well as God's unlimited power. The second creature is like a calf, which is an animal of both service and sacrifice, reminding the reader that God is good (he provides for our needs, like the cow gives milk) and that he is worthy of worship. The third creature has a face like a human, which means that God is rational and wise, as well as relational and communicative, as opposed to some abstract concept of the divine. The fourth creature is like an eagle in flight. The eagle was thought to be the bird that can fly the highest and the farthest, and so represents the unlimited extent of God's reign and providence (see below, under Eagle).[35] Put another way, the lion represents God's omnipotence, the calf represents God's omnibenevolence, the human face represents God's omniscience, and the eagle represents God's omnipresence.

CROWN—There are two kinds of crowns in the book of Revelation. The first is the laurel-wreath crown of the Roman emperors, sometimes translated "diadem." This crown appears in 12:3 and 13:1, where it refers to the rulers of the Roman Empire, and also in 19:12, where it refers to the "many crowns" that Jesus wears. In general, this kind of

---

beings." Therefore, it does not imply anything about their existence as created versus uncreated.

34. Irenaeus had said that the cherubim and seraphim are metaphors for God's word and wisdom. See Irenaeus of Lyons of Lyons, *Proof of the Apostolic Preaching* 10.

35. Irenaeus of Lyons connected the four faces to the four canonical Gospels. The lion represents John (which presents Christ's royalty), the calf represents Luke (which presents Christ's role as priest), the man represents Matthew (which presents Christ's true humanity), and the eagle represents Mark (which presents Christ's role as prophet). Irenaeus of Lyons, *Against Heresies* 3.11.8.

crown represents royalty, and the fact that Jesus wears many crowns shows that his sovereignty is far above that of the earthly rulers: he is the King of kings.

Most occurrences of the image of a crown, however, refer to the victory crown of the saints, especially the martyrs (Rev 2:10; 3:11; 4:4; 4:10, cf. also Rev 6:9; 15:2; and 21:7). Jesus himself wears the victory crown of martyrdom in 6:2 and 14:14. Mary wears a crown of twelve stars in 12:1, and while this is not a crown of martyrdom, it is a crown of victory, signifying her triumph over the dragon (Rev 12:13–17; cf. Genesis 3:15), with the stars symbolizing her ancestry as the descendant of the patriarchs (see above, under Twelve, and below, under Stars and Woman).

In Revelation 9:7, the locusts also wear crowns of gold, which means that they will be victorious in battle. This use of "crown" may also be descriptive, in the sense that it relates to the heads of the "locusts." If this is the case, then verse 7 could be translated, "on their heads they wore something like crowns of gold," which would be an attempt to describe the gleaming helmets of the Roman legions (see below, under Locust).

DISASTERS—In the Old Testament, God's judgment sometimes comes in the form of what would seem like natural disasters (for example, the flood, in Genesis 7–8; the judgment on Sodom and Gomorrah in Genesis 19:1–29; and the plagues in Egypt in Exodus 7–11). In Revelation, the judgment of God is accompanied by earthquakes, thunder, and what appear to be volcanic eruptions and even an eclipse of the sun. When the sixth seal is opened, there is a great earthquake, and the sky becomes dark (Rev 6:12–17). The seven trumpets of judgment begin with an earthquake and burning coals falling from the sky (Rev 8:5). When the first six trumpets are blown, a portion (one-third) of the land, sea, fresh waters, sky, and air are all destroyed in turn, which leads up to the plagues of fire, smoke, and sulfur (Rev 8:7—9:2; 9:13–21). This description sounds very much like a volcano, with a burning mountain hurled into the sea, hail mixed with fire and blood falling from the sky and poison, smoke, and darkness (cf. Joel 2). Of course the eruption of Mt. Vesuvius in August of 79 CE would have been relatively fresh in the minds of Romans, and was considered by many to be God's judgment on the Roman Empire for the destruction of Jerusalem and the temple nine years before. In the year 79, Titus, the Roman general who ordered the attack on the temple, became Rome's newest emperor.

Jerusalem is damaged by an earthquake (Rev 11:13), but unlike the plagues, those not killed do seem to repent, or at least they turn to God in gratitude for having been spared. The destruction of Jerusalem is described as the second "woe" (Rev 11:14; cf. Isaiah 24). The description of this event includes hail (cf. Exodus 9:18–25; Isaiah 28:2; and Ezekiel 38:22), thunder, and lightening, and the temple in heaven is opened, reminiscent of Jesus' crucifixion, when the curtain in the temple was torn in two (Rev 11:19; cf. Matthew 27:51–53).

Rome also suffers an earthquake, called the worst ever (Rev 16:18–21; cf. Jeremiah 51:24–26). This earthquake is also accompanied by hail, thunder, and lightening. The image of the earthquake as a manifestation of God's judgment comes from Old Testament texts like Isaiah 24:17–21. According to Isaiah, the devastation takes place on the earth so that the people are scattered, "the lay person like the priest, the servant like his master, the maid like her mistress, the buyer like the seller, the lender like the borrower, the creditor like the debtor" (Isaiah 24:1–2). In other words, the devastation causes the breakdown of society, which makes everyone equal (cf. the tower of Babel; Genesis 11:1–9). As Jesus said, the last shall be first, therefore the "end of the world" should be understood as the end of the world's reversal of the Kingdom's values.

The mistake that is often made when reading the book of Revelation is to try to connect specific natural disasters in history or in the current headlines with the images of devastation described in Revelation. But with the possible exception of a reference to the eruption of Vesuvius, the images of disaster are there to emphasize God's intervention in human events, and warn of God's punishment; they are certainly not there to give us clues to the timing of God's plan. One must always keep in mind the words of Jesus in Matthew 24:4–8: "Be careful not to let anyone lead you astray ... you will hear about wars and rumors of wars; do not be alarmed, for it must happen, but it is not yet the end. For nation will rise up against nation, and kingdom against kingdom, and there will be famines and earthquakes in many places. But all these things are just the beginning of the labor pains."

DRAGON—The image of the dragon originally comes from Leviathan, the sea monster of Isaiah 27:1 and Psalm 74:13–14 (see also Job 41). In the Old Testament, the sea monster represents Egypt (cf. Isaiah 51:9–10) or Babylon (cf. Jeremiah 51:34). A dragon is also mentioned in Daniel

14, the story of Bel and the Dragon. The monster stands for the nations that held God's people captive. In Revelation, however, the dragon is the devil himself, who is the force behind the oppression and persecutions of the Roman Empire. John tells his readers that the dragon is "that old serpent, who is called the devil and Satan" (Rev 12:9, a reference to Genesis 3:1). The dragon is red, which symbolizes death (blood), and in this context, martyrdom. It has seven heads with seven laurel-wreath crowns, and ten horns, which represent the emperors of Rome who persecuted the Church (see above, under Babylon). The point is that the kings of the earth (i.e., the Roman emperors) are under the dragon's control. The dragon wants to kill the woman's child, which is a reference to the attempt on Jesus' life when he was an infant (Rev 12; cf. Matthew 2:16–18). When the dragon is unsuccessful in killing the infant Jesus, he wages war against the rest of the woman's "children" (Rev 12:17), which refers to the persecution of Jesus' followers.

After the persecution, the dragon will be bound for a thousand years (Rev 20:2–3; see above, under One Thousand). The words ". . . so that he would not deceive the nations any longer" are reminiscent of Isaiah 14:12–15, which is an allusion to the fall from heaven of the angel Lucifer (Rev 8:10; 9:1; cf. also Daniel 8:10). After the thousand years is ended, the dragon will be released and will attempt to deceive the nations again, only to be thrown into a lake of fire and sulfur for eternity (Rev 20:7–10). The reference to Gog and Magog (Rev 20:8) brings the reader's mind back to Ezekiel 38–39 (see above, under Beast).

EAGLE—In addition to being the image used for one of the four living beings (see above, under Creatures), the eagle is a herald of God's judgment in Revelation 8:13 and a symbol of God's protection in 12:14. In 8:13, an eagle flies overhead crying out, "Woe, woe, woe" (the three "woes" or tragedies) because of the coming judgment (Jeremiah 49:22). The eagle is used because it is a swift predator (Jeremiah 48:40; cf. Deuteronomy 28:49), and God's judgment is understood to be swift and deadly. The eagle's ability to fly high and land anywhere describes God's far-reaching influence (from Ezekiel 17).[36]

In Revelation 12, the woman is given the wings of the eagle to escape from the dragon. This refers to the Holy Family's escape from Herod, with an allusion to Exodus 19:4, where the rescue of God's people

---

36. Cf. also 2 Baruch 77.20–26.

from Egypt is described as God bearing them on eagle's wings. John may also have in mind Deuteronomy 32:11, where God is compared to an eagle who protects its young, and also Isaiah 40:31 and Psalm 103:1–5. In general, the eagle is a symbol of God's sovereignty and providence.

FALSE PROPHET—A false prophet is mentioned in Revelation 16:13; 19:20; and 20:10. The false prophet, the beast, and the dragon are the threefold source of evil. Most interpreters associate the false prophet with the revived beast in 13:11–18, based on the connection of 13:13–18 with 19:20 (see above, under Beast). The false prophet of Revelation causes people to accept the mark of the beast, and so the false prophet works hand in hand with the beast. Like the false prophets of the Old Testament, who worked for the kings and told them what they wanted to hear, the false prophet represents the professionally religious of the time, specifically the cults and priesthoods of the traditional Roman religions. The official Roman priests were the ones who declared emperors to be gods and encouraged people to worship them. They also helped to enforce the imperial edicts to make pagan sacrifices, partly out of fear that if Christianity grew, their priesthood would be threatened (cf. Matthew 7:15; 24:24; Mark 13:22; 2 Peter 2:1; 1 John 4:1).[37] Thus the unholy trinity of dragon, beast, and false prophet represent Satan, the Roman emperors, and the pagan priesthoods, respectively.

FIRE—Fire can represent at least three different ideas in biblical thought. In the Old Testament, fire represents the presence and glory of God, or it can represent destruction (often as a form of judgment), or it can represent a refining or purifying agent. John uses all three meanings in Revelation, so we should not expect fire always to represent the same thing every time it is mentioned. The most important thing to remember, however, is that the image of fire in the book of Revelation almost never indicates literal fire, with only a few possible exceptions. When John says an angel has legs that are like pillars of fire (Rev 10:1), it does not mean that they are being burned; it means we should think of the pillars of fire in Exodus 13:21–22, which went before the people of God and guided them on their way (see also Isaiah 4:5). And when John says Jesus had eyes like flaming fire, we should think of the similar vision in Daniel 10:6. There the flaming eyes refer to the glory of the presence of

---

37. Beale, *Book of Revelation*, 831.

the Lord (cf. Ezekiel 1:27–28). Therefore Jesus is understood as divine, the very presence of God. No doubt John also had in mind Jesus' ability to see into people's hearts (Romans 8:27).

A few passages in Revelation refer to fire as destruction, though it is still not always meant to be interpreted literally. Fire symbolizes God's defeat of his enemies (Rev 11:5; 20:9), and the false prophet uses fire to impress the people he deceives (Rev 13:13, in an attempt to copy Elijah; 1 Kings 18:38; and 2 Kings 1:10–12; cf. Luke 9:54). Babylon would be consumed by fire (Rev 17:16; 18:8; cf. Genesis 19:24–28). In fact, Rome was consumed by fire, or at least major part of it was, in 64 CE. This was the fire rumored to have been started on Nero's orders, and was the occasion for Nero's persecution of Christians in Rome. When the city was invaded in 410 CE, it was burned again. In these cases where fire is mentioned, the fire may indicate literal burning, but the bigger picture is that the image of fire represents destruction, and sometimes judgment.

The rest of the passages in Revelation refer to fire as a purifying agent. Since gold was purified by melting it over a fire, allowing the impurities to rise to the top so that they could be skimmed off, the image of fire became a metaphor for trials that, though painful, would serve to strengthen one's character (cf. 1 Peter 1:7). In the letter to Laodicea, Jesus advises the Christians there to buy from him "gold refined by fire" (Rev 3:18). This is an admonition for the Christians of Laodicea to purify themselves from their particular sins. Also, in John's vision of the martyrs in chapter 15, they are standing on a sea of glass and fire (Rev 15:2). The fire in this case refers to the fact that the martyrs were purified by their martyrdom.

However, most of the references to fire as purification are directly related to judgment. The time for judgment is announced by the angel in charge of the fire of the heavenly altar (Rev 14:18). John tells his readers that anyone who worships the beast (i.e., commits apostasy and idolatry by participating in emperor worship) will be tormented in burning sulfur for eternity (Rev 14:10–11). They have committed the unforgivable sin of denying Christ, making the beast their god (Matthew 12:31–32). This knowledge is supposed to strengthen the resolve of Christians, so that they do not give in to the persecution and deny Christ to save their lives (Rev 14:12). On the surface, one might assume that references to the lake of fire are more about destruction than purification. However, if the ones thrown into the lake of fire are said to be there for eternity, then it is clear that they are not destroyed. They continue to exist for eternity, though apparently suffering an endless purification process.

The dragon, the beast, and the false prophet will be thrown into the lake of fire and sulfur for eternity (Rev 19:20; 20:10; cf. Daniel 7:11, where the beast of Daniel's vision is thrown into the fire). All those whose names are not found in the book of life will also be thrown into the lake of fire,[38] along with death itself (Rev 20:14–15; cf. Isaiah 25:8 and 1 Corinthians 15:26). The lake of fire is called the "second death," which refers to spiritual death (as opposed to physical death, which would be the "first death"; see below, under Second Death). Spiritual death is separation from God ("outside" of the heavenly city; Revelation 22:15; cf. Matthew 22:13). However, we must keep in mind that that the lake of fire is not a place, nor does it contain literal fire. The lake of fire is a state of existence, a banishment from the presence of God, in which those who are unfit to enter God's presence are purified in a crucible of regret, which is often characterized by "weeping and gnashing of teeth" (Matthew 22:13).[39]

HEADS—Heads represent rulers, kings, or in the case of Rome, emperors (Rev 12:3; 13:1; see above, under Babylon). In Revelation, the seven heads also represent the seven hills of the city of Rome, connecting the emperors with their capital city (Rev 17:9). Like many of the images in

38. John does not say that this last group of people are to be tormented for eternity. If we are to take the absence of the mention of *eternal* torment in Revelation 20:15 as significant, then it is possible that there is hope for this group. They are thrown into the lake of fire, but perhaps not for eternity, and if we assume that fire in this verse means purification, we may hold out hope that this group will be purified at some point. If this is true, then we have two distinct groups who are thrown into the lake of fire. The first group consists of those who commit the unforgivable sin and deny Christ, those who demand worship of themselves (the emperors), and the devil and his demons, who are all thrown into the lake of fire for eternity. Apparently, they cannot ever be purified, but they will spend eternity in the process of purification. The second group would consist of those whose names are not in the book of life, who are thrown into the lake of fire, but perhaps not for eternity. They would presumably then be purified and eventually allowed to enter the presence of God in the eternal city. If this interpretation is correct, it could also be an early reference to a belief in purgatory (cf. 1 Corinthians 3:15).

39. Other texts which use the image of fire to refer to purification, or speak of a process of purification, include Matthew 3:11; Luke 3:16; 1 Corinthians 3:12–15; 1 Peter 1:7; Proverbs 17:3; Isaiah 1:25; Daniel 12:10; Zechariah 13:9; and Malachi 3:2–3, as well as Wisdom 3:1–9 and Sirach 2:5. If the reader wishes to see in my speculation here a connection to the concept of purgatory, so be it, as long as we agree to remember that outside of the created realm time itself has no meaning.

Revelation, the use of "heads" to represent rulers comes mostly from the vision of Daniel (for example, Daniel 7:6).

HORNS—Horns represent power, since an animal's power to fight and defend itself is in its horns. The Lamb is described as having seven horns (complete power and authority; Rev 5:6), and the dragon and the beast each have ten horns, representing ten future emperors (Rev 12:3; 13:1; 17:12). The image of horns symbolizing kings or emperors also comes from Daniel's vision (cf. Daniel 7–8).

The beast from the earth has "two horns like a lamb" (cf. Daniel 8:3) "but he spoke like a dragon" (Rev 13:11). This beast is imitating the Lamb, but it is a false lamb. The beast demands worship, but it is really only a puppet of the dragon.

The expression "the four horns of the golden altar" in Revelation 9:13 does not refer to horns as images of power but is an ornamental feature of the altar as described in Exodus 30:1–10. In this case, John is simply describing the place of the presence of God, using terms from the Old Testament Holy of Holies.

HORSES—The horse is a symbol of war, as opposed to the donkey, which is a symbol of service. In the Gospels, Jesus rides a donkey into Jerusalem, signifying that he comes to serve humanity, not to start a war (Matthew 21:1–11). But in the book of Revelation, Jesus rides a white horse (symbolizing victory; Revelation 6:2; 19:11–19). He wears a cloak dipped in blood (cf. Isaiah 63:3) and the martyr's crown, and is described as victorious, referencing his defeat of death at his resurrection. In his earthly life and ministry, Jesus was a pacifist. He refused to be the kind of Messiah that many expected, which was a warrior who would lead a rebellion against the occupying forces of Rome. Now the resurrected Christ rides a warhorse, but the war is a spiritual one. He carries a bow, which symbolizes judgment (Jeremiah 51:11). The spiritual warfare goes on behind the scenes, but has consequences on the physical plane, since the other three horsemen represent trouble on earth (cf. Matthew 10:34–39). Though the first of the four horsemen is Jesus, who brings salvation; the last three horses bring suffering. Their riders are not meant to be interpreted as particular individuals, but the colors of the horses are significant. The four colored horses combine the images of four judgments from Ezekiel and four horses as the four compass directions from Zechariah. In Zechariah 1:8 and 6:1–3, there are horses of four different colors: white, red, black, and "spotted," which are clearly the inspiration for John's four horses.

The second horse is red, which is the color of bloodshed (Rev 6:4; cf. 12:3). This horse, its rider carrying a sword, represents actual warfare on the earth. The third horse is black, which represents poverty or famine (Rev 6:5). The rider of the black horse carries a scale, which symbolizes shortage and rationing (cf. Ezekiel 4:16–17). The fourth horse is pale, which is the color of sickness, and which represents plague (Rev 6:8). This horse carries Death personified, and Hades. Not to be interpreted as two riders, this is a Hebrew-style parallelism in which both terms refer to the same thing. Hades does not mean "hell" as we might think of it, but it refers to the underworld, the place of the dead (good or bad) in ancient mythology. The point is that the horse represents death, specifically death by plague. The key to understanding all this is in Revelation 6:8, where John switches from talking about the fourth horse to talking about all of the last three horses. He says, ". . . and authority over one-fourth of the earth was given to them, to kill with the sword, and with famine and with death, even by the beasts of the earth." This refers to the last three horses: red (death caused by war), black (death caused by famine), and pale (death caused by disease).[40] All of this is a reference to the war of 66–70 CE, which ended with the siege of Jerusalem, which would have included rationing and epidemic.

When the four angels who wait at the four corners of the earth are released to kill a third of humanity (Rev 9:16–19; see above, under One-third), they lead an infinite number of cavalry, whose horses have heads like lions and tails like snakes (which means they are deadly). These horses breathe fire, smoke, and sulfur, which refer to three plagues (Rev 9:18–20). The colors of the horses' breastplates refer to the same plagues: fire (red), smoke (blue) and sulfur (yellow). These plagues are part of God's judgment against those who worship idols and commit the sins that go hand in hand with pagan sacrifice (Rev 9:20–21).

---

40. The phrase "even by the beasts of the earth" is often translated "and by the wild beasts of the earth." However, the Greek wording is almost identical to Revelation 13:11, the beast who comes up from the earth. The meaning of the phrase could be that the plague is ultimately caused by the beast of chapter 13, or it could simply mean that animals often carry disease and transmit plague, and the same conditions that would cause famine and plague would also cause animals to become rabid and turn on people.

Jezebel—Jezebel was the wife of King Ahab, and in the Old Testament she is the epitome of those who worship other gods. She convinced not only the king, but many of his subjects, to turn to foreign worship, which may have included ritual prostitution (1 Kings 16:31, 21:25; 2 Kings 9:7; see also 1 Kings 18–19). In the prophetic tradition of the Old Testament, turning away from God to the worship of other deities was described as a kind of spiritual adultery. Therefore, in Revelation the name Jezebel stands for idolatry in general, as it is personified in the Roman Empire.

In addition, there was someone in the church of Thyatira who claimed to be a prophetess but led Christians into idolatrous practices (Rev 2:20–21; see also 2:14). She apparently taught something called the "mysteries of Satan" (literally, the "deep things of Satan"; Rev 2:24, probably a reference to early Gnosticism). Jesus says he will put her children to death (Rev 2:23). Since this clearly does not mean her literal offspring, it probably means that Christ will put an end to the fruits of her labors. John calls this woman a Jezebel.

Rome is also a kind of Jezebel, described as the "great whore" who is drunk on the blood of the martyrs (Rev 17:1–6). She wears purple (signifying royalty) and red (signifying bloodshed), and she is adorned with gold and precious gems (signifying wealth). She is, "The great Babylon, the mother of whores and of the atrocities of the earth," a city of many peoples that will be abandoned by its own emperors (Rev 17:5, 15–18). In fact, Rome was abandoned by its leaders, who put more effort into securing their own power and expanding the borders of the empire than taking care of their people. This eventually led to the downfall of the empire. In a way, the city of Rome itself was abandoned when the emperor Constantine moved the capital to Byzantium (renaming it Constantinople, after himself), opening the way for the barbarian invasions into the western empire.

The place where the original Jezebel met her death is near the site of several significant Old Testament battles. In Hebrew it is called Har Megiddo, or "Megiddo Hill." In Greek is it Armageddon (see above). This place symbolizes the defeat of evil by the forces of good and is used by John in Revelation to describe the final defeat of evil. In 17:16, John says that the fate of the whore is that the beast will "eat her flesh," which is an allusion to the fate of Jezebel in 2 Kings 9:27–37.

LAMB—The Lamb is, of course, the sacrificial animal, especially in the context of the Exodus. The Lamb is the sacrifice that saves the people of Israel from slavery in Egypt, and Jesus is the new Lamb of God who saves all who call him their Savior by the sacrifice of his blood (Rev 5:9; 7:10, 14–17; 12:11; 21:27). He saves the people by taking away the sin of the world (John 1:29; cf. Isaiah 53:4–9). In Revelation, the Lamb who was slain is Jesus, the Crucified One, who is described as having seven horns (complete power, or omnipotence) and seven eyes (complete sight, or omniscience). The Lamb is the only one worthy to open the scroll that begins the unfolding of the final stages of God's plan (Rev 5:6–14). At this point, all of heaven worships the Lamb by singing a new song, in other words, a song of the new covenant.

Reminiscent of the parable of the wedding feast in Matthew 22, in which the king represents God the Father and the prince, or groom, represents Jesus, John presents the return of Christ as the Lamb's wedding day (Rev 19:7). The Lamb's bride is the Church, or more precisely the people of Christ who will live with him in the heavenly Jerusalem (Rev 19:7; cf. John 3:29).

LAMPSTAND—The image of the lampstand comes from the book of Exodus and the description of the sanctuary (Exodus 25:31–40; 37:17–24; cf. also Zechariah 4:2). The lampstand held seven lamps and is commonly known as the menorah. In Revelation, each of the seven lampstands represents one of the seven churches (Rev 1:12, 20; 2:1). Like the stars, though, the lampstands also refer to the leaders of the seven churches (see Rev 11:4, where the two witnesses are called lampstands). The lampstand is the source of light, and since Christians are supposed to be the light of the world, the lampstand represents the source of the light of the gospel: the Church and its evangelists (Matthew 5:14–16). But to the leader of the church of Ephesus, Jesus warns that the lampstand could be taken away (Rev 2:5). The implication is that if a leader falls away from devotion to Christ, his ministry will suffer, or even that he could be removed from his position of leadership.

LOCUSTS—These small, grasshopper-like insects have the ability to swarm and destroy whole fields of crops, causing famine and disease. A swarm of locusts was the eighth plague that God sent to Egypt to convince the Pharaoh to let the Hebrew people go (Exodus 10:1–20). In Revelation, John sees a swarm of locusts that look like horses ready for

battle and sound like rumbling chariots (Rev 9:3–11; cf. Jeremiah 47:3;
Joel 2:4–5). But these locusts have not come to eat the crops. They have
come to torment the people who are not marked with the seal of God
(see below, under Seal/Mark). They have human faces, which means that
John is talking about a human army, not actual locusts. They have hair
like a woman, which may refer to strength (cf. Judges 16:17–19), or it
may refer to the plumes on a Roman helmet. They have gold crowns
on their heads, possibly signifying that they march on the orders of a
king, or perhaps to represent the gleaming bronze helmets of the Roman
legions, but more importantly, this means that they will be victorious
in their campaign. They have lion's teeth (cf. Joel 1:6), signifying the
destructive power of an invading nation; scorpion tails, signifying that
they are deadly; and iron breastplates, signifying that they are invincible.
Though these "locusts" are deadly, they are prevented from killing for five
months, which was the approximate duration of the siege of Jerusalem
by the Roman legions. The legions could torment the inhabitants of
Jerusalem, but could not kill them until they breached the walls at the
end of the (approximately) five-month period. Their orders come from
the emperor, but ultimately they are of the devil (Rev 9:11), who is described as the "angel of the abyss."

MILLENNIUM—The so-called "millennium" is a period of one thousand
years, during which Satan is said to be "bound," or in some way restricted
(Rev 20:1–3; see above, under One thousand). Since biblical numbers are
more symbolic than mathematic, it is not to be understood as exactly
one thousand years but as a relatively long time (a "multitude" of years)
that is characterized by the reign of Christ (Rev 20:4). This is roughly
equivalent to what is called the "age of the Church," during which time
Christianity would become the dominant religion in the known world,
and would shape Western civilization. The Church age actually begins
with the Pentecost event in about 33 CE, but according to Revelation the
"millennium" begins with the triumph of Christianity over its persecutors, and the end of persecution. In the millennium, Christ reigns over
the earth through the Church.

MOUTH—The mouth is generally understood to be the source of one's
words or teaching. In Revelation, a double-edged sword comes from
the mouth of Jesus (Rev 1:16; cf. Isaiah 49:2). This concept is more
clearly spelled out in Hebrews 4:12, which says, "For the word of God is

living and effective and sharper than any double-edged sword, and cutting even to the extent of the separation of life and spirit, of joints and marrow, and is able to judge the thoughts and motivations of one's heart." Interestingly, the Greek word for "double-edged" literally means "two-mouthed." The point is that the words of Jesus are able to discern good from evil and divide truth from falsehood (see below, under Sword).

In the Old Testament, the prophets were ones who spoke for God, and so were considered God's "mouthpieces." In Revelation, the two witnesses function in this way. A protecting fire comes from the mouths of the two witnesses (Rev 11:5; cf. 2 Kings 1:10–12). This means that the "fire" of their preaching destroys the arguments of their adversaries.

Demons come from the mouths of the dragon, the beast, and the false prophet (Rev 16:13). In this case, it is the words of the emperors and the Roman priests that are described as demonic, ultimately coming from Satan.

Finally, fire, smoke, and sulfur come out of the mouths of the horses released from the four corners of the earth (Rev 9:16–19; see above, under Horses). Obviously, this would not refer to any teaching of the "horses," but it may have something to do with God's will being "spoken," or enacted, in the plagues that the horses bring.

RAPTURE—The concept of the rapture does not come from the book of Revelation. The idea actually comes from Paul's words of comfort to the Thessalonian Christians in 1 Thessalonians 4:17. There Paul reassures them that their loved ones who died before the return of Christ will not miss out on the Kingdom of God. In that context, he says that those who are alive at the return of Christ will be "caught up" to meet Christ in the air. This sense of being "caught up" has given rise to the popular notion of the rapture. However, the belief in a future rapture in which believers are "taken" from the earth and non-believers are "left behind" requires inserting the text from 1 Thessalonians into the book of Revelation, where it simply does not belong. It is true that the apostle Paul was telling the Thessalonians that those Christians who happened to be alive when Christ returns would "ascend," something like the way Christ did (cf. Acts 1:9). But Paul does not say that the world as we know it will go on without us, leaving the unbelievers behind scratching their heads. Paul's point was that the Christians who had died would *not* be left behind.[41]

41. Jewett, *Jesus against the Rapture*, 139.

Those who believe in a rapture in the popular sense also refer to Jesus' words in Matthew 24:40–41. In those verses, Jesus refers to a time of tribulation before the end of the age when two people will be working together; one will be taken and one will be left. However, Jesus does not say that the one taken will be taken into the Kingdom, leaving the other one on earth to figure out what happened. In fact, he does not say that it is better to be taken at all. One must read Matthew 24:40–41 in the context of Jesus' words on tribulation in the rest of chapter 24. The verses immediately preceding 40–41 are a reference to the flood, in which those who are "taken away" are the ones who were unbelieving and who were killed by the flood. According to Jesus, "the return of the Son of Man will also be like this" (Matthew 24:37–39). Jesus' words about being "taken" are not a reference to the ascension of believers but refer instead to the unfortunate ones who suffer the disasters that precede the end of the age. This means that it is actually better to be left than to be taken. Therefore, the concept of the rapture, as popularly conceived, especially in end-times fiction, is simply not biblical.

On the other hand, there are references in the book of Revelation to being taken away "in the Spirit." This is a kind of temporary rapture experienced only by John for the purpose of the heavenly vision (Rev 1:10; 4:2; cf. 2 Corinthians 12:2–4).

Finally, Jesus is described as the one who was "caught up" to God (Rev 12:5). This is the only use of the "rapture" terminology in the book of Revelation, and is simply a reference to Jesus' ascension.

RIGHT HAND—The right hand symbolizes power and authority and comes from the image of God's anointed sitting "at his right hand" (Psalm 110:1; Mark 16:19; cf. Matthew 22:41–46; 26:64; Acts 7:55–56). In Revelation, Jesus holds the seven stars in his right hand (Rev 1:16; 2:1). The seven stars are said to be the angels of the seven churches (Rev 1:20; see below, under Stars). Since the Greek word *angelos* simply means a messenger, this refers to the evangelists, or leaders, of the seven churches. That he holds them in his right hand means that he is guiding and protecting them with his power. Jesus also touched John with his right hand (Rev 1:17), which reassures John of Jesus' protection, and that he will survive his mystical experience.

In chapter 13, the reader is told that people will be forced to have the image of the beast marked on their right hand or forehead. The image of the beast is further defined as the beast's name or number (Rev 13:16–18; see above, under Six, and below, under Seal/Mark). Here the right hand is related to authority but has more to do with identification and servanthood (cf. Matthew 25:33). The mark of the beast is the opposite of the seal or mark of God on a person and is a blasphemous version of the Jewish practice of the phylactery (see below, under Seal/Mark). Those who accept the mark of the beast are giving their right hands (or their heads) to him, which means they submit to the power and authority of the beast.

SEAL/MARK—In the Old Testament, the people of God were given the words of the *Shema*: "Hear, oh Israel, Yahweh is our God, Yahweh is one. And you must love Yahweh your God with all of your heart and with all of your soul and with all of your strength" (Deuteronomy 6:4–7). They were told to keep these words in their hearts, teach them to their children, and talk about them every day. As a sign, or seal, of their commitment to these words (which Jesus would call the greatest commandment), the people were instructed, "Tie them as a sign on your hand, and wear them as a headband on your forehead, and write them on the doorframes of your house and on your gates" (Deuteronomy 6:8–9; 11:18; see also Exodus 13:9–16; Ezekiel 9:4; cf. Matthew 23:5). This gave rise to the traditions of the phylactery (leather pouches containing Scripture bound around the arm) and the mezuzah (small boxes containing Scripture on the door frame of a home).

In Revelation, the people who represent the remnant of Israel are marked with the seal of God on their foreheads (Rev 7:3–4). This seal performs the same function as the phylactery—to show the wearer's commitment to God—but this seal is the name of the Lamb as well as the name of the Lamb's Father (Rev 14:1; 22:4). In the early Church, baptism was described as a seal, replacing circumcision as the rite that marked one as belonging to God (2 Corinthians 1:20–22).[42] Irenaeus called baptism in the name of the Father, Son and Holy Spirit the "three articles of our seal."[43] Therefore, to be sealed, or marked, for God is to be baptized.

---

42. Melito of Sardis, *Homily on the Passover* 16–17; Irenaeus of Lyons, *Proof of the Apostolic Preaching* 3 (cf. 24); Clement of Alexandria, *Exhortation to the Greeks* 11; Cyprian of Carthage, *Epistle* 72.9; Eusebius of Caesarea, *Ecclesiastical History* 6.5. See also Martin, *Worship in the Early Church*, 37.

43. Irenaeus of Lyons, *Proof of the Apostolic Preaching* 100.

The opposite of the seal of God is the mark of the beast, the name or number of the beast on the right hand or forehead (Rev 13:16–18). John says that at a certain time, no one would be able to buy or sell without the mark of the beast (Rev 13:17). In fact, during the persecution of the emperor Decius (reigned 249–51 CE), papers were issued to those who complied with the imperial edict to participate in pagan sacrifice. The document was called a *libellus*, Latin for "booklet," and was used to identify one as someone loyal to the emperor. It was expected that everyone in Roman society have one, and failure to comply with the edict made one guilty of treason, a capital offense.[44] Of course, to escape death a person had only to make a pagan sacrifice in honor of the emperor and obtain a *libellus* with a Roman official's signature, or mark, on it. Known Christians would also often be required to take an oath and renounce Christ. The enforcement was not uniform across the empire, but the official requirement was to carry papers with the name of the emperor (signed by a Roman official on his behalf). When we think of this as the polar opposite of a phylactery, it is easy to imagine that the "mark of the beast" describes an element of John's vision that would be fulfilled in the *libellus* of Decius.[45] Anyone who did not comply and make the sacrifice could be martyred (Rev 20:4), but John warns that those who did make the sacrifice and take the mark of the beast would face judgment (Rev 14:9–12). Therefore, the "mark of the beast" is not literally a mark, such as a brand or tattoo, but it is a sign of commitment and dedication to the emperor. If one were to make a sacrifice to comply with the demands of the emperor, that would be tantamount to proclaiming one's allegiance to the emperor over against Christ.

In John's vision, there is a book closed up with seven seals (meaning completely sealed up; Rev 5:1; cf. Ezekiel 2:9–3:3). The book is actually a scroll, and in this sense the seals refer, not to a mark of commitment, but to the wax seals that would have closed the scroll to keep its contents from being revealed. The image of the sealed document is a familiar one in the ancient world. Contracts, deeds, and wills would be written on parchment, rolled or folded and then sealed (see, for example, Jeremiah

---

44. Cyprian of Carthage, *On the Lapsed* 5.6.

45. Dionysius of Alexandria saw in Decius' edict the fulfillment of Matthew 24:24, and understood Decius to be a "false Christ." Eusebius of Caesarea, *Ecclesiastical History* 4.41.9–13 (cf. 6.7, 41). Hippolytus also predicted that the mark of the beast would be connected to the requirement of pagan sacrifice. See Hippolytus, *On Christ and Antichrist* 49. See also Cyprian of Carthage, *On the Lapsed* 10.

32:9–12). In apocalyptic prophecy, the sealing of a document often signifies that the end of God's plan is currently hidden from the people, only to be revealed at the right time (cf. Daniel 8:26; 12:9).[46] The fact that the document is sealed means that it is not to be opened until the right time, and only by the right person. Only the Lamb, Jesus, is worthy to open the seals, which begin the events of judgment (Rev 6:1). John wept when he thought no one would be able to open the book, but the Lamb was found to be worthy, and the seven seals are opened one at a time, revealing the unfolding of God's plan. The point is that the revealing of God's plan for judgment can only be set in motion by Jesus himself. It takes divine intervention in the person of Christ.

SECOND DEATH—The first death is every human being's physical death. The second death is spiritual death, or eternal separation from God. The apostle Paul wrote that spiritual death is the natural result of sin (Romans 6:23). A life of continually separating oneself from God by intentional sin will naturally lead to a continuation of that separation in the afterlife (cf. Matthew 22:13).

In Revelation, the second death is described as a lake of fire (Rev 20:14; 21:8). This is not to be understood as a place, or as literal fire, but as a state of separation from God, with the image of fire representing purification (see above, under Fire). It is to be the eternal state of the devil and his demons, the emperors who persecuted the Church, and those who denied Christ to save their lives (Rev 19:20; 20:10). It is also the state of those whose names are not written in the Lamb's book of life (Rev 20:15). Death itself will also be thrown into the lake of fire (Rev 20:14). This reference to death is the first death, or physical death, which will not exist in the eternal city of God. Those who persevere and do not deny their faith, especially if they are martyred, will not experience the second death (Rev 2:11; 20:6).

SON OF MAN—The image of the Son of Man coming from the clouds originally comes from the book of Daniel, in his apocalyptic vision (Daniel 7:13–14). There the Son of Man is a messianic figure who comes from God and reigns over an eternal kingdom (cf. 2 Samuel 7:12–13). Though the phrase "son of man" originally meant simply "human being" (Psalm 8:4; Ezekiel 2:1), in later prophecy it became a messianic title,

46. Beasley-Murray, *Revelation*, 120–21.

referring to one who was like a human but somehow more than human.[47] The Christian Church understood Jesus as the awaited Son of Man, in large part because Jesus referred to himself as the Son of Man (for example, Matthew 16:13–17; 25:31; and Luke 5:24), interpreted in light of Isaiah's "suffering servant" (Isaiah 53).

There is no doubt that in the book of Revelation, the Son of Man is Jesus, risen and glorified. John quotes Daniel 7:13 in Revelation 1:7, a reference to the coming of the Son of Man "from the clouds," which means that he comes from heaven, that is, from God. The message of the vision that was given to John comes from Jesus, who is found to be in the midst of the lampstands, meaning that he is in the churches (Rev 1:12–13). He wears a gold sash, symbolizing his (divine) royalty, and his hair is white, symbolizing wisdom and moral purity (Daniel 7:9; cf. Isaiah 1:18). His face shone, which means he comes from the presence of God, and is reminiscent of Moses coming down from the mountain (Exodus 34:30–35). He wears the martyr's victory crown (Rev 14:14; cf. 1:18). He has flaming eyes, which represent the glory of God, and which see into the hearts of people (Romans 8:27; cf. Luke 16:15), and his feet are like polished brass, refined in a furnace, signifying that faith in Christ is on a sure and firm foundation (Rev 1:14–16; 2:18). Overall, the elements of this description comes from the visions recorded in Ezekiel 1:26–28 and Daniel 10:5–6. In these apocalyptic visions, the context implies that the one described comes and radiates with the presence of God, and the shining of the metal reflects the glory of God (Ezekiel 1:28).

Stars—In the Old Testament, the star is a symbol for a king (Numbers 24:17; cf. Matthew 2:1–2). However, in the book of Revelation, stars primarily refer to the leaders of churches (Rev 1:16, 20). John is told that the seven stars held in Jesus' right hand are the angels of the seven churches of Asia Minor. Since the word "angel" means *messenger*, this refers to the evangelists, or leaders, of the seven churches.

The "woman" (Mary, see below, under Woman) wears a crown of twelve stars (Rev 12:1), which represent the twelve patriarchs, or the leaders of the twelve tribes of Israel, which is Mary's ancestry.

Later in chapter 12, the stars are angels who followed Satan in his rebellion against God and became demons. Satan is called a fallen star in

---

47. For an example of the extent of the evolution of the term "Son of Man," see 2 Esdras 13:1–5, 25–40.

Revelation 9:1 (cf. Isaiah 14:12; Daniel 8:10). According to pre-Christian tradition, the devil was once an angel called Lucifer, who rejected God's authority and convinced other angels to join in his rebellion. The Isaiah passage above uses the image of a falling star to describe Lucifer being expelled from heaven, banished from the presence of God, only to come to earth to deceive the nations. John picks up this image in 9:1, including the idea that the fallen angel (the devil, Satan) is now the ruler of the underworld.

SWORD—The sword is the word of God (Hebrews 4:12; cf. Isaiah 27:1). The fact that it is a double-edged sword refers to its power to cut in both directions, symbolizing the ultimate power to divide, or discern, between what is true and what is false. It comes from Jesus' mouth (Rev 1:16; 2:12, 16; 19:15, 21; cf. Isaiah 49:2; see above, under Mouth). Even though the sword is said to kill in chapter 19, it would be wrong to interpret this as literal warfare. The battle is a spiritual one and takes place in the spiritual realm (note that this part of the vision begins with "and I saw heaven opened up . . ."; Rev 19:11).

On one occasion, the sword symbolizes warfare in general, and does not represent the word of God. The rider of the red horse carries a sword, which means that the red horse symbolizes war, or more specifically death caused by war (Rev 6:4).

TREE OF LIFE—References to paradise and the tree of life are obviously linked back to the creation accounts in Genesis and to the garden of Eden (Genesis 2:8–14). It is interesting to note that when John mentions the four corners of the earth (a reference to the whole world) he does not place the "corners" of the earth at the far reaches of the known world, but the four "corners" converge at the river Euphrates—the place described by the book of Genesis as the location of the garden of Eden (Rev 9:14). When the Kingdom of God is fully revealed, creation comes full circle to the originally intended state of paradise. Receiving the right to eat from the tree of life (Rev 2:7; 22:14) means living in the presence of God (Rev 21:3; cf. Genesis 3:8). This right is reserved for those who remain pure in their worship of God, some even to the point of martyrdom. However, this right will be withheld from anyone who takes anything away from the words of the book of Revelation (Rev 22:19).

The description of the heavenly city is taken from Old Testament promises of peace and security for Israel (Rev 7:15–16; 21:1-7; 22:1–5;

cf. Isaiah 11:6–9). The heavenly Jerusalem, the tree of life, and the new heaven and new earth all refer to the same concept: the return to paradise in the presence of God, at the revealing of the Kingdom of God.

TRIBULATION—Tribulation refers to times of great distress, trouble, or oppression. John opens the book of Revelation with a reference to the current state of distress in the persecution that the Church was enduring (Rev 1:9). Just as in the Old Testament, when in times of great oppression the prophets promised that someday God would intervene, the prophecy of Revelation balances the warnings of persecution and judgment with the promise of divine intervention in the form of the return of Christ (cf. Acts 14:22).

The concept of tribulation comes primarily from the prophet Daniel, who warned of the trouble to come under Greek rulers, which would eventually lead to the desecration of the temple under Antiochus IV in the second century BCE. In Daniel, tribulation means war, oppression and religious persecution. John is comparing the persecution of his own time, as well as the coming persecutions of the third and fourth centuries, to what had happened before. As the Greeks had done, so the Romans had done after them, including the desecration of the temple in Jerusalem. But the tribulation under the Romans did not end with the destruction of the temple. John warns that more tribulation is coming in the form of persecution against the Church. In this context, John also clearly intends to make a connection with Jesus' apocalyptic preaching in the Gospels, especially Matthew 23–25 (cf. Rev 16:15).

TRUMPET—In general, the trumpet is a herald of divine intervention. The image of the trumpet is used in the Old Testament, most famously in the battle of Jericho—a battle fought, not by a human army, but by God on behalf of his people. When the trumpets were sounded, the walls of Jericho fell (Joshua 6). In Revelation, the trumpets announce the coming of God's judgment, the fulfillment of the promised "day of the Lord" (Rev 8–9; cf. Isaiah 27:13; Ezekiel 33:1–7; Joel 2:1–17; Zephaniah 1:15–18; 1 Thessalonians 4:16).[48]

WHITE ROBE OR CLEAN GARMENTS—The color white symbolizes purity, so that a white or clean robe means the wearer has "put on" purity, not in a superficial way, but in the sense of having taken it up as a lifestyle

---

48. Beasley-Murray, *Revelation*, 153–54.

(Rev 3:18; 19:8; cf. Matthew 22:11–13; Romans 13:14). This is connected to the Old Testament laws of ritual purity, which determined whether one was acceptable to enter into the presence of God in worship. In the heavenly kingdom, only those who are purified can approach God and remain in his presence. The surest way one can be purified is to die as a martyr.

On the other hand, those who wear soiled garments are considered unworthy to walk with Jesus. Walking with Jesus has a two-fold meaning, including following and identifying with Christ in life, and eternal life with him in the Kingdom (cf. Rev 3:4; 22:14). It is clear that John's most pressing concern is that his readers stay pure in that they do not give in to the pressure to participate in idolatrous practices. Those who persevere are worthy (Rev 7:9–14; 22:14), especially the martyrs (Rev 3:5; 6:11; cf. 15:2).

The seven angels from the heavenly tabernacle who pour out the seven bowls of God's anger are described as wearing white linen, which was the dress of the priesthood (Exodus 28:39), as are the heavenly cavalry who follow Jesus into battle on white horses (Rev 15:6; 19:14). The purity of the angelic army is assumed, and yet here it emphasizes that God's judgment is pure and true and righteous. Finally, the bride of the Lamb is wearing white, signifying the purity that Christ imparts to the Church (Rev 19:7–8; cf. Ephesians 5:25–32).

WITNESSES—In Revelation 11, two witnesses emerge, who are described as lampstands and olive trees (Rev 11:3–14). The fact that they are referred to as lampstands means that they are evangelists, or "lights" in the world (see above, under Lampstand; cf. Matthew 5:14–16). It is well attested in the New Testament that, according to the law, at least two witnesses were required to bring a conviction, especially of a capital offense (Numbers 35:30; Deuteronomy 17:6; 19:15; Matthew 18:16; John 8:17; 2 Corinthians 13:1; 1 Timothy 5:19; Hebrews 10:28). These two witnesses would testify, not only to the gospel, but also to the guilt of their killers. The image of a pair of olive trees associated with lampstands comes from Zechariah 4:1–14. In that context, the connection with olive trees (the source of oil for lamps and for anointing) means that the two men in question are anointed by God.[49]

---

49. In Zechariah, the two olive trees represent a priest named Joshua and Zerubbabel, the prince, who would initiate the rebuilding of Jerusalem.

In Revelation, the two witnesses speak with God's authority for three and a half years (twelve hundred sixty days). This time period connects their prophetic mission to the time of the events leading up to the fall of Jerusalem, because this was the approximate length of the war with Rome, which ended with the destruction of Jerusalem in 70 CE.[50]

The two witnesses speak words from God that destroy the arguments of their enemies (Rev 11:5, an allusion to Elijah's ability to bring down fire from heaven to silence the false prophets; 1 Kings 18:22–39; cf. also 2 Kings 1:9–14 and Jeremiah 5:14). They also have the power to stop the rain (Rev 11:6, an allusion to a drought caused by Elijah; 1 Kings 17:1; cf. Luke 4:25 and James 5:17) and to turn water into blood, as well as bring about other plagues (an obvious connection to Moses; Exodus 7:20). It is not clear who the witnesses are, but what is clear is that John wants the reader to think of them in terms that remind one of Old Testament figures whom God had chosen to do his work, such as Moses and Elijah. However, they are not characters from the Old Testament, because Revelation 11:8 describes the city where the two witnesses died as the place, "where their Lord was crucified." Therefore, these are Christian evangelists, followers of Jesus who lived in the first century and who might have been killed by the Roman legions during the fall of Jerusalem (Rev 11:7). There is also a tradition in the early Church that associated one of the two martyrs with James, the overseer of the Jerusalem church, though he probably died in the year 62.[51] It is possible that John's original audience knew exactly who these two apostles were, and that John is memorializing them in this way. On the other hand, the two could simply represent all Christians who were martyred in Jerusalem, with a reference to the tradition that two witnesses were required for a testimony. The exact identification of the two witnesses is not as important as the fact that they were martyred in Jerusalem during the time of the war with Rome, and were remembered by the Church as heroes of the faith.

The witnesses could not be harmed, except by the beast, who finally killed them. Their bodies lay in the streets of Jerusalem for three and

---

50. Court, *Myth and History*, 86–87.

51. Eusebius of Caesarea knew of a tradition that associated the death of the witnesses with the martyrdom of James, the first bishop of Rome. According to Eusebius (following a Christian addition to the writings of Josephus), Jerusalem fell because its people killed James. See Eusebius of Caesarea, *Ecclesiastical History* 2.23.

a half days (symbolizing that their deaths do not mean the end of the story; see above, under Three and one-half), after which time they are raised to heaven. Their resurrection and ascension added to the confusion in the city at the time Jerusalem fell (cf. Matthew 27:51–53). It is important to note that, although it was not yet a technical term when John wrote revelation, the Greek word for "witness" is *martyr*.

WOMAN—The woman who gives birth to the Son is of course Mary, the Mother of Jesus (Rev 12:1–17).[52] She is described as clothed with the sun, with the moon under her feet, and wearing a crown of twelve stars (see above, under Stars). This glorious description of Mary shows the adoration already given to her, especially from the one to whom she was entrusted by her Son (John 19:26–27). The woman is pursued by the dragon into the desert, an obvious reference to the Holy Family's flight into Egypt to avoid Herod's attempt to kill Jesus (Matthew 2:13–23). The exile in Egypt is said to last twelve hundred sixty days, which connects the persecution of Jesus' family by Herod to the oppression by Rome, and therefore to the persecution of the Church by the Roman emperors. The persecution of the Church (called "the rest of her offspring," cf. John 19:26–27) then becomes a reenactment of the persecution of Jesus (Rev 12:17; cf. also Matthew 25:45–46; Acts 9:4). It is the dragon's attempt to hurt Jesus by hurting those whom he loves.

It is clear that the vast majority of the symbols and images in the book of Revelation come from the Old Testament. However, this does not contradict John's statement that the message of Revelation came to him in an ecstatic vision (Rev 1:9–19). Whatever he saw in his mystical experience would no doubt defy explanation in everyday language. Add to this the fact that John's own understanding of the meaning of the vision would be shaped by the tradition of apocalyptic prophecy, and it is no wonder that John would have to turn to his best source for descriptive themes,

52. Many commentators interpret the woman as Israel. It is true that in Jewish thought Israel is sometimes represented as a woman in labor (cf. Isaiah 26:17–18), and it could be said that Israel "brought forth" Jesus. For this view, see Beasley-Murray, *Revelation*, 194. However, to interpret the woman in Revelation as Israel rather than Mary complicates the interpretation of "the rest of her offspring" (Rev 12:17) and amounts to trading the obvious meaning for a more obscure one. More important, the description of Mary in glorious terms makes more sense than such a description used for Israel, especially when one assumes that the author of Revelation is John, Jesus' beloved disciple and the one to whom he entrusted his mother.

the prophetic books of the Hebrew Bible. The realization that John's images can be understood by referring back to the Old Testament does not imply a denial of the inspiration of the book of Revelation—rather it is evidence for the unity of Scripture and the providence of God.

SUMMARY

The list below is a quick reference guide to the numbers and major symbols found in the book of Revelation. Each number or symbol is listed in glossary form, with an abridged definition of the term as it applies to its use in Revelation. For more detailed definitions, refer back to the relevant chapter section above.

- **666**—The emperor Domitian, and secondarily his successors who persecuted the Church

- **144,000**—Representative of those from the descendants of Israel who are faithful to God and have identified themselves with Christ

- **Alpha and Omega**—God the Father, and/or Jesus the Son, as the source and culmination of creation

- **Armageddon**—The final defeat of evil, a spiritual "battle," not actual warfare

- **Babylon**—Rome; either the city of Rome or the whole Roman Empire

- **Beast**—The Roman imperial office, specifically the emperors who persecute the Church

- **Black horse**—Death caused by famine, associated with the siege of Jerusalem in 70 CE

- **Bowl**—An offering poured out: both prayers for judgment and the judgment itself

- **Bride of the Lamb**—The Church, Christians of all time who will be united with Christ at his return

- **Calf**—Symbolic of the fact that God is worthy of worship, also the divine attribute of omnibenevolence

- **Crown**—Usually signifies victory and/or martyrdom, sometimes royalty

- **Disasters**—Divine intervention, judgment
- **Dragon**—Satan, the devil
- **Eagle**—Symbolic of God's sovereignty and providence, the divine attribute of omnipresence
- **False prophet**—The Roman religious system, connected to the imperial government, supporting the worship of emperors
- **Fire**—Usually refers to purification, sometimes the glory and presence of God, or destruction and/or judgment
- **First woe**—The siege of Jerusalem in 70 CE, described as lasting five months
- **Five**—The flesh, in Revelation physical suffering during the siege of Jerusalem
- **Four**—Wholeness, specifically spatial wholeness or geometric symmetry
- **Four corners of the earth**—The whole world
- **Four living beings**—The omnipotence, omnipresence, omniscience, and omnibenevolence of God
- **Head**—A ruler or king, specifically heads in Revelation represent Roman emperors
- **Horn**—Power, usually the reigns of particular Roman emperors
- **Human face**—When referring to God, the attribute of omniscience
- **Jezebel the whore**—The city of Rome
- **Lamb**—Jesus Christ, crucified, risen, and glorified
- **Lampstand**—The churches and their evangelists, the lights of the world
- **Lion**—When referring to God, the attribute of omnipotence
- **Locusts**—The Roman legions that besieged and sacked Jerusalem in 70 CE
- **Mark of the beast**—A document of loyalty to the emperor, proving pagan sacrifice

- **Millennium**—The age of the Church since its legalization
- **Mouth**—The words or teaching of the one whose mouth it is
- **New song**—The song of the new covenant, including worship of Jesus, the Lamb
- **One-third**—A divinely appointed portion, less than half
- **Pale horse**—Death caused by disease and/or plague, associated with the siege of Jerusalem in 70 CE
- **Red horse**—Death caused by war, specifically the Jewish-Roman war of 66–70 CE, and the siege of Jerusalem
- **Right hand**—Power and authority, identification with and/or submission to an authority
- **Second death**—Separation from God, banishment from God's presence in the afterlife
- **Second woe**—The destruction of Jerusalem in 70 CE
- **Seven**—Completion, fulfillment
- **Seven heads**—Seven Roman emperors up to the time of Domitian, when Revelation was written
- **Seven stars**—The leaders of the churches of Asia Minor
- **Silence for half an hour**—The calm before the storm
- **Six**—Imperfection, evil, sin
- **Son of Man**—Jesus Christ, who comes from God, and reflects God's glory
- **Star**—Ruler or leader, used of leaders of churches, Old Testament patriarchs, and sometimes angels
- **Sword**—The word of God, which divides truth from falsehood
- **Ten horns**—Ten Roman emperors who persecute the Church after the time of Domitian
- **Three**—Perfection
- **Three and one-half**—Incomplete, waiting for resolution (half of seven)
- **Tree of life**—Paradise, eternal life in the presence of God

- **Tribulation**—Oppression and/or persecution, especially under a foreign power

- **Trumpet**—Announces the coming of divine intervention

- **Twenty-four elders**—The twelve patriarchs of Israel and the twelve apostles of Jesus

- **Two witnesses**—Christian evangelists who were martyred in Jerusalem

- **White horse**—Victory, specifically in spiritual warfare; the risen and glorified Christ rides the white horse

- **White robe**—A lifestyle of purity, or a purified state due to martyrdom

- **Woman**—Mary, the mother of Jesus

4

The Structure of the Book of Revelation

INTRODUCTION

NOW THAT WE HAVE come to some conclusions about the interpretations of the symbolic images in the book of Revelation, we can begin to put the building blocks together to form a literary unit. However, the nature of the genre of apocalyptic prophecy is such that these building blocks will not necessarily fit together in a neat or orderly way. In particular, we may have to let go of some of our assumptions about the function of narrative in the book of Revelation. The first thing we have to keep in the front of our minds is that the book of Revelation was not written with a chronological storyline as its goal. The goal of Revelation, as we have seen, is encouragement for the Christians of John's own time. Therefore the events described in Revelation are not presented as a story, they are presented thematically, as each theme relates to and revolves around the present situation of the original audience. In other words, past and future revolve around the present, so that the individual elements in the text do not fall in line in chronological order.

In addition, significant sections of the text are John's description of his visions of the spiritual realm, and therefore these images are completely outside of earthly time. In fact, since time itself is a part of the created order (cf. Genesis 1:3, 14–18), visions of heavenly worship, such as are found in Revelation chapters 4, 12 and 15, belong to the realm of eternity, and so they cannot easily be placed into a timeline. Similarly, other sections of the text take place irrespective of the continuum of time, either because they are ongoing or because they are independent of events happening in creation. Sometimes these visions out of time function as transition points in the text, marking the movement from one set of events to another. Other times, they simply blur the lines between past, present, and future.

Even apparent grammatical clues do not help solve the problem. For example, in 11:7–8 the death of the two witnesses is described in the future tense, but in verse 11 their resurrection is described in the past tense. In addition, sometimes the prophetic present is used to convey a warning or promise of the future, for example, "Babylon is fallen" (Rev 14:8). Therefore the tenses of verbs will not tell us whether an event is in John's past, present, or future, since in the context of the vision, the verb tenses bounce back and forth without regard for chronological perspective. Even phrases such as "then I saw . . ." only imply the order in which John saw the images, not the order of their parallels in history or their fulfillment in the future. One final thing to remember is that the chapter and verse divisions were added to the text long after it was written, so we cannot rely on them for guidance in understanding the structure of the book.

In 1:19, Jesus tells John, "Therefore, write down the things that you have seen, and the things that are, and the things that will happen after these things." *The things that you have seen* does not refer to what John has seen so far in the vision, nor does it refer to everything John will see in his vision. It refers specifically to those parts of the vision that relate to events that have already been witnessed in the first decades of the Church, before the time John wrote Revelation. Therefore, *the things that you have seen* are visions of events in John's past that he will describe with prophetic symbols from the Old Testament, but which he and his readers know have already happened. The phrase is similar to "what we have seen" in 1 John 1:1–4 (cf. also John 19:35; 21:24). *The things that are* of course refers to the current events of John's time, including the persecution by the Roman government. *The things that will happen after these things* refers to events in John's future, and includes both warning and promise.

The problem is that, as we have already discovered, the book as it is given to us does not place the events of John's past, present, and future in chronological order. Instead, the vision alternates back and forth. We find painful memories of the past juxtaposed with warnings for the future, present suffering paired with future promise, along with frequent flashbacks to significant past events that might bring hope for the present. Sometimes certain themes are repeated, and the same event is described separately in more than one place. For example, 6:3–8 and 9:1–12 refer to the same event, the war with Rome and the siege of Jerusalem. Other times, John initially gives only a bird's-eye view of something, then comes back to it later to describe it in more detail. For example, the beast is introduced in chapters 12 and 13, but the reader waits until chapter 17 to receive more detailed information about it.[1]

Thus our usual ideas about time and narrative cannot serve as our guide through Revelation. We need another way to put the pieces together. Our method, therefore, is to rely on the interpretations of the symbols and images in the text to dictate where they actually belong in the timeline. In the last chapter, we determined what each symbol stands for. That understanding will allow us to discover the chronological order of the narrative. But before we can do that, we need to understand the tension between the present and future aspects of what Jesus called the Kingdom of God.

THE DUAL NATURE OF THE KINGDOM OF GOD

Because the book of Revelation is about the *revealing* of the Kingdom of God, the structure of the book is related to the early Church's understanding of the Kingdom, which of course was based on Jesus' own teaching. In the prophecy of Jesus' Bible (our Old Testament), the promised future intervention of God was known as the "Day of the Lord," when God would break into human history to judge oppressors and to vindicate the oppressed. However, when Jesus came, his preaching on the Kingdom, and in fact his very presence, effectively split this idea of the Day of the Lord into two separate realities. Jesus proclaimed that the Day of the Lord is here, because the Lord has come to his people (Matthew 4:17, cf. John 1:11–14). However, the Day of the Lord is not yet *fully* here, because judgment is postponed until God's message of reconciliation can be brought to the world and people are given a chance to turn to God. Jesus said there would be a time between his first coming and his return during which the gospel would be preached to the world (Matthew 24:14, cf. 25:5).

According to Jesus, the Kingdom is "among you"[2] (Luke 17:21), but it is concealed, like a mustard seed buried in the ground, or some yeast

1. Court, *Myth and History*, 123.

2. The Greek phrase in Luke 17:21 can also be translated "within you," however, since Jesus was speaking to the Pharisees, the best translation should be "among you,"

folded into dough (Matthew 13:31–33). But Jesus also promised that someday the Kingdom would be revealed, like the mustard bush that flowers or the dough that rises. Jesus' advent two thousand years ago brought the Kingdom of God to humanity, but as an unseen reality. This is why accepting the Kingdom requires faith (cf. Hebrews 11:1). Jesus' promise was that he would return someday to bring the Kingdom in its fully revealed sense. That is what the book of Revelation is all about, and it is written to those who live in the age of the Church, the time between the coming of the Kingdom concealed within us and its full revelation. Therefore *the things that you have seen* includes as its focal point a reference to the birth, death, and resurrection of Christ, when the seed of the Kingdom was planted. *The things that will happen after these things* leads up to and culminates in the *revelation* of the Kingdom of God in its fully realized form.

But the book of Revelation is not intended to give us advance warning when the present age is coming to an end. In Luke's Gospel, Jesus says, "The Kingdom of God is not coming in a way that one could watch for it" (17:20).[3] Rather, the return of Christ will take humanity by surprise, and yet it will be something that no one can miss (Luke 17:24–30; Matthew 24:42–44). In the meantime, we live in the time in between Jesus' first advent and his second coming. As he taught in his parables, we live in a time of waiting, between planting and harvest (Matthew 13:24–30, 36–43; and Mark 4:26–29), between engagement and wedding (Matthew 22:1–14; 25:1–13).

Keeping this in mind will prevent two common misuses of the book of Revelation. On one hand, we cannot use John's visions to try to predict the future or anticipate some supposed time of tribulation right before the end of the age. On the other hand, we also cannot be so proud as to assume that the revelation of the Kingdom is the result of the successful efforts of humans to create a peaceful existence on earth, as if the Kingdom that Jesus preached was only a metaphor for the activity of Christians in the world. The book of Revelation teaches neither a doomsday view of the future nor a utopian view. The truth is somewhere in between those extreme options. Both the book of Revelation,

---

with the sense of "in your midst." This would then be a reference to Jesus himself, as well as the new movement that he was starting. For Christians and for the Church, it is appropriate to say that the Kingdom is "within you" (cf. 1 Corinthians 6:19).

3. The Greek literally says, "The Kingdom of God is not coming with watching."

as well as Jesus' words in the Gospels, tell us that the Kingdom will not be gradually built by the good works of people, but must come as the result of divine intervention and the return of Christ to claim his bride, the Church. In fact, John's visions indicate that the world (i.e., human society) is actually getting worse, which argues against a kind of "city of God built by humanity" view of the Kingdom.[4] One only needs to look at the events of the twentieth century to acknowledge that humanity is not progressing toward utopia. The revealed Kingdom of God is not a heaven on earth, but eternal life in the Realm of God, the re-created paradise that was originally intended, in the new heaven and new earth where God's people will live in his presence.

  Therefore the progression of the visions of Revelation do not reflect a linear timeline, but something more like a downward spiral. The only thing that can stop the downward spiral of human history and vindicate Christ and his Church is divine intervention, when the Kingdom of God will be fully and finally revealed. The structure of the book of Revelation holds in tension the dual nature of the Kingdom of God. It is both here now and not here yet. It is both the Reign of God and the Realm of God. In the present age followers of Christ do their best to live according to the Reign of God, by living by the values of the Kingdom (which will always be counter-cultural in the world) and by extending God's sphere of influence through the Church. But in eternity, God's people will live in the Realm of God, in the new and heavenly Jerusalem. In the present age of the Church, the Kingdom is in us. In the age to come, we will be in the Kingdom.

THE NARRATIVE OF THE VISIONS

The major sections of Revelation include the letters to seven churches; the seals broken open; the trumpets blown; the dragon, the beast, and the false prophet; the bowls and the whore of Babylon; the final defeat of evil; and the return of Christ for the wedding of the Lamb. Only a few sections describe specifically the revelation of the Kingdom. The rest of the book is really about the Church age, the time between Jesus' advent and his return.

  As the visions of Revelation unfold, there are three main series of judgments, described as (1) seals (or more precisely, the *opening* of wax

---

4. Beasley-Muray, *Revelation*, 44.

seals which close up a document), (2) trumpets (the blowing of trumpets announcing God's judgments), and (3) bowls (such as were used in temple worship—the judgments are poured out of the bowls like offerings were poured out on the altar of the temple). These judgments are presented so that each series reveals the next. Therefore, the seventh seal reveals the trumpets, the seventh trumpet reveals the bowls, and the seventh bowl reveals the Kingdom. Before the seventh in each series, there is a pause, an interlude that foreshadows what is to come or reveals some aspect of the spiritual warfare that goes on behind the scenes of history. Finally, the seventh in each series is accompanied by an earthquake, which points to divine intervention, and possibly also connects it to the crucifixion of Christ (Matthew 27:51). But even this progression of three series of seven judgments cannot be understood as a linear timeline, because each series overlaps the others, and includes flashbacks, repetitions, and foreshadowing.

Just as there are three series of judgments (seals, trumpets, and bowls), there are also three "woes," or tragedies, announced by an eagle (Rev 8:13). It is implied that the three woes correspond to the last three trumpets, but because the judgments overlap, the three woes also correspond in general to the three series of judgments. As we will see in chapter 6 below, the first series of judgments (the seals) revolves around the war with Rome that took place in 66–70 CE, up to and including the siege of Jerusalem. In this series, the second seal represents the war with Rome, and the third and fourth seals represent the famine and plague that would go along with the siege of the city of Jerusalem. Therefore the first woe represents the war and the siege of the holy city. Another reference to the siege of Jerusalem is seen in the image of the locusts (the fifth trumpet, cf. Rev 9:3–12).

The trumpet judgments overlap with the seals, in that they include references to the war with the Romans and the siege of Jerusalem, but the trumpets crescendo to the fall of Jerusalem in the sixth trumpet blast (Rev 11:13–14). Therefore the second woe is the fall of Jerusalem, which took place in the year 70.

The third and final woe is not specifically pointed out by John, though we know that there are three of them (Rev 9:12; 11:14). However it is relatively clear that the seventh trumpet reveals the bowl judgments, which revolve around the fall of Rome. Therefore it is easy to see that the third woe is the fall of Rome, the punishment for destroying Jerusalem and for the persecution of the Church. The fall of Rome takes place on two levels, the political and the spiritual. On the political level, the city of Rome did fall to barbarians in the early fifth century, beginning the decline of the western empire. By the end of that century, the western Roman Empire was no more. But the more important fall of Rome for John and his audience came a century earlier—that is, the spiritual fall of Rome, when the pagan (and anti-Christian) nature of the empire was overturned by the Church under the emperor Constantine.

It is important to note that the first two woes have already taken place by John's time, but the third woe has not yet happened at the end of the first century. John tells the reader that the first woe has passed (Rev 9:12), and the second woe has passed (Rev 11:14), but he never says that the third woe has passed, because it has not happened yet from his perspective, and it falls into that part of the book which is in the future for John, even though it is in our past.

Between the time of the first two woes and the third woe, John's vision warns of prolonged persecution of the Church by the empire. The unholy trinity of the dragon, the beast, and the false prophet conspire to draw worship away from God, and in the process, they threaten God's people. But God's victory on behalf of his people is sure. And just as the fall of Rome comes in two parts, so does the victory of God. The Lamb of God claims victory in the human world when the Church overcomes the empire (the spiritual fall of Rome). But finally, the Lamb will claim ultimate and final victory when evil is defeated once and for all, the Kingdom is revealed, and Christ and his Church are united in the New Jerusalem.

As we are finally able to sort out the events of Revelation into a timeline, or something approaching a narrative, we will use the clue in 1:19 as an outline, into which we can place the individual events. This gives us a structure for the book of Revelation that divides it into three main sections: John's past (*The things that you have seen*), John's present (*The things that are*), and John's future (*The things that will happen after these things*).

For the most part, the seals and the trumpets relate to events in John's past, including the birth of Christ, his triumph over death at his resurrection, the war with the Romans, the siege of Jerusalem, and the fall of Jerusalem with the destruction of the temple. In the tradition of the Old Testament prophets, the destruction of the temple is portrayed as both a punishment for the city that murdered prophets and apostles, and a crime for which the Roman Empire would be punished.

The passages relating to John's present are primarily the letters to the seven churches, but also include the spread of the gospel in the early Church as well as references to persecution. In addition, some of the visions of spiritual warfare and worship in heaven are meant to be understood as ongoing, taking place behind the scenes of human history. They are outside of time, and therefore in a sense they are always happening in the present.

When we get to the events in John's future, this third major section must be separated into two subsections. The first subsection contains those events in John's future but in our past, and this includes the persecutions of the third and fourth centuries, the victory of the Church over the empire, and the fall of Rome. The bowls are the plagues of punishment poured out on the empire that sacked Jerusalem, destroyed the temple, and persecuted the Church. This vindication of the persecuted followers of Christ and the punishment of the oppressive empire was a promise of future fulfillment for John and his audience. However, from the perspective of the twenty-first-century reader, all of this is in our past.

The remaining subsection includes the last few events of the visions, which were not only in John's future, but are also in our own future. The age of the Church continues until the Church can no longer influence the world for the Kingdom of God. At that time (and when the gospel has been preached in the whole world), God will intervene to overcome evil once and for all, judge the nations, and reveal the Kingdom in its fullness, and the people of the Lamb will live in the Realm of God for eternity. In the next few chapters, we will look at each phase of the timeline in turn.

The chart in the back of this book entitled "The Structure of the Book of Revelation" lists each passage of the book of Revelation and where it falls in relation to our four sections, based on the interpretations of the symbolism from the last chapter and on comparison with events in the history of the Church and the Roman Empire. The reader will notice that there are also several sections that are outside of time, which sometimes function as literary transitions. There is also a column in the chart labeled "Appendix A Section." This contains the reference numbers in Appendix A, "The Book of Revelation in Plain English."

These section numbers will be helpful to the reader who wants to find particular passages from Revelation in the text of the appendix, since the interpretation has them recast in chronological order. The section reference numbers will also be helpful while reading "The Book of Revelation in Plain English," when a certain part of the interpretation seems unfamiliar and the reader wants to find the corresponding passages in the original text of Revelation.

SUMMARY

- The primary purpose of the book of Revelation is not to predict the future, but to give the readers of John's *present* time encouragement and hope.

- Parts of Revelation take place outside the continuum of time, and do not fit neatly into a chronological narrative. This may be because they function as transition points in the narrative, and/or because they are ongoing realities that take place behind the scenes of human history.

- Chapter and verse divisions do not necessarily help in determining the structure of Revelation.

- We also cannot rely on grammatical clues to tell us where the past ends or the future begins.

- Verse 1:19 provides the key to the structure of Revelation. From John's perspective the book can be broken up into three parts:
  - The things that you have seen
  - The things that are
  - The things that will happen after these things

- From our perspective, the third section above can be further broken into two subsections:
  - The things that were in John's future, but are in our past
  - The things that are in our future

- Past, present, and future are not presented in chronological order in Revelation. They are juxtaposed thematically, and in patterns of unfolding understanding, often from lesser to greater detail. Overall, the book presents human history as a downward spiral toward the eventual intervention of God.

- In general, the seals represent events surrounding the war with Rome of 66–70 CE, and especially the siege of Jerusalem. This was the first woe.

- In general, the trumpets represent the events surrounding the fall of Jerusalem and the destruction of the temple in 70 CE. This was the second woe.

- In general, the bowls represent the events surrounding the fall of Rome. This is the third woe.

- Jesus' advent brought the Kingdom of God in its concealed sense. During the age of the Church, the Kingdom is the Reign of God within us.

- Jesus' return will bring the Kingdom of God in its fully revealed sense. Then, we will live eternally in the Realm of God.

5

Visions outside of Time

INTRODUCTION

SINCE WE ARE LOOKING back on the book of Revelation from the twenty-first century, we need to organize its parts into something like a chronological sequence if we want to understand it. But before we can do that, there are sections of the text (portions of John's vision) that are difficult to fit into the timeline. As has been noted, some of them function as transitions from one part of the vision to another, and others are descriptions of continuous or timeless events that take place in the spiritual realm independent of particular events in human history. In a way, these sections take a step back from the vision and allow the reader to catch his or her breath, take a break from the downward spiral, and be encouraged by the promises of victory and eternal life to come. In this chapter, we will look at these visions outside of the realm of creation and time.

THE SON OF MAN
(REVELATION 1:12–20)

In 1:12–20, John's vision has begun. John hears a loud voice, which he describes as sounding like a trumpet (a herald of divine intervention), and as anyone would, he turns to look in the direction of the voice to see who is speaking to him.[1] John sees the "one like a son of man," a direct quotation from Daniel 7:13, which is meant to convey that the one who is speaking is the Son of Man, Jesus.[2] The description of Jesus with hair

1. Cf. Isaiah 30:21, where the voice of God is described as speaking from behind the hearer, just as John says in Revelation 1:10.
2. Jesus described himself as the Son of Man; see for example Matthew 16:13–20.

like white wool, as well as references to "white as snow" and "blazing fire" also come from Daniel's vision, except that there it refers to God, the "Ancient of Days." Thus, John's vision makes a clear connection between Jesus the Son of Man and Yahweh God (the Father), implying the belief in the divinity of Christ. In Daniel's vision, the one like a son of man is given authority by the Ancient of Days (Daniel 7:13–14). In John's vision, the Son of Man holds the seven stars in his right hand, which means that he has authority over the leadership of the churches and that he protects them (cf. Matthew 16:18).

In John's vision of Jesus, we read that he is among the seven gold lampstands, which means that he is present in the seven churches (Rev 1:20; cf. Matthew 18:20; 28:20). The lampstands represent the seven churches in particular, but taken as a unit they represent the whole Church, and the seven churches are representative of all churches. The fact that there are seven of them adds to the interpretation of the lampstands as an image of the complete Church universal. The image of the robe, while it is not described as white in this context (the robe in Daniel's vision is white, so it is probably assumed) still signifies Jesus' perfect purity, and especially his priestly office.[3] The golden belt or sash implies royalty, and the white hair wisdom. The shining face and flaming eyes are the presence of the glory of God (cf. Exodus 34:29; Matthew 17:2; John 1:14), as well as divine judgment, the fact that Jesus sees into people's hearts.[4] The bronze feet symbolize the radiance of the glory of God, and reassure the reader that faith in Christ is on a solid foundation.[5] The voice like rushing waters means that the voice of Jesus is also the voice of God (Ezekiel 1:24; 43:2), and that the words of Jesus are the word of God. Finally, John says that a sharp, double-edged sword was coming out of the mouth of Jesus. This is the word of God, which Jesus speaks, and with which he judges (Hebrews 4:12).

When John recognizes that it is Jesus who is speaking to him, he falls at the Lord's feet in fear and reverence. Jesus reassures John with a touch of his right hand, which further confirms the image of Jesus' protection over the leaders of the churches, of which John is the over-

3. Irenaeus of Lyons, *Against Heresies* 4.20.11.

4. Beale, *Book of Revelation*, 209.

5. The reference to the furnace might also be a reference to Jesus' purity, which makes him worthy of our faith. It is as if he has already been through the purifying fire, not because he needed purification, but because he has always been perfectly pure.

seer, and adds an element of blessing to the scene.[6] Jesus' words, "Do not be afraid," are reminiscent of Matthew 14:27 and John 14:27, as well as God's similar reassurance to Isaac in Genesis 26:24. The reason that fear is not necessary is, of course, that the very presence of Jesus on the scene is divine intervention, and divine protection is implied (cf. 1 John 4:18–19). But these comforting words are not only for John in his vision—they are for all the churches, especially during persecution, and in this way they are a theme for the entire book of Revelation. Jesus' own resurrection (verse 18) provides hope for those who risk their lives for his sake.[7] Jesus describes himself as both immortal and eternal, and in fact he has authority (keys) over death itself.

Verse 19 is both the reason for the vision and the key to the structure of the book. John is to write down what he sees in the vision. It is a message for the whole Church, not just for him, and the vision that he sees and records will include reminders of the past, encouragement and admonitions for the present, as well as promises and warnings for the future.

A VISION OF HEAVEN
(REVELATION 4:1–11)

Revelation 4:1 is the beginning of the vision proper. What comes before is introduction, as well as John's "pastoral epistles" to the churches in his area. Now begins the vision that is the rest of the book of Revelation. John sees an open door in heaven and is invited in to witness "the things that must happen."[8] But this does not mean that everything that follows, to the end of the book, is in John's future. We know that this is not the case. John will see things that have already taken place, along with things that must take place (promise), and possibly things that might take place (warning). The words of Jesus in 4:1 are a general reference to the vision as a whole and to a certain extent refer specifically to the more apocalyptic portions of it, but they are not meant to limit the interpretation of the rest of the book to John's future only. The proof of this is that

6. Mounce, *Book of Revelation*, 80.

7. Beale, *Book of Revelation*, 206, 214–15.

8. The phrase is slightly different from the phrase in 1:19. Here it is not necessarily meant to be equated with John's future only, as opposed to his past and present as in 1:19. Rather, the phrase in 4:1 probably refers to everything that John is about to see in his vision.

the very next verse begins a description of the setting in the heavenly realm, where the events described are ongoing and take place outside of creation and time.

John, like only a few before him, is privileged to see God and live to tell about it.[9] He sees the throne of heaven, and the One sitting on the throne. The description of the "sea of glass" (Rev 4:6) is based on the idea of the heavens as a "firmament" and conveys the feeling that in the floor of the heavenly throne room one looks down at the sky. God is described as seated on a throne, surrounded by twenty-four other thrones, on which sit the twenty-four elders: the twelve patriarchs of Israel and the twelve apostles. The reader is not meant to ask whether John saw himself among the twelve apostles. This is not the point. In fact, we must keep in mind that this is a vision outside of time, or even a vision of eternity beyond time, so the content of John's vision cannot be compared to the circumstances of John's presence as a witness, as if they are happening concurrently. Certainly, John would have to be one of the twelve apostles, and yet their individual identities are not the issue here, only their number. As the first leaders of the Church, they represent all Christians, who are promised to reign with Christ in eternity (Matthew 19:28; 2 Timothy 2:12; cf. Rev 20:6). Their white robes represent their status as martyrs and saints, and their crowns represent their reward, the victory of resurrection.

The throne of God is described in terms reminiscent of the temple of Jerusalem. The jewels and the thunder and lightening symbolize both the supreme authority and the divine power of God (Ezekiel 1:26–28).[10] The seven lamps are the churches, the light of the world. Because the Holy Spirit empowers the churches for their mission, the lamps are also described as the "sevenfold Spirit of God." Some translations render this phrase as "the seven spirits of God," however this translation risks confusing the symbolic number seven, which means complete, for some

9. According to Irenaeus of Lyons, John sees the "throne," not God himself, for in spite of the descriptions of experiences of Moses and Ezekiel in the Old Testament, not to mention the phrase "and the One seated on the throne" in Revelation 4:2, "no one has ever seen God" (John 1:18). The understanding of the early Church was that seeing Christ was as close as anyone would get to seeing God, and that in fact even when people in the Old Testament thought they were seeing God, they were really seeing the pre-incarnate Christ. Irenaeus of Lyons, *Against Heresies* 4.20.11.

10. Mounce, *Book of Revelation*, 134; and Beale, *Book of Revelation*, 320–21. Cf. also Exodus 28:15–21; Psalm 104:1–4; 1 Timothy 6:15–16.

kind of divine plurality. The meaning here is that the Holy Spirit of God is present in all the churches and that the Spirit is God's omniscient presence in the worldwide Church.[11]

The descriptions of the four "living beings" are really descriptions of the attributes of God, using images taken from the visions of Isaiah and Ezekiel. God is omniscient (covered with eyes) and omnipresent (three pair of wings). There are four beings, which means that God's influence reaches to the four corners of the earth. There is no place on earth outside of God's reach, and there is no room for other gods because God is omnipotent and all-sufficient. The four living creatures proclaim God's holiness and eternal nature. God is ultimate wisdom and is relational (the human), God's sovereignty is over all creation and throughout all time (the eagle), God is the ultimate power and authority (the lion), and God is ultimate good in his providence and is worthy of worship (the calf). In other words, God's attributes witness to his character as omniscient, eternally omnipresent, omnipotent, and omnibenevolent.[12]

God is also described as "the one who is and the one who was and the one who is coming." This phrase, related to God's self-revelation in Exodus 3:14, presents God's perfect eternality in the past, the present, and the future. The fact that God is the one who "is coming" points to more than God's eternal nature, however. In addition to meaning that God will of course continue to exist in the future, it also reminds us of the promise of God's' intervention in human history on the Day of the Lord. God will come to his people.[13]

Just as God's own attributes continually proclaim his greatness, the living beings are said to give him glory, honor, and thanks. This should

11. Some interpreters have connected the "seven spirits" with the seven sacraments of the Church, or the seven traditional gifts of the Holy Spirit. In this context, the sea of glass was also seen as a metaphor for baptism. Cf. Primasius, *Commentary on the Apocalypse* 4.5.

12. Many early Church writers saw in the four living beings a reference to the four Gospels, or the four evangelists. While there was no universal agreement on which beings represented which Gospels, most saw the lion as a reference to John (thought to be the Gospel that most clearly portrayed Jesus' divinity, and therefore his role as King), the calf as a reference to Luke (which was understood to emphasize Jesus' priestly office), the human face as a reference to Matthew (thought to be the Gospel of Jesus' humanity), and the eagle as a reference to Mark (the Gospel that was seen as most clearly revealing the work of the Holy Spirit in Jesus' ministry, and therefore emphasized his role as prophet). See Irenaeus of Lyons, *Against Heresies* 3.11.8.

13. Beale, 332–33.

not make us reluctant to interpret the living beings as descriptions of the attributes of God. The image simply means that it is God who is credited as being the source of all goodness. Glory, honor, and thanks are due to God alone, and it is God's character, perceived in God's activity on earth, that witnesses to this fact. As the living beings sing "Holy, Holy, Holy," it is God's very attributes that proclaim his divine nature, the threefold acclamation signifying perfect holiness.[14]

The twenty-four elders respond to this witness by worshipping God. We should not be too concerned with the fact that the living beings sing their *Sanctus* without stopping, and yet the elders are said to worship God "whenever" the living beings do. This is a general picture of ongoing worship in the heavenly realm, and it is not necessary to try to dissect the grammar as if two different activities of the living beings are intended. The elders present their martyrs' crowns to God and confess what the living beings have proclaimed: that God is indeed worthy to receive glory and honor. Interestingly, where the living beings give God glory, honor, and *thanks*, the elders have replaced *thanks* with *power*. This can be confusing at first glance, for why would God's own attributes thank him, and how can God receive power? However, it just shows that no one can give God anything God does not already possess, including glory and honor. What God receives are not really the glory, honor, and power in themselves, but the acknowledgment of them. When we worship God, we admit that God is holy (and that by comparison, we're not!), and we acknowledge that God is the source of glory, honor, and power, and that God alone deserves thanks as the source of all creation. According to the elders, the reason that God is worthy is that he is the Creator (Rev 4:11).

To be reminded that God is almighty would be comforting to a persecuted Church. In fact, the phrase "our Lord and God" (Rev 4:11, cf. John 20:28) was similar to the title that the current emperor Domitian assumed for himself, *dominus et deus*. Therefore, as the vision begins in earnest, the suffering Church is reminded who is the true Lord and God, and that this God reigns over all creation.

---

14. Some interpreters see in the threefold "holy" a reference to the Trinity, as if the living beings sing one "holy" to each of the three persons of the Trinity. Athanasius, *On Luke* 10.22. However, it probably simply means that God is perfectly holy.

THE FIRST INTERLUDE: THE CALM BEFORE THE STORM
(REVELATION 7:1—8:6)

Four angels stand at the four corners of the earth, holding back the four winds. The repeated use of the number four represents the whole earth, indicating that this is not a localized event but something that hovers over the whole world, in the same way that the Spirit of God hovered over the unformed world at its creation (Genesis 1:2). In fact, since the number four is used three times (four angels, four corners, four winds), there is a sense of perfect wholeness, both spatially and geographically. It is a three-dimensional wholeness, which encompasses not only the horizontal plane of the earth's surface but also the vertical space as well. The winds are prevented from blowing, and in a sense, time itself stands still; this is the calm before the storm. Another angel arrives on the scene, coming from the east. The east is the direction of the rising sun and represents a change, a radical newness that is about to dawn. But first, the angel must put a seal on the servants of God, who will be marked as belonging to him.[15] This seal of God is reminiscent of the phylacteries of the Old Testament and is the opposite of the mark of the beast (Rev 13:16–18). The seal also brings to mind Genesis 4:15; Exodus 12:13; and Ezekiel 9:4, in which a mark (in Ezekiel, the mark is on the forehead) would spare one from judgment and punishment. The angel with the seal of God comes with God's authority to designate those who are God's own. The mark implies that God knows who are his own, and protects them (Matthew 10:29–31). The angel warns the four angels holding back the winds not to release these winds (which we now learn are to be destructive; cf. Jeremiah 49:36) until the servants of God from the people of Israel are marked. The seal, or mark, of God sets apart those who bear it as belonging to God and thereby saves them from the coming judgment. In the early Church, the seal was baptism.

The number of descendants of Israel who are sealed is 144,000, which is twelve thousand from each of the twelve tribes. But these are not the actual twelve tribes, which would have included the two tribes named after Joseph's sons instead of Joseph and Levi. In fact the twelve tribes named here include both Levi and Joseph, as well as Manasseh, one of the tribes named after Joseph's sons. The tribe of Dan is missing from the list, probably because of a tradition that the tribe of Dan was

15. Beale, *Book of Revelation*, 410–11.

associated with idolatry.[16] In reality, ten of the twelve tribes had ceased to exist as discernable ethnic distinctions because their lands had been conquered and colonized by the Assyrians in the eighth century BCE. And yet, Jews were still considered descendants of the "twelve tribes" (James 1:1). All of this shows that we are not to interpret the sealed remnant of Israel as a particular group of people, much less an actual headcount, but as a representative number of descendants of the people of Israel. In other words, twelve multitudes of descendants from the twelve sons of Jacob represent the Jewish Church. The point is that there is a large but finite number of Christians from among the people of Israel.

Next, John's attention is turned to a countless number of souls from every nation. These are the Gentile Christians. They are presented to God the Father (the throne) and Jesus the Son (the Lamb). John is told that they have come through the great tribulation, presumably without succumbing to the temptation to commit apostasy to save their own lives. Their white robes signify that they have kept themselves pure for Christ and have not committed idolatry. Many of them are martyrs, but they are not necessarily all martyrs. Their robes are washed in the blood of the lamb, not in their own blood.[17]

We should not make too much of the fact that John does not specifically say that the multitude are sealed or marked like the 144,000 were. Some interpreters have speculated that the sealing of the 144,000 saves them from the tribulation to come, but the text does not say this. It only says that what is to come must wait until those who are God's own are marked as such. Furthermore, the text does not mean to imply that the 144,000 are sealed while the countless multitude is not. Both groups can rightfully be considered marked for God—the Jewish Church is said to be sealed by an image that relates to their tradition, and the Gentile Church is sealed by the blood of the Lamb. Both images of identification are theologically related to the Exodus and the marking of doorways with lamb's blood, and the two groups together make up the Church that is saved by the Lamb of God, Jesus.

Just as the 144,000 represent the whole Jewish Church, the multitude from the nations is representative of the whole Gentile Church, regardless of whether every one of them personally experienced persecution. What matters is that the Church as a whole went through persecution,

16. Mounce, *Book of Revelation*, 169–70.

17. Ibid., 174.

and now John sees the cumulative membership of the universal Church receiving its reward in heaven. They wave palm branches, reminiscent of Jesus' triumphal entry into Jerusalem, and sing a song of praise and thanksgiving for their salvation.[18] The angels in the heavenly court join in the worship of God with those who "worship him day and night in his temple" (Rev 7:15). It is at this point that one of the elders speaks words of peace and hope to John, words that would bring comfort to John's readers in the midst of persecution. Though they might give their lives on earth for their faith in Christ, God will "cover them with his tent," and they will never again know hunger, or thirst, or the oppressive heat of the sun, or sorrow. Their God "will wipe away every tear from their eyes." In a paradoxical twist, the Lamb will be their Shepherd, and they will be led to the heavenly oasis. These images of paradise come from the Old Testament promises of the land, both the original entry into the Promised Land and the return to it after the exile (Isaiah 49:8–13).[19]

With the opening of the seventh seal, there is silence in heaven. This is the grand pause before the crescendo. Seven angels prepare to blow seven trumpets, which herald divine judgment. But before the judgments begin, another angel presents the prayers of the people to God. Presumably the prayers here are the same as in Revelation 5:8 and 6:9–11. The answer to those prayers now comes in the form of fire from the altar of heaven, hurled down to the earth. This image brings to mind the punishment of Sodom and Gomorrah, as well as the judgment of Ezekiel 38–39, with thunder, lightening, and an earthquake to signify divine intervention and impending judgment.[20] The angels prepare to sound their trumpets as the judgments are about to begin.

THE EAGLE
(REVELATION 8:13)

After the sounding of the fourth trumpet, a flying eagle comes to announce the sounding of the last three trumpets, and pronounces a threefold woe to those on earth. Although it is not made clear at this point, the three woes correspond to three events in the unfolding of God's judgment. By John's time, two of the woes have already taken place,

18. Beale, *Book of Revelation*, 428.

19. Mounce, *Book of Revelation*, 175.

20. Beale, *Book of Revelation*, 459.

namely the siege of Jerusalem (Rev 9:1–12) and the fall of Jerusalem (Rev 11:1–14). The third woe is yet to come but will be fulfilled with the fall of Rome (Rev 18).

The Greek word translated "eagle" actually just means a bird of prey, and could also be translated "vulture."[21] Just as in caricatures of the American Old West, the vulture would signify impending doom. But the eagle is a better image here because of its symbolism of God's omnipresence, and its connection with God's providence in the Old Testament (Exodus 19:4; Deuteronomy 32:11).[22] In this context the eagle represents God's sovereignty over all creation and is a herald of God's coming judgment on the two great cities, Jerusalem and Rome.

THE SECOND INTERLUDE: SEVEN THUNDERS (REVELATION 10:1–11)

Before the sounding of the seventh trumpet, there is another interlude, with another heavenly scene involving an angel. This time, however, what the angel reveals is not to be written down. The angel is curiously described in terms that sound like the description of Jesus in Revelation 1. This means that this "mighty angel" is Christ himself, and his "coming down from heaven, clothed with a cloud" is both a sign of the end of the great persecution (cf. Rev 6:10–11) and a foreshadowing of his second coming. The image of Christ coming from the clouds is echoed in Ezekiel 1:26–28; Daniel 7:13; Matthew 24:30; and 1 Thessalonians 4:16–17. Therefore, the reason that the words he speaks are not to be written down is that no one is to know "that day and hour" (Matthew 24:36).

Interestingly, there is a well-known tradition that in 312 CE, just before the battle at the Milvian Bridge on the northern edge Rome, the emperor-to-be Constantine saw a vision in the sky, which consisted of a sign of Christ and the words, "By this sign, you will conquer."[23] Constantine instructed his soldiers to inscribe the sign on their stan-

21. Mounce, *Book of Revelation*, 189.

22. Beale, *Book of Revelation*, 490–91.

23. The sign of Christ was probably the Chi-Rho monogram, which looks like the letter "P" with an "X" superimposed over it. These are actually the first two letters of the Greek word *Christos*, or Christ. Some versions of the story say the sign was a cross, but this is unlikely, since the cross was still being used as a method of execution at this time.

dards, and marched into battle under the banner of Christ. He won that battle, which made him emperor of the western Roman Empire and allowed him to issue the Edict of Milan in 313, effectively ending the persecution of the Church in the west. He would go on to become the sole emperor of the entire Roman Empire and make Christianity a legally recognized religion. In a sense, the great persecution ended because Christ "came from the clouds" to Constantine, who certainly attributed his victory (and his reign as emperor) to divine intervention.

The angelic Christ lands with one foot on the sea and one foot on the land, signifying his authority over the whole earth.[24] He holds a small scroll in his hand, and when he shouts, his shout is like the roar of a lion (omnipotence) and is described as the voice of seven thunders (complete authority). He swears by God that "there will be no more delay." The Greek text here literally says, "time shall be no longer," which has a curious double meaning, including the implication that at some point time itself will cease to exist. Jesus promises that when the seventh angel blows the seventh trumpet, "the mystery of God will be accomplished, just as he proclaimed to his servants the prophets." This can only be a reference to the Old Testament concept of the Day of the Lord. The persecuted Church has prayed for vindication (Rev 6:10), and it seems that it is about to come. More important, the mystery that is to be revealed is the Kingdom of God. What was concealed will now be revealed (Matthew 13:31–33).

At this point, John is instructed to take the little scroll, which it is safe to assume contains the coming judgments, and he is told to eat it. This image comes directly from Ezekiel 2:7—3:4 (cf. also Psalm 119:103 and Jeremiah 15:16). Before the prophet can speak the words of God to the people, he is told to eat the scroll that contains the words.[25] This places John as a prophet in the tradition of Ezekiel, taking God's word "to heart." John is warned that it will taste sweet but will turn sour in his stomach. In other words, the coming judgments will be bittersweet. The persecuted Church is vindicated in the destruction of Jerusalem and Rome, and yet these punishments themselves will cause great suffering. The promise includes an implicit warning that Christians not become too triumphant over the punishment of their oppressors.

---

24. Mounce, *Book of Revelation*, 208.

25. Ibid., 214.

WAR IN HEAVEN: SATAN'S REBELLION
(REVELATION 12:7–12)

The dragon, of course, represents the devil Satan. The army of Satan is made up of rebellious angels, and they fight against the army of God's loyal angels, led by the archangel Michael. According to Jewish tradition, this took place before the creation of the world, when time itself had not yet been created. The angel Lucifer had convinced a portion of the angels to reject God's authority (Luke 10:18; Rev 12:4a), and heaven was split between those who were loyal to God and those who were not.[26] We should not take the image of war literally, as if there were actual weaponry or military maneuvers in the spiritual realm. The war is a vivid image of rebellion, but it is only a symbolic picture. Just as the demons flee before the authority of Jesus in the gospels, we can safely assume that the "fight" in heaven was over before it began, with no actual struggle required of Michael and the angels loyal to God's authority. They simply represent defiant resistance to Lucifer's rebellion, and the resulting banishment from the presence of God.[27]

According to the book of Daniel, the angel Michael is apparently the chief angel and therefore is the one most likely to lead the army of God (Daniel 10:13; 12:1). But even the image of an army of God is only symbolic and simply refers to those angels who were steadfast in their loyalty to God. One assumes that the number of angels who remained faithful to God vastly outnumbered those who rebelled. Revelation 12:4a implies that the number of rebellious angels was one-third, though this simply means that it was a portion less than half. The tradition assumes that these rebellious angels, once banished from heaven, are now the demons, some of whom encountered Jesus in his ministry recorded in the Gospels.

The good news is that the devil lost the rebellion. The bad news is that he was cast out of heaven, coming down to earth, where he has been deceiving humans, tempting them and turning them away from God, then accusing them before God of the very sins he has seduced them

---

26. Cf. 2 Enoch 29. This Jewish apocalyptic text of unknown origin places the rebellion and fall of Satan between the second and third days of creation. See Beasley-Murray, *Revelation*, 193.

27. The question of how it is possible to be banished from the presence of an omnipresent God will have to remain outside the scope of the present study. However, Jesus did teach that some would find themselves outside of the Kingdom (Matthew 22:13).

into committing. But with the final trumpet, the Messiah will exercise his authority over Satan, and with his martyrs he will trample the devil (cf. Genesis 3:15). Therefore the heavens rejoice because Satan is cast out, but woe to the earth to which he has fallen. At Satan's initial rebellion, it was Michael who conquered him for God, perhaps because it was before the creation of humanity. Now, Christian believers conquer the devil by the blood of Christ (cf. John 12:31).

Here we see the far distant past (time before time) juxtaposed with the coming future in a vision that defies placement on a historical timeline. In the context of the vision, John sees the fall of Satan in the midst of Satan's attempt to destroy Jesus as a child, with a promise that the devil will be finally defeated once and for all.

THE REMNANT REVISITED
(REVELATION 14:1–5)

Once again John sees the Lamb of God with the 144,000 from Israel who are marked with the seal of God. In this passage we are told that they have on their foreheads the name of the Lamb (Jesus) and of his Father. It is clear from this that these are descendants of Israel who have accepted Jesus as their Messiah. The name written on the forehead again reminds us of the phylacteries of Jewish tradition, and the marking of the foreheads in Ezekiel 9:4. It is not meant to be understood literally, as if these people have tattoos on their foreheads, it is meant to be taken as a metaphor for their identification with Christ in baptism.[28] Their salvation is sealed by their relationship with God through Christ and through his Church. This was realized through baptism in the name of the Father and the Son (and the Holy Spirit), followed by a confirmation of anointing with oil on the forehead.

Now the heavenly orchestra begins to accompany the 144,000 in the singing of a new song, which only they could learn. This is a song of thanksgiving for those who are redeemed by the blood of Christ. The angels and other heavenly hosts cannot sing this song, since they have never been outside the realm of God and have not needed salva-

---

28. Another sign of identification with Christ is the sign of the cross, or "crossing" oneself. When done with holy water, it is also an acknowledgment of one's baptism, in which one symbolically identifies with Christ. Going under the water of baptism symbolizes following Christ in death, and coming up from the water symbolizes following Christ in resurrection.

tion. Only those who are saved can sing a song of thanksgiving for their salvation (cf. Psalms 40:1–4; 98:1–3). More specifically, only those who understand the significance of the old covenant first hand can sing the song of the new covenant.

We are now apparently told that the 144,000 are all celibate men (that they did not "defile themselves" with women assumes that they are men). They are described as "unblemished," like the sacrificial animals of the Old Testament. Some translations render this word "blameless," which is a fair interpretation, however it loses the connection to the Old Testament and the requirement that the sacrificial animals be perfect. In this context, "unblemished" means that "no lie was found in their mouths." This is a reference to apostasy, that they did not lie by denying Christ (or by accepting heresy), and therefore they remain "unblemished." Therefore, to be undefiled and blameless does not mean that they were without sin; it means they have not committed the particular sin of idolatry, that is, they did not commit spiritual adultery by worshipping other gods (cf. 2 Corinthians 11:2).[29] The specific mention of defilement with women may also refer to the practice of temple prostitution in certain cults, but in any case it does not mean to imply that any man who is married to a woman is defiled.[30] The 144,000 are representative of all who have kept themselves *spiritually* pure. It may also mean that they have remained *doctrinally* pure, in the sense that they have not accepted any heresy. It would be a mistake to interpret these verses as having to do with literal celibacy, much less sinlessness, since such a large number of celibate men would defy any meaningful interpretation.

The fact that all of this takes place on Mount Zion simply represents a gathering of God's people at God's holy place, that is, in God's presence. It is not meant to make a connection with the actual city of Jerusalem at any particular point in the narrative.[31] The 144,000 gather at Mount Zion because they are an offering to God. They are said to be purchased for God and are the "firstfruits" of humanity, offered to God and to the Lamb. The key to interpreting this passage is in the fact that they are the

29. Apart from the context of persecution, the early Church also interpreted this spiritual chastity as avoiding heresy.

30. Mounce, *Book of Revelation*, 270.

31. Ibid., 267. Mt. Zion was traditionally thought to be the place of the return of God's Messiah, however the text in question refers to heavenly Zion, the new Jerusalem (cf. Rev 21:2).

firstfruits, which means that they are representatives of the families of
God's people. The firstfruits of a human family would normally be the
firstborn son, who would be dedicated to God. As such, these 144,000
are those who are dedicated to God. Also, just as the head of a household
would represent the whole family, these 144,000 represent the whole
faithful (i.e., Christian) "remnant" of Israel, and in a more general sense
the image is expanded here to also represent the whole Church.

THE VICTORIOUS MARTYRS
(REVELATION 15:2–4)

In these verses, John sees a vision of the martyrs of the persecutions of
the Church. This is a foreshadowing of the vindication of those who will
die for the faith. They are standing beside what is described as a sea of
molten glass. As in chapter 4, here also the sea of glass is simply the floor
of the throne room of God, the topside of the firmament of the heavens.
The fire in this context is a reference to the purity of the martyrs, they
have been purified by their tribulations, like gold in a fire.

The martyrs are given harps from God, so that they can join in the
heavenly song of praise to God (cf. 1 Chronicles 25:1). There is evidence
that lyres, a harp-like instrument, were in fact used in early Christian
worship. The song acknowledges God's omnipotence, as well as his holiness, and praises his great activity in human history. The song ends with
the conviction that all nations will submit to God because his "justice
has been revealed." This is, in fact, what is happening in the revelation.
God's activity, his sovereign plan, indeed his Kingdom, is in the process
of being revealed, and when it is fully revealed, "every knee will bend
. . ." (Philippians 2:10–11).

THE THIRD INTERLUDE: ARMAGEDDON
(REVELATION 16:13–16)

Just as we have seen with the seals and trumpets, we also see a departure
from the narrative between the sixth and seventh bowls. The reader may
find it curious that the "battle of Armageddon" should be included in the
chapter of visions outside of time, when most interpreters of the book
of Revelation have seen this as the climactic event of human history and
the culmination of time itself. However, when one looks closely at the
text, it becomes clear that this battle takes place entirely in the spiritual

realm, much like the first battle when Satan rebelled against God and was expelled from heaven. Despite the interpretations of some end-times fiction, there is no particular earthly war going on concurrently with the spiritual warfare that is described here. Of course, there will always be "wars and rumors of wars" (Matthew 24:6), and peace on earth will always be elusive, yet it is a mistake to try to read World War III into the text of Revelation, and it is even more dubious to try to find the machinery of contemporary warfare hidden between the lines of the text.

John sees the unholy trinity of the dragon, the beast, and the false prophet. As we have seen, these are the devil Satan, the Roman imperial government, and the Roman priesthood, respectively. Out of their mouths come evil spirits, which John describes as looking like frogs. The frogs are clearly meant to bring to mind the plagues of Egypt, which were a refutation of the gods worshipped by the Egyptians. The Egyptians venerated frogs, and the plague of frogs shows that the God of the Hebrews has power over the frogs, and indeed over all the gods of the Egyptians. Therefore the evil (or "unclean") spirits that come from the mouths of the "unholy trinity" are the false gods and the false worship of the Romans, all of which is supported, encouraged, and even demanded by the Roman government. The power of the Roman state is used to seduce the nations (the "kings of the whole world") to its worship. The evil spirits are even said to perform signs that bring the kings to their side (cf. Matthew 24:24; Rev 13:13).[32] As the Roman Empire expands, it spreads its influence over the world. This worship of false gods and emperors is an act of rebellion (war) against the one true God. But this is spiritual warfare. While the powers of the earth compete for the souls of people, the spiritual forces behind the scenes anticipate a climactic confrontation.

The fact that they are said to gather at the place called Armageddon is more a statement about the outcome of the confrontation than it is about the location. Armageddon is, in Hebrew, Har Megiddo, or "Megiddo Hill." It is a place of decisive battles in the Old Testament, and it is near the place where the idolatress Jezebel met her death. Jezebel was the great spiritual adulteress of the Old Testament, who convinced many of God's people to turn to false worship, and in the book of Revelation she becomes a symbol for Rome. So the place where Jezebel met her end is a sign of the coming of the end of Rome and its false worship.

32. Mounce, *Book of Revelation*, 300.

Therefore, in the book of Revelation, Armageddon is not a place, it is a promise: first, that Rome and its idolatry will fall; and second, that the army of God will certainly win the final battle against evil.

Inserted in these verses is a word from Jesus, "Look, I am coming like a thief . . . ," which is related to Matthew 24:42–44 (cf. also 1 Thessalonians 5:2). There is a definite connection between the final defeat of evil and the coming of Christ. It is the divine intervention of the second coming of Christ that brings about the decisive end to the spiritual warfare. Just as in Matthew's Gospel, Jesus advises his followers to be in a state of readiness. And just as in the Exodus, being ready means being ready to travel, to follow him "wherever he may go" (Rev 14:4).

All of these sections of John's vision occur irrespective of time, and yet there is a connection between what goes on in the spiritual realm and what happens on earth. Both the forces of evil and the power of God break through into human history, with Satan seducing people away from God, and God calling them back. The devil is portrayed as the unseen puppet master, working the strings of the Roman Empire, especially its emperors and priests. The resulting effect is a struggle between humans that puts the lives of believers at risk. In Appendix A, "The Book of Revelation in Plain English," the visions outside of time are inserted into the chronology based on their relationship to the events in the narrative, conveying a sense of cause and effect wherever appropriate.

SUMMARY

- The message of the vision of Revelation comes from Jesus, the Son of Man.

- Jesus is the tangible presence and glory of God, which justifies the worship of Jesus. In fact worshipping Jesus is worshipping God.

- Jesus' words "Do not be afraid" are a theme for the book of Revelation, and are a message of comfort to a suffering Church.

- All attempts to turn people away from God ultimately come from Satan, but John's vision promises that Satan will be defeated for all time, just as sure as he was once defeated when he first rebelled against God.

- Those who follow Jesus in death will follow him in resurrection.

- Scenes of heavenly worship remind a persecuted Church that God is the Creator, and is all-powerful, and will come to vindicate them.

- The mark of God means that God knows who are his own, and protects them, and that they are to receive the victory of eternal life.

- The resurrection life will be without pain or suffering or sorrow.

6

Visions of John's Past

The things that you have seen . . .

INTRODUCTION

AS WE ENTER THE timeline of the visions of Revelation, we begin with John's past. This chapter will survey those parts of Revelation that relate to events that have already taken place by the time John sees them represented in the vision. The meaning of the images John sees and the symbols John employs in Revelation would have been immediately clear to John and his readers because they relate to events familiar to them.

It should be pointed out before we begin that these visions of John's past are not unconnected to those of John's future, and when past events appear in the text they do so because they have significant relevance to the present situation of John and his readers or to the warnings and promises for their future. As we discern the meaning of each event we will, as much as possible, take into account its context within the overall vision, and its relevance for John's audience. We will take the visions we consider in this chapter in historical order, not necessarily in the order they appear in the book of Revelation.

THE FALL OF SATAN
(REV 8:10–11; 12:3–4A, 7–12)

We have already discussed the fall of the angel Lucifer as an event that occurs outside the realm of time. While it clearly belongs in that context, the fall of Satan is treated in the text as a past event, in the sense that it has already taken place and has implications for the present and future of the people of earth. In 12:4a, we are told that the dragon's tail swept away one-third of the stars from heaven and threw them to earth. These stars represent a portion of the angels in heaven who (according to Jewish tradition) joined Lucifer in his rejection of God's authority. Presumably, they would now be the demons who tempt and torment the people of earth (cf. Daniel 8:10).[1] It is not necessary to interpret these angels as exactly one-third of all the angels in existence. The fraction simply means that a portion (perhaps even a divinely appointed portion) joined Lucifer's rebellion. The number is not significant, except that it is less than half, a minority, as opposed to the majority of the angels who remained faithful to God. Later in that same chapter, John goes into more detail about the "war" in heaven and Satan and his angels being cast out (Rev 12:7–9). The fact that the army of heaven is led by the archangel Michael and not by Christ shows that it is "pre-history," or at least before the time of the incarnation. If this were a vision of a future battle, Christ would certainly be the leader of the angelic army, as he is depicted in 6:2 and 19:11.

In 8:10–11, the effect of the fall of Satan to earth is that a portion of the earth's waters were poisoned. This has a double meaning. In addition to reminding the reader of one of the plagues of Egypt (Exodus 7:17–21), this is an image of the poisoning effect that the presence of the devil will have on the people of the earth.[2] He will be a tempter, seducing people away from their God, causing spiritual death.

In 12:10–12, the fall of Satan is presented as an event in the far distant past, and yet the heavenly voice proclaims, "*Now* the salvation and the power and the kingdom of our God and the authority of His Christ have come, for the accuser of our brothers and sisters has been cast away." This connects the expulsion of Satan to his final defeat by Christ, meaning that as surely as he was cast out of heaven, Satan's plans for deceiving the people of earth were thwarted by the death and resurrection of Jesus (cf. John 12:31). It is through the blood of the Lamb that the followers of the Lamb will overcome Satan, and this passage is an encouragement and a promise of that fact. Those who follow the Lamb even to death can rejoice in the fact that their Savior has already overcome death.

1. For a New Testament understanding of the state of fallen angels, see 2 Peter 2:4 and Jude 6.

2. Some early Church writers interpreted the images of poisoning and darkness as various heresies that existed in their own times.

The seed of the future is planted in the present, just as the seed of the past has come to fruition in the Christ event (cf. Matthew 13:31–33). "Woe to the earth," states the heavenly voice, "because the devil has come down to you" *in the past—but now,* "the salvation and the power and the kingdom of our God and the authority of His Christ have come," and the devil knows he has only a short time left (Rev 12:12).

THE BIRTH OF CHRIST
(REV 12:1–2, 4B–6, 13–17)

At the midpoint of the book of Revelation the text is grounded in the birth of Christ. The woman is Mary, who is depicted as being clothed with the sun, the moon at her feet, and a crown of twelve stars on her head. Assuming that the man writing this vision down was the same one to whom Jesus himself entrusted the care of his mother (John 19:26–27), the apostle not only knew and cared for Mary, he was probably with her to the end of her life.[3] Here in his words we see the beginning of the great respect and admiration that the Church would have for the mother of Jesus. The crown of twelve stars represents her legacy as a daughter of Israel (understood as twelve tribes) and as the first one to accept her Messiah (Luke 1:38), as well as her victory over Satan (Genesis 3:15).

Some have interpreted the woman as a reference to Israel, but that is trading an obvious meaning for a more obscure one. It is true that there are references in the Old Testament to Israel described as a woman in labor (for example, see Isaiah 26:18), but it is not the labor here that is important, it is the birth. Even interpreters who say that the woman represents Israel usually agree that the child born is Christ.[4] Others have said that the woman's son represents the church, but again this is making the meaning more complicated than it needs to be. If the son that is born represents the church, then what would be the meaning of the woman's other offspring? Here, at least, we can say that the simplest interpretation is the best one. The woman is Mary, and her Son is Jesus. The other offspring then represent those who believe in Christ, because they are his

3. According to tradition, Mary only lived a few years after the death and resurrection of Jesus.

4. Mounce, *Book of Revelation*, 236–38. On the other hand, the third-century writer Hippolytus said that the woman represents the Church (mother Church). Hippolytus, *On Christ and Antichrist* 61.

brothers and sisters, adopted children of God (John 1:12–13; Matthew 12:48–50; cf. also John 19:26–27).

The dragon comes from the Old Testament image of the sea monster, leviathan, and usually represents the enemies of Israel.[5] Here it represents the devil himself, as the demonic force behind the enemies of the Church. The reference to seven heads with seven crowns and ten horns in this context makes the point that the same evil force that is behind the current persecuting empire was also behind Herod when he attempted to kill Jesus by murdering all the infants in and around Bethlehem (Matthew 2:16–18). Note that the beast does not have seven horns—it does not have complete power, nor is it an equal opposite force to God. There is no hint that the beast's power rivals God, only that the beast's agenda opposes God's own. In Judeo-Christian thought, good and evil are not equal opposites in balance. The clear message of hope in the book of Revelation is that good and evil are at odds and, in the end, evil doesn't stand a chance. When the dragon tried to destroy the Son, Jesus was protected by God and, after his resurrection, he returned to the Father. That he "was caught up to God and to his throne" is clearly a reference to the ascension (Acts 1:9).

The woman gives birth to Jesus, and as soon as he was born, Satan was poised to try to kill him. Revelation 12:6 and 12:13–16 refer to the same event, the flight of the holy family into Egypt. Here the woman represents the holy family by a figure of speech known as *synecdoche*, in which the whole is represented by a part. The flight of the woman into the wilderness is the flight of the Mary and her family, who went into Egypt to escape Herod and his plan to get rid of the infant Jesus. There they were guided and protected by God, and according to verses 6 and 14, they spent about three and a half years in Egypt. There is no record of the amount of time the holy family actually spent in Egypt, so this approximate time frame may be accurate, but more important is the symbolic significance of this length of time. It is the same amount of time as the activity of the beast, that is, the war of Rome against the people of Judea. It is significant to note that during the time of the war with the Romans, many Christians of Judea escaped to Pella, in the region of the Decapolis (in modern Jordan).[6] So the length of time that the Christians fled the Romans is also said to be the same amount of time that the

---

5. Mounce, *Book of Revelation*, 237.

6. Eusebius of Caesarea, *Ecclesiastical History* 3.5. Cf. Mark 13:14.

holy family fled from Herod. It is also the same amount of time that is described in the book of Daniel as a great tribulation interpreted as the reign of Antiochus IV. Connecting all of these events in this way signifies that the same satanic force that was cast out of heaven also caused the oppression of historic Israel, tried to kill the infant Jesus, was behind the Roman war against the Jews with the subsequent destruction of the temple, and will be behind the continued persecution of the Church. Just as there is a continuity to God's activity in history, there is also a historical continuity to the activity of Satan on the earth.

The rescue of the holy family is compared to the Exodus and the walk through the Red Sea in John's water imagery of 12:15–16.[7] Just as the people of Israel were led out of Egypt through the waters of the Red Sea, so the holy family was saved by being led into Egypt and then out again. The image of eagle's wings in this context signifies divine providence and protection.[8] The connection of the Exodus to the holy family in Egypt goes back to the Gospel of Matthew, where the author quotes the prophet, "Out of Egypt I called my son" (Matthew 2:15; Hosea 11:1).

THE DEATH AND RESURRECTION OF CHRIST
(REV 5:1—6:2)

Chapter 4 is a vision of heaven, and chapter 5 is a continuation of that vision. However, chapter 5 is bound to one all-important event in time, the passion of Christ. In John's vision, he sees God holding a scroll in his right hand. This is the scroll that contains God's judgments as they are about to unfold. The scroll is sealed with seven seals, the opening of which unleashes the judgments themselves.[9] But until the time of Christ, no one has ever been worthy to break the seals and open the scroll (cf. Luke 24:25–27). We could ask why God the Father was not considered

---

7. There may also be a connection with the rescue of Moses in the Nile (Exodus 1:22—2:10). Cf. Mounce, 245.

8. Mounce, *Book of Revelation*, 245.

9. The image of the scroll with seven seals seems to be a combination of two kinds of ancient documents. There is the ancient will or testament, which would be sealed seven times by seven witnesses. All surviving witnesses had to be present for the seals to be opened. There is also the ancient contract, which would be written on both sides, one side to be sealed on the inside, and the other side to be visible on the outside to summarize the contents of the contract. John's vision of the scroll comes from these ancient examples, but it is also based on Ezekiel 2:8–10. For a more detailed explanation, see Beasley-Murray, *Revelation*, 120–22. See also Mounce, *Book of Revelation*, 142.

worthy to do this, but that question seems unnecessary. Obviously, the Father would be worthy, except for some reason he is excluded from the survey (verse 3). We can only assume that what is meant here is that no human being was found worthy until Christ. Also, since the scroll contains judgments, only one who is without sin can open it (cf. John 8:7). In other words, Jesus Christ is the Savior of humanity precisely because he is both human and divine. As the Church has taught from the beginning, only a human being could be the representative of humanity, and yet only God is perfectly holy enough and has the authority to initiate judgment. Because Christ is both human and divine, he is the One who is able to be the substitutionary sacrifice for the rest of humanity, without having to atone for any sin of his own. He is the promised Messiah, the root of David (Isaiah 11:1–10) and the Lion of Judah (Genesis 49:8–11; Ezekiel 19:2–9). Here the image of the lion represents royalty and power, and is related to God's omnipotence. Therefore, not only is Jesus worthy in the sense of being perfectly pure and holy, but he is also worthy in the sense of having the authority to open the scroll.

The key to this chapter is verse 6. John sees the Lamb, standing, yet as if slain, next to the throne. The Lamb has been slain, but now stands (is resurrected) at the right hand of God. The Lamb has all power and authority from God (seven horns), is omniscient (seven eyes), and the Holy Spirit of God proceeds from him to the Church.[10] It is because of Christ's sacrificial death and his victory in resurrection that he is worthy and able to open the scroll. He accepts the scroll from his Father, and all the inhabitants of heaven break into a new song of praise. It is significant that this is a "new" song. Like the new song of the 144,000 in chapter 14, this is a song of the new covenant.[11] Unlike the songs of chapter 4, which we can assume have been sung for eternity and are in fact part of the vision outside of time, the song of chapter 5 has not been sung before because it is only made possible by the death and resurrection of Christ. In fact, the song bears similarities to the song of chapter 4 (verse 11), but

---

10. In the Eastern (original) version of the creed, it is said that the Holy Spirit proceeds from the Father. The Cappdocians had also said that the Holy Spirit proceeds from the Father *through* the Son. In the Western version of the creed, we say that the Spirit proceeds from the Father *and the Son*. While this distinction contributed to the split between East and West in the eleventh century, the motivation for the Western change was to highlight the equality of the Father and the Son against the heresy of Arianism. It is, therefore, primarily a difference of emphasis.

11. Mounce, *Book of Revelation*, 147.

now with the added element of praise and worship to the Lamb. Before this time, people only worshipped God the Father; now both God the Father and Jesus the Lamb are worshipped and glorified. The heavenly host numbers thousand upon thousands (an image from Daniel 7:10), and the sound of their new song is mingled with the perfume of the prayers of the saints, which rise up to God like incense (Psalm 141:2).[12] Finally, Revelation 5:13 foreshadows what is promised in Philippians 2:9–11, that "every knee will bend . . . and every tongue will admit that Jesus Christ is Lord." And they all said . . . "Amen!"

As the Lamb opens the first seal, John sees Christ in another form, dressed for battle riding a white horse.[13] He wears the victory crown of his resurrection and carries a bow, which symbolizes judgment (cf. Jeremiah 51:11; Zechariah 9:13). He goes out "conquering and to conquer." The conquering does not refer to the successful spread of the gospel, as some have suggested. It refers to the two bookends of Christ's victory over evil: the resurrection (cf. Rev 5:5) and the final defeat of evil at his second coming. The apparent redundancy is simply another way to say that he goes out already victorious (in his resurrection) and to conquer again in the coming judgments and the final confrontation with evil.

This section marks a transition in the vision from the scenes in the heavenly throne room to the beginning of the sequence of judgments.

---

12. Cf. also Tobit 12:12–15.

13. While some interpreters have denied that the rider of the white horse in chapter 6 is Christ, it is clear that the rider of the white horse in chapter 19 is Christ, so it could hardly be otherwise here. Also note that there are no disastrous effects of the coming of the white horse, unless one interprets "conquering" as war on earth, but in that case there is nothing to distinguish the white horse from the red horse. A few commentators have tried to distinguish the white horse from the red horse as war with a foreign foe and civil war respectively, but that is reaching. Some also interpret the bow as a reference to the Parthians, who were known as accomplished archers, and who did defeat the Romans in a battle in 62 ce. However, they did not "conquer" the Romans, and while such a reference is possible, it seems far too tangential to the broader trajectory of the book as a whole. Its only function in the narrative could be to foreshadow the fall of Rome, which would not explain the prominence (or indeed the color) of the white horse. It should go without saying that the color white can only symbolize something good and pure. Finally, note that the words translated "conquering" and "to conquer" share the same Greek root with the word translated "overcome" in 5:5. The implication of this is that the "conquering" of the rider of the white horse refers to the resurrection, not to any actual warfare. The early Church writers were virtually unanimous that the rider of the white horse is Christ, though some went farther, saying that the white horse itself represents the Church. A few went on to say that the red horse would then represent persecution of the Church.

It is important to note that it is Christ who inaugurates the judgments, and in fact the beginning of the revelation of the Kingdom goes all the way back to the death and resurrection of Jesus.

THE ROMAN EMPERORS AND THE ROMAN WAR OF 66–70 CE (REV 6:3–4; 13:1–7)

The Lamb breaks the second seal on the scroll and the second horse, the red horse, goes out to bring war to the earth. Specifically, this is the war between the Romans and the Jews that began about thirty years before John wrote Revelation. A slightly more detailed vision of the war is recorded in 13:1–7.

As chapter 12 comes to a close, and chapter 13 opens, the dragon that pursued the woman and her Son is pictured standing at the seashore, as if calling the beast up from the sea. John's beast combines the characteristics of all four beasts in Daniel, where the four beasts represent four ancient empires leading up to and including the Greek Empire under Alexander the Great. John's beast is the culmination and the successor of those four great empires.[14] The beast is the Roman Empire, or more precisely, the Roman imperial office and the Roman emperors themselves.[15] It is the emperors of Rome who wage war against God's people the Jews, and it is the emperors of Rome whom Satan will use to persecute the Christian Church, described as the rest of Mary's offspring (Rev 12:17) since they are the brothers and sisters of Christ (cf. Mark 3:35; John 1:12–13).

The fact that the beast comes from the sea is, as we have already acknowledged, reminiscent of the leviathan of the Old Testament, which is also equated with the dragon, Satan. In addition, the Roman Empire surrounded the Mediterranean Sea, and whenever Roman troops arrived in Palestine, they usually arrived by the sea. The seven heads with blasphemous names are seven emperors up to the time of John who expected to be worshiped as gods. The one that had been slain was the

---

14. Beasley-Murray, *Revelation*, 208.

15. While the word "antichrist" does not actually appear in the book of Revelation, if there is an antichrist reflected in the text, it would be the beast, i.e., the Roman imperial office, specifically whichever emperor might be persecuting the Church at any given time (cf. 1 John 2:18; 2 John 7; 2 Thessalonians 2:1–44). Mounce, *Book of Revelation*, 254. See also Beasley-Murray, *Revelation*, 206. Note that the emperor Caligula had planned to set up a statue of himself in the Jerusalem temple during his reign (about 40 CE), Josephus, *Antiquities of the Jews* 18.8.

emperor Nero, the first to persecute Christians. In John's day, the present emperor, Domitian, was considered by many to be a reincarnation of Nero.[16] This is the meaning of the mortally wounded head that was healed—Domitian represents Nero come back again from the dead, both in his ruthless insanity and in his treatment of the Christians. Domitian took for himself the title *dominus et deus noster*, which means "our lord and god."[17] This would, of course, be seen as the height of blasphemy by both Christians and Jews. The ten horns are ten emperors who will persecute the Church after John's time (Rev 17:12). The beast is further described as being like a leopard (swift in its attack), with feet like a bear (fierce, with razor-sharp claws), and a mouth like a lion (strong and deadly). What's more, the empire acts and moves on the authority of the dragon, Satan. For forty-two months the beast is given authority to act, and to make war against God's people and defeat them.[18] The actual war, from the revolt of the Zealots to the beginning of the siege of Jerusalem, was closer to four years long, however John is using the three-and-a-half-year time frame to connect this event (and the evil force behind it) to similar events in the past. Through the cult of the emperors, the beast is worshipped, and indirectly Satan is worshipped. By demanding worship, and by demanding the cultic loyalty of Christians, the Roman emperors commit blasphemy against God.

THE FIRST WOE: THE SIEGE OF JERUSALEM 70 CE (REV 6:5–8; 9:1–12)

The war that began in the year 66 came to a standstill in 70 when the Roman legions surrounded the walls of Jerusalem. In Revelation 9 (the fifth trumpet) John describes the Roman legions in apocalyptic terms as a swarm of locusts; and in chapter 6 (the black and pale horses) John describes the effects of the siege on the city: famine and disease. This is a case where there is significant overlap from one series of judgments to the next, so that the third through sixth seals and the fifth trumpet refer to the same event in history.

16. Beasley-Murray, *Revelation*, 210–11.

17. Mounce, *Book of Revelation*, 250–51.

18. When verse 7 states that the beast "was allowed to wage war against the holy ones and overcome them," this is probably a general reference to the persecution of the Church, not a specific reference to the war of 66–70 CE.

At the beginning of chapter 9, as the fifth trumpet is blown, John again sees Satan as a fallen star. The same rebellious angel who called the beast up out of the sea now calls a swarm of locusts up out of the abyss. These locusts are described in military terms, with human faces, like horses ready for battle, with golden crowns and hair like women (Roman helmets) and iron breastplates (Roman shields). They sound like chariots and have the ability to sting like scorpions, but unlike actual locusts, they were not to consume the grass or other vegetation.[19] It is clear that the image of the swarming locusts represents the Roman legions, and their marching orders come (indirectly) from the devil himself, whose name is "Destruction" (*Abaddon* in Hebrew, *Apollyon* in Greek[20]). Their orders are to hurt, but not kill, for five months. This is almost exactly the length of time of the historical siege of Jerusalem, before the city fell. During this time, the people of Jerusalem would suffer from hunger and disease, but the killing would be delayed until the breech of the city's walls.

The locusts were to attack only those who did not have the seal of God (i.e., those who were not Christian). In one sense, the connection of the death of the two witnesses with the fall of Jerusalem (Rev 11:12–13) may reflect an understanding in the early Church that the fall of Jerusalem was God's punishment for the crucifixion of Jesus and the death of James and other martyrs (Acts 12:1–2). If this is the case, it would reflect the Old Testament understanding that the suffering (and conquering) of Jerusalem by a foreign power was divine judgment for the unfaithfulness if its inhabitants. Thus, the fact that the leaders of Jerusalem had rejected Christ and harassed the Church (cf. Acts 6:8–8:1) may have been seen as a reason for the fall of the city, and could partially explain the reference to those in the city at the time of the siege as being without the mark of God.[21] However, we must not read into this any kind

19. Many interpreters relate various traditions of descriptions of locusts in which they are said to be armored, with heads like horses and antennae like hair. However, this is merely coincidental. The fact that they do not harm the grass but attack people is a clear indication that they are not to be interpreted as actual locusts. Locusts as a symbolic image represent destruction. For examples, see Deuteronomy 28:42; 1 Kings 8:37 (where the locust is mentioned in close proximity to a siege); Psalm 78:46; and Joel 1:4, 10–11 (cf. 2:4–11, where the description sounds like John's description of the locusts). Note that in all these examples, the destruction of the locusts is God's punishment. Mounce, *Book of Revelation*, 193–94.

20. Apollyon may also be a play on words with the name of the god Apollo, a favorite deity of both Nero and Domitian. Beasley-Murray, *Revelation*, 162.

21. Cf. Mounce, *Book of Revelation*, 155. Josephus said that the fall of Jerusalem was God's punishment for civil war within the city. He blamed the warring factions for

of anti-Semitic argument, since John himself was a Jew, as were many (if not most) Christians of his time. It is not implied that all Jews were unfaithful to God, since indeed many of them had become followers of Christ. It simply means that there were many who, by rejecting Jesus and persecuting the early Christians, were actually making themselves enemies of God. This being said, the more concrete meaning of this limitation of the locusts, however, is that God had spared the Church from the siege. In fact, most of the Christians of Jerusalem had left the city by the time the war came to its walls, leaving almost no Christians in the city, with the notable exception of the two witnesses. According to the fourth-century historian Eusebius, the Christians of Jerusalem were warned by God to leave the city, and fled to Pella.[22]

For approximately five months, the people of Jerusalem were surrounded by the Romans and confined within the city.[23] Using the prophetic voice of the future tense, John wrote, "And in those days the people will look for death but they will not find it, and they will long to die but death flees from them" (Rev 9:6). Of course this does not mean that no one died during the siege. But as the months dragged on, it is easy to imagine that some would have accepted an end to the suffering at any cost.

The third seal, which is also the black horse, represents famine. With no way to bring supplies into the city, the inhabitants of Jerusalem had to hold out as long as they could on whatever was already within the city walls when the Romans began the siege. Food would be rationed (cf. Ezekiel 4:9–17) and would be extremely expensive. The prices mentioned in Revelation 6:6 are over ten times the normal rate.[24] For the Romans' part, they would be careful not to destroy sources of food outside the city walls that they would need, such as olive trees and vineyards (Rev 6:6). In fact, it was common in times of battle for orders to be given not

---

destroying provisions and causing the famine during the Roman siege. Josephus, *Wars of the Jews* 5.1.4, see also 5.6.1 and 5.13.6.

22. Eusebius of Caesarea, *Ecclesiastical History* 3.5. Some contemporary interpreters have speculated that this passage means that the Church will be spared from some future tribulation, or part of it, however it is not necessary to project the fulfillment of this passage into our future, when it has already been fulfilled in our past.

23. Beasley-Murray points out that in Genesis 7:14 the waters of the flood took five months to subside. Beasley-Murray, *Revelation*, 161.

24. Mounce, *Book of Revelation*, 155. See also Eusebius of Caesarea, *Ecclesiastical History* 3.6; Josephus, *Wars of the Jews* 5.13.7.

to harm the olive trees and vineyards, since these took a long time to cultivate, and a conquering army would not want to have to start over with those commodities in their new colony.

The fourth seal is the pale horse, which represents death, primarily by plague. There are three causes of death mentioned in 6:8: war, famine, and plague (which are actually a summary of the last three horses). The war had already caused much death, and the siege had brought famine and plague. Even domesticated animals could become wild during the siege and might attack people if they were hungry enough. But John sees even more death coming. However, a close reading reveals that John does not actually say that a fourth of the world would be killed, just that Death and Hades were given authority over a fourth of the earth, to kill (apparently) at will. The fraction one-fourth serves the same function as one-third, except that since it is the geographical world that is in question, the number four is operative. The implication is simply that an important part of the (known) world would be affected. As the narrative approaches the unthinkable, the fall of Jerusalem, the death toll rises. The series of judgments represented by the seals revolves around the siege of Jerusalem, which is the first woe (Rev 9:12), and the second is coming close on its heels, when the city falls.

MARTYRDOM AND THE TWO WITNESSES
(REV 6:9–11; 11:3–12)

In chapter 11, John describes two "witnesses" who will "prophesy" for about three and a half years. The Greek word translated "witness" here is, of course, the word "martyr." In John's time it is too early for the term to have its later meaning of "one who dies for the faith," though this passage certainly contributes to that. Primarily the word means "one who gives testimony." The testimony given is a witness to the death and resurrection of Christ (as in Acts 2:14–36). "Prophecy" in this context could simply refer to the preaching of the gospel, though if the tradition related by Eusebius is correct, they may have predicted the siege and the fall of Jerusalem as well (cf. Matthew 24:15–21). That these witnesses are Christians is clear from Revelation 11:8, which says that they died in the same city where their Lord was crucified. The time frame is not literal, it simply connects the ministry of these martyrs to the time of the war with the Romans, but it may mean that the two witnesses preached the gospel during the time of the war, and possibly also that they died as a result of the war itself or during the siege and fall of Jerusalem.

The two witnesses are described as lampstands and olive trees. This means that they are evangelists, and possibly considered apostles. The fire that proceeds out of their mouths is the gospel message, which is powerful (Romans 1:16). Their arguments are not only persuasive; they are so powerful as to cause their enemies to fear what might happen if they are opposed (cf. Acts 12:3–19; 16:23–34). They are described as having similar powers as Elijah and Moses (Rev 11:6).[25] Eventually, they were killed by the beast (John's choice of language in verse 7 comes directly from Daniel 7:21), though this does not necessarily mean that they were killed by the Romans directly. Revelation 11:13 seems to imply that they died in the city of Jerusalem at or just before the city fell to the Roman legions. If this is the case, they may have died in the famine during the siege, thus their deaths would be indirectly attributed to the Romans. Indeed we know that many who died this way were not buried, and many bodies did lie for days in the streets of Jerusalem during this time.[26]

The exact identity of these two martyrs cannot be known for certain, but their identity is not as important as the fact that they represent the first-century Church leaders who were persecuted and martyred. It doesn't seem to matter to John whether they were killed by authorities in Jerusalem or by the Roman state, for the same evil force is behind any who would persecute the Church.[27] In fact, it is not even required that this passage refers to two particular martyrs at all. Since at least two witnesses were required to bring testimony in a capital offense (Deuteronomy 19:15), the two witnesses could simply be representative of all the martyrs, whose blood cries out against their murderers, but who have found victory in resurrection and eternal life. In addition, their resurrection foreshadows the resurrection of all believers, and may simply be a symbol of that promise.

The deaths of the apostles probably did bring a certain joy to their persecutors, who were annoyed by their preaching. But of course their

---

25. Mounce, *Book of Revelation*, 222–25. A less likely, but possible, connection is Elijah and Enoch. Beasely-Murray, *Revelation*, 183. Others have speculated that the two witnesses represent John the Baptist and Jesus.

26. Josephus, *Wars of the Jews* 5.1.5.

27. Mounce, *Book of Revelation*, 225. Cf. also Beasley-Murray, *Revelation*, 183–84.

deaths were not the end of the story. The fact that the bodies of the two martyrs lay unburied for three and a half days means that there was an anticipation of resolution, a time of waiting for the other shoe to drop. When God intervened and that resolution came, the martyrs were resurrected and called to ascend into heaven in the sight of their enemies (cf. John 5:28–29). It is not clear from the text whether "the ones who saw them" heard the loud voice from heaven, or only the two witnesses heard it.[28] The verb "they heard" in verse 12 is ambiguous, but probably refers only to the two witnesses, who are consistently referred to as "they" in the rest of verses 12–13. In the context of John's vision, he heard what they heard, but it is not necessary to interpret this as a voice heard by all. It is simply God calling his witnesses home. The image of resurrection and ascension is reminiscent of Jesus' own (cf. also Ezekiel 37), and emphasizes that the followers of Christ who die for their faith in him will also follow him in resurrection and eternal life (Matthew 16:25).

We can safely assume that the two witnesses join the other souls who have been martyred. In chapter 6, John sees the souls of the martyrs under the altar of heaven.[29] The fact that they are "under" the altar is a reference to the Old Testament practice of pouring out the blood of the sacrifice on the base of the altar (Exodus 29:12; Leviticus 4:7).[30] Interestingly, the Christians would later develop the tradition of building churches so that the altar was directly over the tomb of a martyr or other saint. To this day, the tomb of the apostle Peter is directly beneath the altar of St. Peter's Basilica in Rome.

The martyrs cry out for justice, asking God, "How long . . . ?" How long will God wait to avenge their deaths? The answer comes: they must wait "a little while longer." Like many such phrases in biblical texts, this one gives us very little to go on if we are trying to determine what the timing will be. To God, "a little while longer" could mean a moment, or a millennium (cf. 2 Peter 3:8). While the fall of Jerusalem is about to take place, and not too long after that, the fall of Rome, there is yet a greater vindication coming at the Day of the Lord, the end of the age, at the revealing of the Kingdom of God. So the martyrs are told that

28. Mounce, *Book of Revelation*, 228.

29. It need not concern us that the martyrs who die in chapter 11 are in heaven in chapter 6. In the downward spiral of the Revelation, many events are not presented in chronological order.

30. Mounce, *Book of Revelation*, 157.

they must wait until the full number of martyrs is completed. Just as the gospel must be preached to all the world before the end (Matthew 24:14), so the world must do its worst to the saints of God before the Kingdom is finally revealed. It must be acknowledged that even now, in the twenty-first century, there are places in the world where the Church is persecuted and where Christian leaders and evangelists risk their lives to spread the gospel. Apparently, the full number of martyrs has not yet been reached.

THE SECOND WOE: THE FALL OF JERUSALEM
(REV 6:12–17; 8:7–12; 9:13–21; 11:1–2, 13–14)

The reader will probably begin to notice that there is a lot of overlap from one section of Revelation to another. Specifically, several significant portions of the book of Revelation are related to this one event, the fall of Jerusalem. One of the keys to interpretation here is the mention of a great earthquake. As already noted, it is a mistake to try to connect the earthquake(s) mentioned in the text to any particular earthquakes in history. Certainly there have been many actual earthquakes, both before and after John's time. However, a better approach is to assume that the earthquake is symbolic, and that each mention of an earthquake in the text of Revelation is actually a reference to one of two similar catastrophic events, both the product of divine intervention and judgment. Taking this approach, the earthquakes mentioned in 6:12 (the sixth seal), 8:5 (the seventh seal, revealing the seven trumpets), and 11:13 (after the death and resurrection of the two witnesses) all reflect the same event, the fall of Jerusalem.[31] The other two earthquakes mentioned (11:19 and 16:18) refer to the fall of Rome.

    The fall of the city of Jerusalem, with the destruction of the temple, was an event so shocking that it takes up much of the focus of the book of Revelation. As such, it is described in terms borrowed from the destruction of Sodom and Gomorrah and the plagues of Egypt, as well as apocalyptic imagery that would be familiar to John's audience. When the Lamb opened the sixth seal, the earthquake was accompanied by a darkened sun and blood on the moon. The stars fell, the sky split open and the mountains were moved. People from every walk of life, from kings to slaves, hid in caves and prayed that the mountains would

31. Cf. Josephus, *Wars of the Jews* 6.5.3.

fall on them to hide them from the anger of God. This is exactly what Jesus said would happen at the time of the desecration of the temple (Matthew 24:15–29; Mark 13:24–25; Luke 21:20–26; 23:28–30).[32] Jesus recalled Daniel's description of the desecration of the temple (interpreted as that of Antiochus IV in the second century BCE) as a warning that it would happen again.[33] In fact, the temple was desecrated for the last time at the fall of Jerusalem in 70 CE.[34]

The first four trumpets also reflect the fall of Jerusalem. The first trumpet blast heralds a Sodom-and-Gomorrah-like hailstorm of fire and blood, which burns a third of the earth. While the Roman war machines did have the capability to hurl burning projectiles from catapults at the walls of Jerusalem, it is not necessary to find military parallels to every symbol in John's description. In 9:17, John reminds the reader that this is a vision, which functions as a warning not to try to interpret the symbolism too literally.[35] The imagery that John uses successfully conveys the terror and confusion of the end of the siege and the sack of the city. When John says that one-third of the earth is destroyed, this is a hyperbole to describe the great devastation. There is no need to look for parallels in history or anticipate the future destruction of major portions of planet earth. The list of natural disasters John describes would have been a familiar catalogue of apocalyptic events that signify the "labor pains" that anticipate the end times.[36] John's use of them, taken as a whole, points to the earth-shattering nature of the fall of Jerusalem.[37] More important, the fraction one-third implies that it is a divinely appointed portion, and that since it is less than half, more of the earth is spared than destroyed. We are to understand that even in this time of

---

32. Mounce, *Book of Revelation*, 163, 188. See also Beasley-Murray, *Revelation*, 138. Cf. Isaiah 2:10, 19–21; 34:4; Ezekiel 32:7–8; 38:19; Hosea 10:8; Joel 2:10, 30–32; Amos 8:8.

33. Mounce, *Book of Revelation*, 221.

34. Some interpreters speculate that the Jerusalem temple will be rebuilt, so that the prophecy of its desecration can be fulfilled in the future. Not only is this highly unlikely, given the fact that Islam's Dome of the Rock is now on the site of the temple, but such speculation is unnecessary. The prophecy was fulfilled when the temple was destroyed (for the second time).

35. Mounce, *Book of Revelation*, 202.

36. Ibid., 161.

37. N. T. Wright uses the same phrase, "earth-shattering," to explain the symbolic nature of apocalyptic images. See, for example, Wright, *Jesus and the Victory of God*, 362.

great suffering and tragedy, which was interpreted as judgment by many, God's mercy is greater than his anger.

When the second trumpet sounds, the same thing happens to the seas that has happened to the earth. From this we can gather that the "earth" in 8:7 does not mean the whole world, but the land. Therefore it is not necessary to interpret this as an event that affects the whole planet, but simply one that would change the world as John's audience knew it. This section of the text may also recall the whole war with Rome, going back to 66 CE, and not just the fall of Jerusalem itself. Also, if one wanted to find a natural parallel to the events described here, 8:8 sounds like the description of a volcano erupting. This could be John's way of reminding the reader that Mt. Vesuvius erupted in August of 79 CE, destroying two important cities of the Roman Empire less than a decade after it had sacked Jerusalem. In fact, Titus, the Roman general who led the attack on Jerusalem and authorized the destruction of the temple became emperor the same year Vesuvius erupted, and thus for many the volcano may have been a sign and foreshadowing of God's punishment of Rome.

The third trumpet sounds, and the waters become poisonous. This is a picture of the fall of Lucifer, but the effect of the falling star is that it turns the waters bitter. Implicit in these verses is a reminder who is behind all these events: Satan, who has poisoned the world with his evil.[38] On the other hand, safe drinking water would most definitely become an issue during a siege, and it is likely that some people had died from a lack of fresh water during the siege of Jerusalem.

The fourth trumpet brings darkness for one-third of each day. It should go without saying by now that we are not looking for a literal fulfillment of this verse. Were this to happen literally, with one-third of the sun, moon, and stars destroyed, the universe would be one-third darker all of the time, not completely dark for one-third of the time (Rev 8:12). This is simply more apocalyptic imagery, borrowed from the plagues God brought on Egypt during the time of Moses, to show both the cataclysmic nature of the event taking place, and also to show that it is part of the unfolding of God's judgment.

---

38. Wormwood is mentioned in the Old Testament as a source of poison in water, in Jeremiah 9:15 and 23:15. However, wormwood would not actually make the water poisonous, but simply bitter. Furthermore, in these verses the bitterness is a punishment from God. Mounce, *Book of Revelation*, 187–88. Cf. also Proverbs 5:3–4, where the wormwood is described in terms reminiscent of John's little scroll, which tastes good at first, but in the end is bitter.

Following on the heels of the fifth trumpet, which, as we have seen, is a description of the (approximately) five-month siege of Jerusalem, the sixth trumpet sounds, and John describes the sack of the city by the Roman legions. What had previously happened to the land and the sea now happens to the people—one-third of them are killed. While many English translations of 9:18 have one-third of humanity dying ("a third of mankind"), the Greek text does not necessarily say that. The Greek actually says, "one-third of the men were killed." It is probably safe to assume that "men" is meant inclusively, to refer to people in general, although it could also refer only to the men who fought against the Roman legions. Still, it seems best to interpret this as a reference to one-third of the people in the city of Jerusalem at the time of the breach of the city walls, not one-third of all of humanity. This becomes even clearer when we recognize that the reference to the death of one-third of the people comes from Ezekiel 5:12, which is a description of the first fall of Jerusalem, in 586 BCE.

At the sound of the trumpet a heavenly voice is heard authorizing the four angels from chapter 7 to release the destruction that was waiting for this appointed time (cf. Matthew 24:36). However in this passage the angels are not said to be at the four corners of the earth, but at the river Euphrates. Remember that the image of the "four corners of the earth" does not need to imply the farthest reaches of the world, but in fact the "corners" converge at the biblical cradle of human life on earth, the Euphrates River. The destruction of human life seems to come from the same place as the creation of human life. The destruction that is unleashed comes in the form of a vast number of Roman cavalry, which brings with it fire and smoke and sulfur. The horror of the battlefield is brought inside the city walls and no one is safe from its devastation. Many people died in the fall of Jerusalem, mostly the inhabitants of the city. The historian Josephus recorded his eyewitness account of the siege and fall of Jerusalem, noting that there was so much blood spilled when the city fell that the flowing blood actually put out some of the fires.[39]

In chapter 9, John tells us that those who survived did not turn away from their false worship or repent of their treatment of the Christians in their midst. However, in chapter 11, those who witness the martyrs' resurrection and ascension do seem to repent. This does not prevent us from interpreting both passages as related to the fall of Jerusalem.

---

39. Josephus, *Wars of the Jews* 6.8.5.

In 9:20–21, we are told that the rest of the people of the city (not "the rest of mankind," as some translations render it) who were not killed by the plagues of fire, smoke, and sulfur did not stop committing idolatry and other sins. This means that many of those who survived the fall of Jerusalem became collaborators with the Romans, participating in their false worship and other blasphemous practices (cf. Rev 18:3). It does not necessarily mean every last person, but in general the majority of the survivors. Therefore it does not rule out the possibility that some, who had heard the witness of the martyrs, could have turned to God when the city fell.

After the city was taken by the legions, the temple was looted and burned. In John's vision, he is given something like a yardstick with which to measure the temple. The measuring of the temple foreshadows its destruction. As in Ezekiel 40–48, the temple is measured to preserve its dimensions in the event that it can be rebuilt after its destruction.[40] This is not meant to imply that the temple will be rebuilt again, it is simply a way to signify the destruction of the temple that had been destroyed and rebuilt once before. At one end of the ancient forum in Rome stands a triumphal arch, which commemorates the victory of the Romans over Jerusalem. It is called the Arch of Titus, in honor of the general who led the attack on Jerusalem, and who became emperor in 79 CE. Inside the arch is a sculpted scene depicting the parade of the spoils of war. To this day, the temple's menorah is clearly seen among the looted treasures.

Revelation 11:13 says that seven thousand people (seven multitudes) were killed by the "earthquake," while 9:18 says one-third of the people died. These refer to the same event, and as we have seen, we are not required to reconcile the numbers. Some commentators point out that seven thousand people was about one-tenth of the population of Jerusalem at that time.[41] But it is not clear that "one-tenth of the city" necessarily refers to people. It may refer to the physical structures of the city. More importantly, the number seven thousand primarily means a complete number of multitudes. Even though in chapter 11 John may be giving us a more accurate representation of the death toll, in chapter 9 we are told that it is one-third, meaning a divinely appointed portion

---

40. Beasley-Murray, *Revelation*, 181. Cf. Amos 7:7–9. See also Beale, *Book of Revelation*, 20–21.

41. For example, see Beasley-Murray, *Book of Revelation*, 187.

that is less than half the total population.[42] Once again, God's mercy is the overriding factor, in that most of the people survive. Nevertheless, the fall of Jerusalem and the destruction of the temple is the second woe (Rev 11:14).

Although the book of Revelation is considered prophecy, we cannot let that skew our assumptions about the interpretation to the point where we expect everything in the book to be about John's future. In truth, events in John's past make up a large portion of the book, because they are so significant for God's people. Therefore, the birth of Jesus, his death and resurrection, the beginning of persecution of the Church, the Jewish-Roman war, and the fall of Jerusalem are all presented in apocalyptic terms, because they are the labor pains of the end times. Just as labor pains only signal the beginning of labor, which does not end until the birth, these events signal the beginning of God's unfolding plan, which ends with the full revelation of the Kingdom. The fact that John's readers know that these events are all in their past does not diminish the significance of the events for the overall message of John's vision. Just like the Old Testament tradition of remembering the past to encourage faith and hope for the future, Revelation presents these images as a way to remind the Christians of John's time that God is still active in human history, and even though evil seems powerful, God is infinitely more powerful.

SUMMARY

- The first two woes, the siege and fall of Jerusalem, are in John's past—John finds himself between the time of the second and third woe.

- Events in the past often give encouragement and hope in the present, much like the Jewish tradition of remembering the Exodus and other acts of God in history to strengthen faith in the face of uncertainty.

42. On the other hand, Josephus estimated that there were three million people in Jerusalem during the time of the siege, which would have included people from the surrounding areas who fled into the city to escape the Roman legions. Though most scholars today say that Josephus' estimate is high, he did say that the death toll was over one million, which is about one-third of his total estimate. Therefore, in general Josephus' account is consistent with Revelation 9:18. Josephus, *Wars of the Jews* 5–6. See also Eusebius of Caesarea, *Ecclesiastical History* 3.6–7.

- According to a pre-Christian understanding that John accepts, evil exists on earth because the angel Lucifer (Satan, the devil) was expelled from the heavenly realm.

- All tribulation is ultimately caused by the devil—the oppression and exile during the time of Babylon, Herod's attempt to kill Jesus, the Roman war, the siege and fall of Jerusalem, the destruction of the temple, and the persecution of the Church were all energized by the same source of evil.

- Most of the Christians of Jerusalem were spared from the siege and fall of the city because they had fled before the Romans began the siege.

- Jesus defeated Satan before (at his resurrection) and he will do it again. The resurrection contains within it the promise of the final victory of Christ.

- Only Jesus Christ is worthy to set God's judgments in motion because he is both human and divine.

- Christian worship is the singing of a new song, new praise for the new covenant, in which is it appropriate to worship Jesus.

- Those who follow Jesus in martyrdom will also follow him in resurrection.

- Even in the midst of judgment, God's mercy is more prevalent than his anger.

7

Visions of John's Present

The things that are . . .

INTRODUCTION

WE NOW TURN TO those parts of the book of Revelation that relate to John's present situation. The main portions of Revelation's
present circumstances are reflected in the letters to the seven churches
in chapters two and three. We will treat the letters as independent units,
as though they are John's "pastoral epistles" to the churches in his area,
even though the message itself comes from Christ. Most of the letters
have a twofold format. Beginning with "I know your works. . . ," most of
the churches are praised for their faith and good deeds, which sets them
up to receive criticism and words of admonition or warning, beginning
with "But I have against you . . ." In each case the message is meant to
strengthen the church for the continued persecution that is anticipated.

The letters are addressed to the "angel" of each church, which as
we have seen means the leader, or presider, of the local church (what we
would now call the "pastor" of the church). Since these early congrega-
tions were house churches, it is possible that the presider of each church
was simply the owner of the house. There may have been more than
one house church in each town, and if that were the case, the message is
addressed to all the Christians of the town. The letter (indeed, the whole
book of Revelation) would have been passed around from house church
to house church.

In each letter, there is an apocalyptic description of Jesus as the
one from whom the message comes. At the end, each letter contains a
message of hope and encouragement for "whoever overcomes," meaning that any who keep the faith and refuse to submit to idolatry, even

though they may die, they will be granted eternal life. Finally, every letter ends with the words, "Whoever has an ear, let him hear what the Spirit says to the churches." It is clear from this statement that the message to each church is not for the Christians of that town only, but for the whole Church at large.

Other portions of John's present situation include the introduction to Revelation, which describes his exile, an angelic announcement of the spread of the gospel, and a section about the persecution itself. We will begin with these.

THE INTRODUCTION TO THE BOOK OF REVELATION
(1:1–9)

We have already covered much of John's introduction in chapter 2 above. However, a few things are relevant at this point. John begins the book of Revelation by telling his readers of his current situation. He is in exile on the Island of Patmos, which is off the coast of what is now southwestern Turkey, in the Aegean Sea. John acknowledges in verse 9 that he is there because of his testimony to Christ during a time of persecution. To his readers, he refers to himself as their brother and fellow partaker in the "tribulation" (i.e., persecution) and in the Kingdom (i.e., the present Reign of God: the mission and ministry of spreading the message of Jesus) and in the "endurance in Jesus" (i.e., perseverance in the faith; cf. 2 Timothy 4:7). It is within this context that the book of Revelation was written: to encourage Christians in the midst of persecution, to encourage them to continue the ministry of the Kingdom, and especially to encourage them to persevere, in other words, to resist the temptation to give up the faith to save their lives.

On a Sunday (verse 10), John had the vision, or series of visions, that would be the book of Revelation. The content of the vision is the message about the revealing of the Kingdom. It is not that a secret message is revealed in the pages of the book, but that the book promises (in language understandable to its original audience) that the Kingdom which is now concealed will be revealed. The message ultimately comes from God, but through Jesus Christ and by angelic messenger, to John. The purpose of the vision is stated in verse 1: "to show his (Christ's) servants the things which must happen soon." Verse 3 is a blessing on those who read the words of Revelation (that is, read the words aloud in worship) and on those who hear the words and take them to heart, "for the time is near."

Verse 4 almost seems to begin the book again with the formal greeting of a letter. Even though John has already introduced himself and his subject, as well as given a blessing on the recipients of the letter, he formally begins with verse 4, stating who he is and to whom the document is written. He writes to the seven churches in the province of Asia (now western Turkey). These are the house churches in the seven cities, which are individually addressed in chapters 2–3. However, it is safe to assume that the message of Revelation is meant to go beyond these cities to the Church at large. Verses 4–5 sound very much like the beginning of a Pauline letter, with the wish for God's grace and peace to be with the recipients.

The triune God is described by John as follows: "the one who is and the one who was and the one who is coming" (that is, God the Father, one and the same with Yahweh, the God of the Old Testament), and "Jesus Christ, the faithful witness, the first-born from the dead, and the ruler of the kings of the earth" (in other words, he is the Risen One who by his resurrection is vindicated as the King of kings). The Holy Spirit is called "the seven Spirits facing his throne," though a better (albeit less literal) translation is "the sevenfold Spirit" (meaning the all-encompassing, omnipresent Spirit; see Rev 3:1; 4:5; 5:6; cf. Isaiah 11:2). However, John does not list the three persons of the Trinity in the traditional order. For John, the Holy Spirit is almost an extension of the Father. This is what John means when he says the sevenfold Spirit is "facing his throne." So the Trinity for John is God the Father, often described in terms of the heavenly throne with the "sevenfold" Spirit, and Jesus Christ the Son, the Lamb of God.

John gives glory to Christ, for his love for us, for his sacrifice that frees us from our sins, and for making us holy priests and partakers of his Kingdom. John then quotes Daniel's vision of the Son of Man, "coming from the clouds," (Daniel 7:13; cf. Matthew 24:27–31). Verses 6 and 7 of chapter 1 both end with "Amen," which means "So be it—it is true." Thus John begins the book of Revelation with what it all is leading up to: the return of Christ, almost as if the rest of the book is a prophetic flashback, showing how God's sovereign plan leads up to the second coming of Christ. God is, after all, the beginning and the end, the source and culmination of all things (verse 8).

THE SPREAD OF THE GOSPEL
(REVELATION 14:6–7)

In Revelation 14:6–13, three angels bring proclamations. Here we will include only the first one, since the second and third announce events in John's future. For John's present time, he sees an angel, flying through the heavens, who brings "an eternal gospel to preach to those on the earth; to every nation and tribe and tongue and people." Obviously, the spread of the gospel has been going on since before the time of the Revelation, but given the fact that evangelism has become a dangerous enterprise, the Christians of John's time would want to know that their efforts are not in vain. This passage is a promise of the success of the gospel, which is meant to encourage the Christians of that time to continue the mission and not lose heart. The promise that God made to Abraham in Genesis 12:3 is being fulfilled. Through the descendants of Abraham, all the people of the earth are blessed. The gospel that began among the Jews has opened up to include the Gentiles.

The angel then proclaims, "Fear God, and give him glory . . . and worship the One who made heaven and earth and the sea and the springs of water." This message implies that people should give glory *only* to God and worship God *alone*, because he is the Creator and they must not trade worship of the Creator for worship of that which is created, including human beings. The urgency of the angel's message is that "the hour of his judgment has come." This is a warning to avoid apostasy and idolatry during the persecution, and the force of the warning is not diminished by the fact that the final judgment did not come in John's time. Just as Jesus proclaimed that the Kingdom had come when it had not yet been fully revealed, so the angel announces that the beginning of God's judgment has been set in motion, though the final consummation must wait. In this way, the message proclaims the prophetic "now," which promises that the seeds of the future have already been planted in the present. The message delivered by the angel may also be a reference to (and foreshadowing of) God's judgment on the Roman persecutors of Christians, since the fall of Rome is announced by the second angel in the very next verse.

THE PERSECUTION
(REVELATION 13:8–15, 18)

The number of the beast refers to the name of the emperor during John's exile, Domitian. His imperial title was Emperor Caesar Domitian Augustus Germanicus. This would have been abbreviated to fit on coins minted during his reign. As several historians have already pointed out, the letters of the abbreviated version of Domitian's name, the name that would have appeared around his image on coins during John's time, add up to 666.[1] Domitian took the expectation of emperor worship to new heights during his reign, and it was their refusal to participate in this worship that put Christians in danger. Such refusal could be taken as a form of treason, a crime punishable by death.

Virtually everyone in the empire engaged in the imperial cult in some way. Not to do so would have been seen as antisocial behavior. The primary exceptions to the norm were Christians and Jews. John tells his readers that everyone whose name is not in the Lamb's book of life will worship the emperor (represented by the beast, verses 8 and 12). In fact, those names in the book have been there "from the foundation of the world" (cf. Rev 17:8). The idea that the book existed before those whose names are written in it is not meant to imply a predestination of their eternal fate. Rather, it simply affirms God's foreknowledge of those who will remain faithful (Romans 8:29).[2] In fact, in the letter to Sardis (Rev 3:1–6), it is implied that a name can be removed from the book (verse 5).

Characteristic of the letters that relate to John's present time is the phrase, "Whoever has an ear, let him hear what the Spirit says to the churches." This is a warning to John's audience to be careful not to compromise one's faith, because the road of compromise leads to apostasy, especially when faced with a life or death choice. That is exactly what would face many Christians, during John's time and even more so afterward. But John says that if it anyone is meant to be captured, he should

1. See Mounce, *Book of Revelation*, 264n58 for additional sources. Note also the references to this number in 1 Kings 10:14 and 2 Chronicles 9:13.

2. The concept of election in Paul's letter to the Romans must be understood in the context of the early Church's understanding that the Church was the new "chosen people" of God. We must not read Augustine's double predestination back into Paul. For Paul, the Church constitutes the "elect" precisely because it is the new Israel, and God's "election" is based on his foreknowledge of each person's acceptance of the faith by free will.

not try to avoid it (verse 10). In other words, one should not try to escape arrest and possible exile or even torture by giving up the faith. John goes on to say that even if one faces execution, it is better to be executed than to renounce Christ and lose one's eternal reward (cf. Matthew 10:28).[3] Note that verse 10 is not saying, "whoever lives by the sword dies by the sword," nor is this a commentary on the fate of those who kill Christians. The first two phrases of verse 10 are a Hebrew-style parallelism, in which both phrases mean basically the same thing, but the second one takes the idea a step further. So the meaning is, whether the authorities take you away to be imprisoned or to be executed, do not give up your faith, even to save your life. This is the faith of the saints who persevere.

Next in the vision John sees another beast come up from the earth.[4] The image of this other beast is a symbol that has three levels of meaning. First, the emperor Domitian was seen by some as a reincarnation of Nero, or at least a revival of Nero's ruthless spirit. The beast that comes up from the earth is the beast that rises from the dead. Like Nero who reigned before him, Domitian speaks the words of the devil but wants to be treated as a god. In this way, he is "like a lamb but spoke as a dragon." He is a false lamb, demanding worship when none is due him. As such, this is the closest we get to the concept of an antichrist in the book of Revelation, though as noted previously, the word "antichrist" does not appear in the text. The mention of fire may be a reference to the fire in Rome in 64 CE, which many believed was started by Nero to make room for a new palace he wanted to build. The fire was Nero's justification for the first imperial persecution of Christians.

The second level of meaning is that the beast from the earth represents renewed persecution. This means that the present persecution under the emperor Domitian is a revival of Nero's persecution, but it also foreshadows more persecution to come in the future. This functions as a warning that persecution may subside for a while but will come back again, each time more dangerous than before. Therefore the Church is not to become complacent and drop its guard when the persecution subsides temporarily. For Christians of the Roman era, the two most wide-

3. The phrasing of this passage is based on Jeremiah 15:2 and 43:11.

4. Some Jewish apocalyptic literature assumed the existence of two beasts, one of the land, and one of the sea. The beast of the land was the male beast, behemoth; and the beast of the sea was the female beast, leviathan. While John's vision shows no such distinction between the two beasts, this background contributes to the imagery. Mounce, *Book of Revelation*, 258.

spread revivals of persecution would come in the middle of the third century and at the beginning of the fourth century. The persecution of the third century was the result of the emperor Decius, who wanted to restore Roman society and religion to its glory days. The so-called Great Persecution began in 303 CE and was led by the emperor Diocletian and his right-hand man and son-in-law, Galerius. The two horns of the second beast could be taken as a prediction of these two waves of persecution under Decius and Diocletian, or they may refer to the Great Persecution and its two most notorious persecutors, Diocletian and Galerius.

The third level of meaning is that the second beast is related to the false prophet mentioned in 16:13; 19:20; and 20:10. In this context, the second beast represents the Roman imperial cult—the religious system of temples and priesthoods that supported and was supported by the imperial government. Like the Old Testament false prophets, who were the yes-men of the idolatrous kings of Israel, the false prophet or second beast of Revelation is the Roman religious system that supports the worship of the emperors. In this way, the second beast makes everyone worship the first beast, authorizes the making of images of the beast, and encourages the condemnation of any who do not engage in the imperial cult. The signs that are performed to deceive the people bring to mind the signs that the Pharaoh's magicians produced to compete with Moses and Aaron (Exodus 7–8; cf. also Deuteronomy 13:1–4; 2 Thessalonians 2:8–12). Though the emperors had supreme authority in the empire, they could not be everywhere at once. Their will was enforced in part by their officers in the provinces but also by the collaboration of the priests, who operated across the empire and who exercised control over the people through their religion. John says that the second beast, or the false prophet, will perform signs, even to the point of giving breath to the image of the beast, which will be able to speak and will cause those who do not worship it to be killed. By their influence at the local level, the priests reinforced the power of the Roman officers, who in turn enforced the emperor's wishes. In this way, they gave voice to the image of the emperor in each city or town. We can assume that in many places there were literal images of the emperors. In John's own town of Ephesus there was a statue of Domitian set up as a daily reminder of who held the authority. Therefore, on this third level of meaning, the two horns could represent the two unified powers of the empire that conspire to persecute the Church—the imperial office (the emperors) and the Roman priesthood.

We now turn to the letters to seven churches of Asia Minor. As the resident apostle, John would have functioned as the "overseer," or bishop, of these churches. Even if we assume that each city had multiple house churches with their own bishop, it is possible that John's role was something like a metropolitan, with authority over the city churches in a certain area.[5] However, it is more likely that at this early date each of these cities had only one house church and were connected to each other through the ministry of their apostle/bishop. Therefore these letters serve as episcopal letters, analogous to the Pauline pastoral epistles, in which John writes to the leaders of the churches under his authority, and conveys to them the messages that Jesus gave him to pass on.

THE LETTER TO EPHESUS
(REVELATION 2:1–7)

The One who holds the seven stars in His right hand, the One who walks in the midst of the seven golden lampstands, says these things . . .

The city of Ephesus was the capital of the province of Asia and was situated on the coast of what is now Turkey, on the Aegean Sea. Ephesus was the most important city in ancient Asia Minor, both in terms of economy and Greco-Roman religion.[6] It had a population of about 250,000 and boasted a famous temple of Diana (the same goddess is called Artemis in Acts 19:23–41).[7] It was also the place where John had lived with Mary, the mother of Jesus. As the resident apostle and bishop of the seven churches, John's see would have been Ephesus. In this letter he delivers a message in which Christ commends the church members for their ability to discern true apostles from false ones. Over thirty years before, the apostle Paul had written to the church in Ephesus, a church he had

---

5. The letter of 1 Clement was written by Bishop Clement of Rome at about the same time as the book of Revelation. It demonstrates that the office of bishop had evolved at least to the point where an overseer might write letters giving advice to the Christians of another city.

6. Beasley-Murray, *Revelation*, 72–73.

7. Mounce, *Book of Revelation*, 85–86.

founded.[8] Paul predicted that false teachers would come to the church of Ephesus, and by the time of John's letter they have (Acts 20:25–31; cf. Matthew 7:15). One group of false apostles is mentioned by name, a group known as the Nicolaitans, who apparently taught a form of dualism that allowed them to practice sexual immorality on the assumption that what they did with their bodies did not affect their souls.[9]

The Ephesian Christians are also commended for their work on behalf of the gospel and for their perseverance in the face of persecution. The "work" to which John refers is not simply good works in general, but labor "because of My name," in other words, evangelism.[10] Not only have the Ephesian Christians not given up their faith in the face of persecution, they have continued to spread it.

"But I have against you . . . ," says Christ. He is disappointed with the church of Ephesus because they have "left [their] first love." This probably means that they have lost the devotion to Christ and the enthusiasm for worship that they once had. While Jesus praises them for not having grown weary (they have not given up the faith; verse 3), perhaps the Christians of Ephesus have lost the joy and enthusiasm they once had when their faith was new (cf. Psalm 51:12). This has led to a degradation of their worship and devotional life, which Christ wants them to regain. He admonishes them to remember where they came from ("from where you have fallen"), and to go back to the way they did things at the begin-

8. Acts 19. Admittedly, the Pauline authorship of the letter to the Ephesians is debated. However, that question is not of critical importance to our current discussion.

9. Beasley-Murray, *Revelation*, 74. Nicolaitanism was apparently an early form of Gnosticism, a heresy that denied that Jesus was truly human, and would later separate from the Church and produce such documents as the so-called *Gospel of Thomas*. Their denial of Christ's true humanity was based on a dualism that assumed all matter was evil, or at least inferior to (and detached from) the spiritual realm. This led some, like the Nicolaitans, to practice a form of libertinism, a lifestyle of indulgence that assumed one could remain spiritually aloof from the world while still physically participating in its basest pursuits. Early Church writers associated the Nicolaitans with a deacon named Nicolaus, mentioned in Acts 6:5. Some said Nicolaus was a heretic, but others said that he was misunderstood by some of his followers who strayed from the Church. There is no early evidence for the Nicolaitans' connection with the deacon of Acts other than the similarity of names. In the third century, Hippolytus knew that the Nicolaitans were Gnostics (Hippolytus, *Refutation of All Heresies* 7.24), but the sect had died out by the time of Eusebius of Caesarea in the early fourth century (Eusebius of Caesarea, *Ecclesiastical History* 3.29). See also Irenaeus of Lyons, *Against Heresies* 1.26.3; and Clement of Alexandria, *Stromateis* 2.118.

10. Beasley-Murray, *Revelation*, 74.

ning. If they do not repent (turn back to the direction they started on), he warns that he will visit them and remove their lampstand from its place. In other words, the leadership of the church is in jeopardy. Jesus warns that the current leader(s) of the church will be replaced if the church does not turn itself around (repent) and regain its former worship and devotional life.

THE LETTER TO SMYRNA
(REVELATION 2:8–11)

The first and the last, who died and then lived, says these things . . .

Smyrna is modern Izmir, and was the second most important city in Asia Minor after Ephesus.[11] In the second century (sixty years after John wrote Revelation), the bishop of Smyrna, Polycarp, would become one of the early Church's most famous martyrs. But the church in Smyrna was already suffering persecution at the time John wrote Revelation. When this letter begins with a description of Jesus as the One "who died and then lived," this reminds John's readers that if they follow Jesus in death they will follow him in resurrection as well. The Christians of Smyrna are poor by the world's standards, probably because of the persecution they are enduring, which would already be having an effect on the economic status of those who refused to participate in the imperial cult.[12] However, what is more important is that they know what is of ultimate value and do not give in to the values of the world, so that in spite of their poverty, they are spiritually rich.

The Lord says, "I know your tribulation . . ." and then tells them that they will continue to suffer persecution, and even martyrdom, for his sake.[13] The persecution will last "ten days." This is a reference to the testing of Daniel at the court of Nebuchadnezzar (Daniel 1:8–16). Daniel and his friends refused to eat meat that might have been sacrificed to

11. Mounce, *Book of Revelation*, 91.

12. Ibid., 92. See also Beale, *Book of Revelation*, 240–41.

13. The fact that "tribulation" (suffering, affliction, oppression) is a present phenomenon in John's time emphasizes that it is not to be thought of as a particular future time of suffering. Many interpretations of Revelation, and especially much of the popular end-times fiction, make far too much of the English word "tribulation," as if it is a technical term (i.e., *the* tribulation). I am tempted to translate these passages with a more common English word, like "suffering" or even "persecution," however I use the word "tribulation" here to show that in John's mind it is not limited to the future.

idols, because this would have been like participating in idolatrous worship. However, their desire to avoid offending God was perceived as disrespect toward the king. Ultimately this was a choice similar to the one faced by many Christians of John's time, a choice between loyalty to the emperor or loyalty to God.[14] The point of the message to the Christians of Smyrna is that they, too, will be faced with this choice. But for those who keep the faith, who do not make pagan sacrifices to save their lives, there awaits for them the martyrs' crown of victory and eternal life. They may die for their faith, but they will not experience the "second death," which is separation from God (Rev 20:6).

Interestingly, the persecution is not explicitly attributed to the Romans but is associated with "the slander [literally "blasphemy"; cf. Mark 3:29] of those who call themselves Jews, but they are nothing but a synagogue of Satan." We have to keep in mind when we read harsh statements such as this that many, if not most, of John's audience are themselves Jews. This is not an anti-Jewish argument, rather it is meant to convey that a few who should know better (because they are God's people) are conspiring against their own brothers and sisters and reporting them to the Romans. The conflict in Smyrna is not between Jews and Gentiles, but between Christians (many of whom are Jews and may still be attending the synagogue) and a few antagonistic non-Christians. The fact that John points out that they "call themselves Jews" probably means that they are harassing the Church in the name of Judaism because they were scandalized by the worship of Jesus in their community, and saw followers of Jesus as leading people astray. But John says that they are not really Jews because they are not acting like people of God. It was probably especially painful to know that some within their own ethnic community were responsible for the persecution of innocent Christians. Also, blaming these antagonists is consistent with John's desire to keep the book of Revelation benign from the Romans' point of view, should any of them ever read it.

However, the persecution itself cannot be blamed on anyone but the Roman emperors (the beast) who demanded cultic loyalty. In making the reference to Daniel, it would have been clear to the readers of Revelation that their loyalty was to be tested. They were going to have to choose between their emperor and their God. Unfortunately, their em-

---

14. Beale, *Book of Revelation*, 242.

peror held the power of life and death. The letter to the church of Smyrna is a reminder that Christ holds the key to eternal life (Rev 1:18).

THE LETTER TO PERGAMUM
(REVELATION 2:12–17)

The One with the sharp double-edged sword says these things . . .

The Christians of Pergamum live "where Satan lives" and "where Satan's throne is." As the former capital of the province of Asia (before Ephesus), Pergamum would have been, until recently, the seat of the Roman governor in the area, and therefore would have retained a culture highly influenced by Rome and its religion. Pergamum would still have been a relatively important site for the Roman imperial cult (the false prophet). As such, it would be seen by the Christians as a center of satanic activity. In spite of living in a pressure cooker of paganism, the Christians of Pergamum had kept faithful to the gospel, even when one of their own, someone named Antipas, was martyred. Antipas was very likely a beloved leader of the church in Pergamum, whose martyrdom was especially traumatic. It is possible that Antipas was the only Christian of Pergamum to have been martyred up to this point. If that was the case, it would be safe to assume that more martyrdoms were coming.

Though the Christians of Pergamum have kept the faith, there are those in the church there who are "holding the teaching of Balaam," as some translations render it. In Numbers 22–24, Balak, king of the Moabites, tried to hire the prophet Balaam to curse Israel. However, Balaam refused. Revelation 2:14 should probably be translated, ". . . you have there some who accept the instruction that Balak instructed Balaam, to throw a stumbling block in front of the children of Israel." In other words, what Balak wanted Balaam to do (but Balaam refused), there are now some among the church in Pergamum who are willing to do: to be (paid?) informants against the followers of Christ. Later in the book of Numbers, Balaam is held responsible for the idolatry of Israelite men who are tempted by Moabite women (possibly temple prostitutes) to worship their gods (Numbers 25:1–9; 31:7–16). Therefore, the "error of Balaam" (2 Peter 2:15; Jude 11) is seen as a kind of collaboration with the enemies of God, which can include sexual immorality with unbelievers (temple prostitution) and eating food that has been used in pagan sacrifices (Acts 15:20; 1 Corinthians 10:19–31).[15]

In the context of Pergamum, the teaching of Balaam is probably a reference to participation in celebrations that included rituals of the various Roman cults. Trade guilds and other membership organizations would sponsor festivals, the ancient world's equivalent of the office party. Even the public spectacles, like games and the theater, often included elements of pagan worship. To go to the party meant participation in this worship, feasting on the meat that had been sacrificed to Roman deities, and whatever drunken reveling might follow. Mention is also made of the Nicolaitan heresy in the church of Pergamum. The Nicolaitans are not necessarily the same people who follow the teaching of Balaam, but the two are related in that they advocate a lax morality, believing it has no bearing on their faith. Since idolatry is often symbolized as spiritual infidelity, there is a close relationship between sexual immorality and apostasy.

Christ warns that if those who engage in these errors do not repent he will visit the church of Pergamum and "will fight them with the sword of [his] mouth." Those who have made friends with Roman religion and immorality will find that Jesus is now their enemy, and his word is against them. It is interesting that the command to repent is directed, not just at the traitors and heretics, but at the whole church of Pergamum. There is a sense in which the whole church is responsible for these elements within it, and the whole church must take responsibility for correcting them. Of course Christ's fight will be with the traitors and heretics, but the responsibility for repentance lies with the whole church, and especially with the church leader (the "angel" of the church).

To the one who overcomes, Jesus promises "hidden manna," the sustaining bread of life (John 6:31–68), which is an image of eternal life. The manna is to be contrasted with the meat sacrificed to idols, which is eaten by those who stray from the Church.[16] Christ also promises a white stone with a new name written on it, known only to the one who receives it. It is well known that significant people in the Bible were given new names when God had chosen them for himself. Abram became Abraham,

15. Ibid., 248–49.

16. Mounce, *Book of Revelation*, 99. Eating meat sacrificed to idols has apparently become more of an issue since the time of Paul (cf. 1 Corinthians 8), probably due to the circumstances of the persecution.

Sarai become Sarah, Jacob became Israel, Simon became Peter, and Saul became Paul. However, in this case it is not a new personal name for the believer, it is God's name attached by identification, like a bride who takes the groom's last name as her own, or an adopted child who receives a new last name. The new name is the name by which an adopted son or daughter of God becomes an heir of God with Christ (Isaiah 56:5; cf. John 1:12–13), and the new name of the believer is equivalent to the mark of God, securing the believer as God's own (Rev 3:12; 14:1; 22:4; cf. also 19:12).[17] The white stone refers to the white and black stones used by a jury to vote on the verdict in a trial.[18] Thus the faithful are promised a favorable verdict in the final judgment where God the Father is the judge, and Jesus is a jury of one.

THE LETTER TO THYATIRA
(REVELATION 2:18–29)

The Son of God, whose eyes are like a flame of fire and whose feet are like polished brass, says these things . . .

The church of Thyatira was a church of service and action. The Christians there are praised for their good works, which have increased since the church was founded. But as is sometimes the case with churches that emphasize the social gospel, the Christians of Thyatira are too tolerant of unorthodox theology in their community. There is a woman there who is called a Jezebel, after the idolatrous queen of Israel (1 Kings 16:31; 21:25; 2 Kings 9:7, 27–37). In the Old Testament, idolatry is spiritual adultery, and this woman of Thyatira is leading Christians away from God just as Jezebel did in her time. We can assume that the Thyatiran woman in question is not really named Jezebel, but she is called by this name to emphasize the effect she is having on the community. She is the polar opposite of one Thyatiran woman whose name we do know, Lydia (Acts 16:14).

The Jezebel of Thyatira advocates participation in pagan celebrations and Roman immorality, as we have already seen in Pergamum, but what is worse, she claims to be a prophetess, and is teaching something John calls "the secrets of Satan" (literally the "deep things" of Satan). This

17. Beale, *Book of Revelation*, 253–55.

18. Cf. Acts 26:9–10, where Paul would have used a black stone to vote for the execution of Jesus' early followers.

may be a form of early Gnosticism, which was based on the concept of secret knowledge, but Gnostics would have attributed the knowledge to Jesus, not Satan. John's reference to Satan is probably his way of saying that what the proto-Gnostics attribute to Jesus really comes from Satan. Whatever the "secrets of Satan" really meant, John understands it to be a heresy that led believers away from the truth of Christ. Since this woman has refused to repent, Jesus says that he is planning to put an end to her teaching. He will discipline her and her followers with some form of suffering which will hinder her "ministry." Interestingly, the Greek word used for "suffering" or "affliction" is the same word used for "tribulation" in other passages where we interpret tribulation as persecution. It is possible that the Roman authorities, not knowing or caring whether a teacher was orthodox, could arrest "Jezebel" and her followers and remove them from the church. Without going too far into speculation, "throwing her onto a bed" could even refer to a form of torture at the hands of the Romans.[19] The point here is that Christ promises to stop the spread of the heresy in the church.

When Jesus says he will "kill her children," this does not refer to any actual offspring of hers. The "children" mentioned here are the fruits of her labors, possibly her disciples, but this is not necessarily a reference to human beings. It probably means simply the effects of her teaching. Her legacy will die and will not outlive her. Some translations render the Greek phrase, "I will kill her children *with pestilence*," or something similar. The Greek actually says, "I will kill her children *with death*." The point is not how the death occurs (which would assume human death); rather, the point is that the death causes something to come to an end. In other words, the emphasis is not on the killing, as if Jesus were to take someone's life. The emphasis is on the death of the "fruit" of this woman's life.

The effect of the suffering of the Thyatiran Jezebel and her followers is that everyone will know that Christ is the one who searches hearts and minds.[20] Knowing human hearts and minds, Jesus rewards each one

19. Some interpreters refer to 1 Corinthians 11:27–30, making the connection between those who would lead Christians astray and what Paul seems to imply, that disrespecting the body of Christ could lead to actual physical sickness. Thus to be "thrown onto a bed" would imply some kind of illness. Cyprian, a third-century bishop of Carthage, saw the image of Jezebel thrown onto a bed as an ironic twist, given her reputation as an adulteress. Cyprian, *Epistle* 55.22.

20. The Greek literally says "kidneys and hearts." In the ancient worldview, kidneys (i.e., guts) were the origin of emotions and passions, and so the word is best translated

according to his or her works. In other words, he will destroy the works of this Jezebel, but he will reward the works of those who keep the faith until he returns for them (Rev 2:25). Specifically, the works of the follower of Jesus means doing the works of Jesus (Rev 2:26). The reward, or at least part of it, is that Christ will share his inheritance of the Kingdom with those who overcome and remain faithful to the end (Psalm 2:8–9; Isaiah 30:14).

Finally, there is the curious phrase, ". . . and I will give him the morning star." In Revelation, the "morning star" is a reference to Christ himself (Rev 22:16). The star of the morning would bring to mind both the star of Bethlehem (Numbers 24:17; Matthew 2:2) and the dawn of Easter morning. Therefore the "bright Morning Star" of Revelation is Jesus, born of the Virgin Mary and risen in glory. However it is not clear how Christ would give himself to the believer who overcomes. It would seem that, by definition, the believer who overcomes does so because he or she already has Christ. Perhaps it means that in eternal life, believers are rewarded with an intimate relationship with Christ, which could not have been known in this life (cf. 1 Corinthians 13:12; Rev 3:20).

THE LETTER TO SARDIS
(REVELATION 3:1–6)

The One who has the sevenfold Spirit of God and the seven stars says these things . . .

There is no praise for the Christians of Sardis. They have a reputation for being alive, but they are spiritually dead. They are told to wake up and to strengthen what they still have before that dies, too.[21] Somehow, they have tried to do the work of the gospel, but that work remains incomplete, because in their attempt to do the work they have forgotten the gospel itself. They are like Martha of Bethany, busy doing work that they think will please God (and give them a good reputation) when all the while they have forgotten that the most important thing is to hear the words of Jesus and "sitting at the feet of the Lord" (Luke 10:38–42). They

---

"hearts" to convey the meaning to our way of thinking. The "heart" in ancient thought was the seat of the will, the place where decisions are made, and so I have translated this as "mind."

21. The admonition to "wake up" may be a reference to an early Christian hymn. Part of this hymn is preserved in Ephesians 5:14.

have forgotten that one must seek Christ before one can serve him. Jesus tells them, "Therefore, remember how you received and heard [the gospel], and go back to keeping it." If they do not repent ("wake up"), Jesus warns, when he comes they will not be found ready. The implication of this warning is not *if you do not repent, then I will come,* but *if you do not repent, then you will not be ready when I come.* In other words, Christ's coming is not dependent on their repentance, or lack of it, as if this were a reference to another visitation from Christ before his expected return. The time of Christ's return will be unknown, like the thief who comes in the night (Matthew 24:36; 1 Thessalonians 5:2; 2 Peter 3:10; Rev 16:15). Those who are not spiritually alive when he comes will not be ready. No matter what works they have done, their works will remain incomplete if they have forgotten the gospel—which should be the very reason they do the works in the first place (Matthew 5:16). The image of incomplete works would have been especially vivid to the Christians of Sardis, since their town had in it an incomplete temple of Diana.[22]

Still, there are some Christians in Sardis who have not forgotten what they had originally received. They are the ones who did not "defile their garments." The image of the defiled garment is the opposite of the white garment, which represents purity. The defiled garment, by contrast, is therefore a life that is somehow impure. To say that one has defiled his garment is basically the same as saying he has defiled himself in the sight of God. This may be because of immorality, or idolatry, but in general those who have defiled their garments have diluted the message that they had once believed by making concessions to the culture around them.

Christians are called to be counter-cultural, not to conform to the culture (Romans 12:2). Paul encouraged the Roman Christians to avoid immorality and to "put on the Lord Jesus Christ" (Romans 13:11–14). Putting on Christ is related to the white garment, because ultimately we trust in the purity of Christ for salvation, not in our own purity. But there is an intimate connection between identification with Christ (putting on the Lord Jesus Christ) and avoiding the things that defile a person, such as immorality and idolatry. Those who persevere do not defile themselves, especially by idolatry, even in the midst of persecution. Living as a Christian during a time of persecution would mean enduring intense pressure to conform to the culture, and even to renounce one's faith in

22. Mounce, *Book of Revelation*, 109, 111.

favor of personal safety. Whoever will overcome these temptations wears
the white garment of purity and has a place in the Kingdom of heaven
(cf. Matthew 22:11–14).[23]

Jesus says of the one who overcomes, "I will confess his name before
my Father and before His angels" (cf. Matthew 10:32–33; Luke 12:8–9).
He also says, "And by no means will I remove his name from the book of
life." This implies that it is possible for a person's name to be in the book
of life, and then removed from it. In other words, this text is evidence
of the possibility of losing one's salvation.[24] However, the cause for loss
of salvation would not be accidental. It would be a deliberate rejection
of Christ (defiling one's garment) through a lifestyle of immorality that
amounts to a denial of Christ, or through apostasy and idolatry. The
Christians of Sardis, with a few exceptions, are being warned that if they
continue down the path they are on, they risk losing their place in the
Kingdom.

The contrasts related to the book of life can be compared in this
way:

Those Whose Names Are in the Book of Life	Those Whose Names Are Removed
Alive	Dead
Awake	Asleep
Strong	Weak
Work completed	Work incomplete
Remember/keep what was received	Forget/leave behind what was received
Repentant	Unrepentant
Ready	Not ready
White garment	Defiled garment
Counter-cultural (overcomes)	Influenced by culture (succumbs)
Acknowledged before God	Denied before God

There is a clear connection between this letter and the parable of
the ten bridesmaids (Matthew 25:1–13). The Christians of Sardis are
like the bridesmaids—some are wise, but some are foolish. The foolish
among them are not prepared for a prolonged delay of the bridegroom,

23. Tertullian understood the white robes as a reference to the resurrection body (cf. Matthew 17:2). Tertullian, *On the Resurrection of the Flesh* 27.

24. See Cyprian of Carthage, *On the Unity of the Catholic Church* 20.

and the more they flirt with Roman culture, the more they risk giving in and giving up their faith when the persecution heats up and the Lord does not return.

THE LETTER TO PHILADELPHIA
(REVELATION 3:7–13)

The holy One, the true One, the One who has the key of David, the One who opens and no one closes, and who closes and no one opens, says these things . . .

Philadelphia is modern Alashehir, in Turkey. In ancient times it was called "little Athens" because of its many pagan temples. The story goes that it was founded by two brothers, and it was the younger brother's loyalty to the older that gave the city its name. It was not the "city of brotherly love" as in love for one's fellow human beings. It was literally the city of the love between two brothers.[25]

Unlike some of the Christians in Ephesus and Sardis, the church of Philadelphia has not left the gospel behind, nor have they diminished in their devotion to Christ. Though they are small and their works are modest (they "have a little power"), their priorities have held fast, and they have not denied Christ but have kept his word. Therefore he says, "I have presented you with an open door that no one can close." Based on the introduction to this letter it is evident that Jesus himself has opened this door, and that is why no one can close it. The door represents an opportunity for sharing the gospel (cf. 1 Corinthians 16:9; 2 Corinthians 2:12), in particular with antagonistic Jewish neighbors, like the ones in Smyrna. Jesus promises the Christians of Philadelphia that those in the synagogue will come to know that he loves the Church, and that they will someday submit to it. The phrase translated "bow down at your feet" or "fall down at your feet" may imply that someday the Jews will beg the Christians for forgiveness, but the Greek word translated "bow down" or "fall down" could also mean "worship," which, if interpreted as such, would mean that someday the Jews with whom they are in conflict will accept the authority of the Church, and join them, as the apostle Paul once did.

Jesus also promises that because the Christians of Philadelphia have kept the faith, he will protect them from "the hour of trial, which is about

25. Mounce, *Book of Revelation*, 115.

to come to all the world," which implies that the church of Philadelphia will be spared from a coming persecution.[26] This probably means that it will be isolated from the enforcement of the persecution because it is a smaller town and is less likely to have zealous Roman officials residing in it. Also, if the Jews who are currently causing trouble for the Christians were to become Christians, or at least to be reconciled to their neighbors, the Roman officials in this town could afford simply to ignore the church altogether.

As he says three times in the last chapter of Revelation, Jesus now states, "I am coming quickly." Of course, "quickly" is a relative term, and it is apparent that by the time the present book is printed, over nineteen hundred years will have gone by and Jesus will not have returned yet. With a promise like this, we have three interpretive choices: (1) we can say that the prophetic promise recorded here is a reflection of the hope of the Church in John's time; (2) we can broaden the definition of "coming" and say that Jesus did indeed return, perhaps many times, in some spiritual sense; or (3) we can broaden the definition of "quickly" to see it from the viewpoint of eternity, so that what takes thousands of years on earth may in fact be relatively soon for God (cf. 2 Peter 3:8–9), meaning that Christ's promised return is still yet to come. The most correct interpretation is the third one, though there is an element of truth in the first two as well. The point of saying that Jesus is coming quickly is to give the Christians in Philadelphia a sense of a light at the end of the tunnel, to encourage them to keep the faith. They are told to hold on to what they have, so that no one takes their crown away. Here again, we have the implication that salvation may be lost, especially if a Christian were to deny Christ to save his or her life. In this view, apostasy could even be considered the "undoing" of conversion (cf. Hebrews 6:4–6). To deny Christ is to erase one's acceptance of him (like a name erased from

---

26. Some interpreters take this to mean that all Christians will be removed from the earth by a "rapture" so that they may be preserved from some great persecution to come, but the text does not say this. Jesus actually prayed that his followers would *not* be taken out of the world (John 17:15), which is much stronger evidence against a rapture than the present passage would be for one. See Mounce, *Book of Revelation*, 119. In fact, this is just one of several places in the text of Revelation where some have tried to insert a rapture. However, the concept of the rapture, as it is popularly understood, is not present in the book of Revelation (or anywhere else in the New Testament, for that matter). And while it is true that in many ways these letters are for the whole Church, this particular promise of Jesus is given to the church of Philadelphia only, not to all of Christianity.

the book of life), and to renounce Christianity is the rejection of one's profession of faith (cf. Matthew 10:33). The choice between one's life and one's soul was, unfortunately, a very real choice many Christians had to make, and in some places in the world, continue to make (Matthew 16:24–26).

Finally, there is the promise of eternal life for those who overcome the persecution and its temptations. Jesus tells the Christians of Philadelphia that he will make the one who overcomes a pillar in the temple of God. The temple pillar is a reference to a local custom of dedicating temple pillars to important people. The Christians of Philadelphia would know of this custom and would hear Jesus saying to them: though you are not prominent in the eyes of your community, you are important to God. The promise is that those who keep the faith will have a pillar dedicated to them in the heavenly temple of God (not that they will be made *into* pillars, or *become* pillars). This is much like saying that they will be marked for God (cf. Exodus 28:36–38) and will be fixtures in the New Jerusalem, "pillars" of the Church in the kingdom of heaven, and will remain there forever.

THE LETTER TO LAODICEA
(REVELATION 3:14–22)

The Amen, the Witness who is faithful and true, the source of God's creation, says these things . . .

Laodicea was the sister church of Colossae. The two towns were relatively close, and letters from Paul were exchanged between them (Colossians 4:16).[27] The church of Laodicea is famous as the "lukewarm" church. Jesus says that he would rather they were hot or cold, for anything would be better than lukewarm. However, it is clear from verse 19 that the desired temperature for one's faith is hot. The phrase "be zealous" in Greek is a play on words because "zealous" could also be translated (figuratively) "hot." Therefore, hot faith is enthusiastic faith. Still Christ would apparently prefer cold faith (such as in Ephesus?) to lukewarm faith. In several of these letters, there are details which show that John (and Jesus?) is familiar with the town where the church is situated, and it may be that this passage is also a reference to the water of Laodicea, which came

27. Mounce, *Book of Revelation*, 123.

into the town by way of a crude aqueduct that could only deliver tepid water. Looked at this way, cold water is good to drink, hot water is good for bathing, but lukewarm water is good for nothing.[28] The point is that the state of faith in the Laodicean church makes Jesus say, "because you are lukewarm, and neither hot nor cold, I am going to spit you out of my mouth" (verse 16). The Greek word translated "spit" in most versions literally means "vomit." Christ is sick to his stomach over the church of Laodicea. Apparently, the persecution has not affected this church much (yet), and the Christians there seem to have the luxury of relying on their material wealth rather than on their faith. Their comfort has led them to put their faith on the back burner of their lives. They are just keeping it warm, just going through the motions. But though they think they are rich (and they probably were in a material sense), they are spiritually poor. In fact, they are spiritually naked and blind.

The solution to their spiritual poverty, nakedness, and blindness is given in verse 18. Jesus advises the Laodicean Christians to "buy" (an ironic reference to their reliance on their money) gold purified by fire, white garments, and eye salve. The gold purified by fire is symbolic of a purified lifestyle. Gold would have been refined by melting it over a fire, allowing the removal of impurities that would rise to the top of the molten gold. To buy gold purified by fire would mean getting rid of the things in life that devalue the pure gold of Christian spirituality; in other words, to get rid of distractions that come between the believer and God, especially immorality, and to live a more pure lifestyle. The white garment also refers to a purified lifestyle, and as it has been noted above, it can also imply a desire for a deeper commitment to Christ and a greater reliance on him rather than one's own sufficiency (cf. verse 17). The salve for eyes is a reference to a major industry of the city of Laodicea. The city was known for producing an eye medicine, and though it would not have actually cured blindness, the counsel of Jesus to buy it is his way of using irony to convict the Christians of this town, as if to say, "You're famous for your eye salve, but you're blind to how your prosperity has compromised your faith."

Interestingly, though they make him sick, Jesus lets the Laodicean Christians know that he still loves them. "I reprimand and discipline the ones I love" (verse 19; cf. Proverbs 3:12). Now they have been reprimanded. If they fail to repent, then they run the risk that they will

28. Beale, *Book of Revelation*, 303–4.

be disciplined. What this might mean, however, is left to the imagination. Rather than give a direct warning, Jesus gives them an invitation. The well-known passage reads, "Look, I stand at the door and knock. If anyone hears my voice and opens the door, I will go in, and we will dine together" (the Greek actually says, ". . . and I will dine with him and he with me," reminiscent of John 6:56). Revelation 3:20 is often interpreted as if Jesus is knocking on "the door of our hearts."[29] This may be true, but it is not as if it is a call to let Jesus into one's life for the first time. This invitation is given to Christians, people who have believed in Christ, though their faith has become lukewarm. The invitation is clearly to deeper fellowship with Christ, in the sense of increased devotion, probably at the table of the Eucharist (which explains the reference to "dining" in verse 20). One might speculate that the Christians of Laodicea have fallen away from the practice of liturgy (cf. Hebrews 10:25), and that is why they are lukewarm. They may have become nominal Christians, Christians in name only, and like so many Christians who live with an illusion of self-sufficiency, they may have stopped going to church meetings and discontinued the practice of prayer and studying the faith. They may claim they are too busy, but all that means is that something else has taken the place of Christ in their lives, and given the emphasis on their wealth, it is probably the business of making money that has occupied the place of honor on the list of their priorities. But whoever makes Christ their priority, they will share his resurrection and his reward of eternal life (2 Timothy 2:12; cf. Matthew 19:28).

As I have noted already, the letters to the seven churches of Asia Minor were primarily pastoral epistles from John their overseer, speaking prophetic words from their Lord Jesus. However, these letters also contain messages for the whole Church, and for the Church of any time. Therefore, in the summary below, I will draw out the meaning of the promises and warnings for the contemporary Church. We now turn to the last segment of Revelation in John's present time, the conclusion at the end of the book.

---

29. This idea goes back at least to Jerome, *Homilies on the Psalms* 9.

THE END OF THE VISION
(REVELATION 22:6–21)

In this last section of the book of Revelation, the vision comes to an end, and closing comments are given to John's readers. Since "the time is near," and these things "must happen quickly," John is not to keep the words of Revelation a secret (as the Gnostics claimed secret revelation) but to make them a warning to the Church. It is clear in this section and at other places in the text that the book of Revelation was meant to be read aloud in the churches that received it.[30] They are assured that the words are "faithful and true," a description used of Jesus himself earlier in the book (Rev 19:11), and that the message comes from the same God who inspired the prophets and from Jesus who is the "root and the offspring of David." Here one more opportunity is taken to assure the readers that this Jesus whom they worship is God's Messiah, coming as both the origin (the "root") and the promised descendant of King David.

The quotations in verses 7, 12–13, and 16–17 are the words of Jesus in the first person, but the angel speaks in verses 9–10, and it is not clear who is speaking in verses 6, 11, and 14–15. Perhaps this confusion led John to attempt to worship at the feet of the angel, but the angel instructs him not to do so. In an example of hyperbole, the angel (or Jesus?) says, "Whoever commits injustice, let him continue to commit injustice . . . ," because when Jesus returns he will reward each person according to his or her actions. This is the opposite of Paul's instruction in Ephesians 4:28, but it is an exaggeration meant to emphasize the immanence of Christ's return. It might even be seen as a bit of reverse psychology, as when a parent says to a child, "keep doing that and see what happens!" The point is that Christ wants his Church to be always living as if his return is near.[31] In reality, though, as long as Jesus waits there is time to repent, and all are invited to "freely accept the water of life" (verse 17; cf. 2 Timothy 2:13).

As the book draws to a close, Jesus repeats what he said at the beginning: "I am the Alpha and the Omega, the first and the last, the beginning and the end." He is the source of all things (John 1:3; Revelation 3:14) and the final consummation of all things. And at that final consummation, which is the revelation of the Kingdom, those who wear the white

---

30. Beasley-Murray, *Revelation*, 342. See also Mounce, *Book of Revelation*, 390.

31. Mounce, *Book of Revelation*, 390–91.

robes of purity will enter the paradise of heaven. Those who do not wear the white robes will be "outside" (verse 15; cf. Matthew 22:11–13).

Several categories of those "outside" are mentioned, the first of which are the "dogs." In the ancient world, dogs were scavengers, not pets, though in some cultures they may have been used for sacrifices and for food. The word "dog" used as an insult implied a male prostitute.[32] Peter used the term to mean false teachers who lead Christians back into paganism (2 Peter 2:22), and Paul used it of those who would make Christians follow the whole Jewish law (Philippians 3:2). Even Jesus used the word, though somewhat sarcastically. For him it meant Gentiles (Matthew 15:26). Though it may be impossible to determine whether John has any particular people in mind when he mentions the "dogs," it is clear that the insult could apply to any number of groups who were seen as living outside the will of God, especially if there was a risk that they might lead Christians away from the true worship of God. The term probably refers to any heretics in general, including, but not limited to, the Nicolaitans.

Others condemned at the end of Revelation are more easily identifiable. The term "sorcerers" probably refers to the priests of the Greco-Roman cults, who encourage emperor worship and persecution of Christians (with a possible reference to Exodus 7:11). The "fornicators" are the prostitutes (possibly temple prostitutes) and those who visit them (the English word "fornicate" comes from the Latin word *fornix*, which was the arch of a city gate, where the prostitutes could be found). The "murderers" are the persecutors. The "idolaters" are those who renounce their faith to save their lives, and those who "love to tell lies" are those who accuse Christians in order to turn them in to the authorities. All of these groups are associated with the time of persecution, either directly or indirectly, and in the end, John says, all will be outside the heavenly Jerusalem.

To be outside the heavenly city is the same fate as the lake of fire (Rev 20:15), but the image of fire is not to be interpreted literally.[33] From the parable of the wedding banquet (Matthew 22:1–14) we get the image of the "outer darkness," which speaks of separation from God, who is light. From other Gospel passages (such as Matthew 5:22; cf. 2 Peter 2:4) we see the image of the fires of Gehenna, which was the place outside

---

32. Ibid., 394. The Hebrew text of Deuteronomy 23:18 uses the term in this way.
33. Beasley-Murray, *Revelation*, 341–42.

the walls of Jerusalem where garbage was burned. Therefore both images are seen as outside the city; one speaks of the darkness and one speaks of the fires of destruction. Both are New Testament images commonly understood as hell, and both find their way into the visions of Revelation. However, we must resist the temptation to read popular conceptions of hell (which come more from medieval sources like Dante and Milton than from the Bible) into the images of Revelation. Hell is not so much a place as it is a state of being, a state of ultimate separation from God. No matter how bad the persecution gets, this is a warning that something worse awaits those who deny Christ to save their lives. Therefore the Holy Spirit inspires the bride of Christ, the Church, to say, "Come . . . Come Lord Jesus." Come soon and end this tribulation.

Finally, verses 18 and 19 are a warning that is meant to preserve the integrity of the text. No one must add to or take away from the words of Revelation (cf. Deuteronomy 4:2). The warning is formulaic in ancient documents and applies specifically to the copying and transmission of the text itself, not to its interpretation, though it could be argued that the attempt to insert a rapture into the book of Revelation does constitute adding to "the words of the prophecy of this book." The last words of Jesus in the book of Revelation are the words repeated three times in this section: "I am coming quickly." The promise of Jesus' return at the end of the age is reiterated, and John responds with, "Amen."

So ends the section of John's revelation that describes events his readers already know. So far they have been given encouragement from their past, and warnings for their present situation. They have also been given a few promises for the future, but these have mostly been generic promises of eternal life. As we turn to the next section, we begin to see those parts of the book that include what is commonly expected of prophecy: predictions of the future. But before we can look into our own future, we turn to those events that were in John's future, but are in our historical past.

SUMMARY

- The book of Revelation was written for the Christians of John's own time, to encourage them to keep the faith and continue the ministry, even though they were being persecuted.

- John begins Revelation by foreshadowing the end—the return of Christ.

- John understood the Trinity as Yahweh God, Jesus Christ the Lamb of God, and the sevenfold Spirit of God.

- There will be times when we as Christians face choices of loyalty, choices of priority, when the false gods of the world attract our attention. These are the times we are called to make our relationship with God in Christ the number one priority in our lives.

- All Christians are encouraged to "remember your first love," that is, remember the enthusiasm for worship and devotion that naturally accompanies a newfound faith. Do not let yourself become lukewarm by neglecting worship, prayer and devotion. Remember to seek Christ before you try to serve him.

- Churches should not let an emphasis on the social gospel, or even the compassion that motivates it, become a tolerance for heresy.

- Compromising one's faith by making concessions to culture, especially when that entails immorality, is the first step toward idolatry and apostasy.

- Material wealth has a way of tempting people to believe they are self-sufficient, and to forget their dependence on God.

- To give up the faith is to give up eternal life. It is better to follow Jesus into martyrdom, and then follow him in resurrection, than to preserve one's earthly life.

- No matter how long the Lord waits to return, we ought to live in readiness, as if he could return at any time.

8

Visions of John's Future (Our Past)

The things that will happen . . .

INTRODUCTION

THERE HAVE BEEN OVER nineteen hundred years since John wrote Revelation, so it should not be surprising that most of the prophetic warnings communicated in the book have already come to pass, especially when one remembers that these are things that were supposed to happen "soon." In general, the warnings of John's prophecy were about continued persecutions, which came to a peak in the Great Persecution of the early fourth century. The promises are, for the most part, of a much more eschatological nature, and therefore are yet to be realized. We turn now to those elements of the book of Revelation which were in the future from the perspective of the time of the vision, but which have been fulfilled in the time before the present day.

THE MARK OF THE BEAST
(REVELATION 13:16–17; 14:9–13)

John warns that there will come a time when everyone will be required to have a mark, which is the name of the beast (the emperor), and that no one may buy or sell without this mark. To begin, we need not look for a mark that is literally on the right hand or the forehead.[1] The reference to the right hand and the forehead calls to mind the practice of using phylacteries to "bind" the word of God to oneself, marking one as God's

---

1. Hippolytus, *On Christ and Antichrist* 49. Hippolytus, writing only about two decades before Decius' persecution, understood that the mark of the beast would be connected to imperial edicts demanding sacrifice.

own (Deuteronomy 6:4–9; cf. Isaiah 44:5).[2] The meaning is that just as one can be sealed or marked for God (cf. Ephesians 1:13–14; 4:30), one can be marked as belonging to the beast, and the obvious implication is that to be marked for the beast is to make oneself an enemy of God.

In late 249 CE, the Emperor Decius issued a decree that required all inhabitants of the empire to show their loyalty by making a sacrifice to the Roman gods and to the emperor.[3] Those who refused were accused of treason, a crime punishable by death. Those who complied were given a certificate, called a *libellus*, which would prove that they had made the required sacrifice and would attest to their loyalty to the emperor. This *libellus* would include the emperor's name, with his imperial titles, and would be signed by witnesses. One could be required to produce the document at any time. Where enforced, one could not participate in commerce without it. This was the mark of the beast described in John's vision. By making a sacrifice and holding the certificate, a person "marked" himself as belonging to the emperor. For a Christian to do this would amount to a rejection of Christ in favor of the emperor and his gods. In some places, Christians were in fact required to renounce Christ in addition to making the sacrifice.

Under Decius, the persecution was, for the first time, systematically enforced across the empire. Christians who did not comply risked arrest, imprisonment, torture, and execution. However, the Roman officials generally did not want to execute Christians. They would rather make apostates than martyrs, so they made it very easy to comply with the emperor's orders. All one had to do was take an oath of loyalty to the emperor, possibly also renouncing Christ in favor of the Roman gods, and offer a sacrifice on an altar of Jupiter. There were a significant number of Christians who submitted to these requirements. Others paid sympathetic (but non-Christian) neighbors to take their place and make the sacrifice for them. Still others were able to bribe the Roman magistrates and avoid the sacrifice, in effect buying a *libellus*. However, most Christians held fast, and many died as a result. In Rome, the bishop Fabian was martyred and it was a year and a half before a new bishop

---

2. Head and hands can also represent mind and activity, respectively. Beale, *Book of Revelation*, 717.

3. Cf. Victorinus, *Commentary on the Apocalypse* 17.2. Though Victorinus does not mention Decius by name, he is probably referring to the edict, which was issued when Victorinus was a young boy.

could be elected. Since there was no way to keep the name of the bishop a secret in Rome, and since the persecution specifically targeted church leaders, electing a bishop at that time would have been to consign him to certain death.[4]

The mark of the beast is, in essence, a test of ultimate loyalty. As Jesus said, a person cannot serve two masters (Matthew 6:24), and the warning of Revelation is that one must not obey the emperor if it means participating in idolatry. One cannot be marked for both God and the beast. One must remain loyal to Christ, even if it means risking physical death (Matthew 10:28).

In Revelation 14, three angels fly through the heavens, each one bringing an announcement. The first angel brings good news, proclaiming the spread of the gospel to the nations. The second angel announces the fall of Rome, and it is on this basis that the third angel brings a warning. Because Rome will fall, the Church must not give in to the emperors' demands of worship. They are temporary, and even the Imperial dynasties are temporary. The angel warns that if anyone does give in by making the sacrifices and accepting the mark of the beast, that person will drink from the cup of God's anger. The reference to fire and brimstone (sulfur) means that apostates will suffer the fate of Sodom and Gomorrah—not only that they will be judged and excluded from eternal life in the presence of God, but that they will also be made an example for future generations (2 Peter 2:6; Jude 1:7).

As it happened, those who did make the sacrifice and accept the *libellus* found that they could not easily come back to the Church when the persecution subsided. Their fate was ultimately decided by the election of a new bishop of Rome who was sympathetic to their situation. However, severe penance was required for any who wished to return to the Church. These people were called the "lapsed" because they had renounced the faith for a time, and they became an example of what not to do in a persecution. Because of them, far fewer people gave in the next time persecution reared its head. Far more people held fast to

---

4. During the time that there was no bishop of Rome, the priest Novatian served as the chair of the council of priests, and was, in effect, acting bishop. However, though he was a brilliant theologian, he did not want to allow apostates back into the church when the persecution subsided, and therefore Novatian was not elected bishop. In a tragically ill-advised move, he was consecrated as a rival bishop of Rome by some sympathetic bishops from the countryside, and was thereafter known as an "anti-pope." To get the full story, see Papandrea, *Trinitarian Theology of Novatian* and "Between Two Thieves."

the faith, and far more became martyrs. This is the perseverance of the saints (Revelation 14:12–13): that those who are marked for God refuse the mark of the beast, even if it means their death, for those who die in the Lord are blessed.

THE ANGER OF GOD: THE BOWL PLAGUES
(REVELATION 15:1; 15:5—16:12)

Chapter 15 introduces seven bowls containing plagues, which are given to seven angels to be poured out like offerings on the altar of God. They are said to be the last of the plagues, because in them the anger of God is completed. As we will see, it is not necessary to find seven distinct events in the seven bowls. The anger of God in general is poured out against certain people and is described in terms reminiscent of the plagues of Egypt. The number seven is symbolic of the completion of God's anger and serves to make the bowls symmetrical with the seven seals and seven trumpets witnessed by John (cf. Leviticus 26:18–28).

Since the seven bowls describe the completion of God's anger, one might wonder why this section appears in the chapter about prophecies already fulfilled. But the bowl plagues are not about the final judgment that comes at the end of the age. These plagues are warnings of punishment for particular people who bring God's anger on themselves, and since these people are all in our past and have already died, the bowls of God's anger are in our past. Final judgment, on the other hand, has to do with justice, not anger. With this distinction in mind, the vision of Revelation implies that God's anger was complete with the punishment that was poured out from the bowls, but God's justice has yet to be completed in the final judgment still in our future (cf. Luke 13:6–9).

The bowl plagues begin with a heavenly scene in which the tabernacle is opened and seven angels emerge dressed as Old Testament-style priests.[5] Each of the angels is given a golden bowl full of the righteous anger of God (metaphorically described as plagues), which is to be poured out on the earth. This is another indication that the bowl plagues are not the final judgment—the scene begins in heaven, but the plagues

---

5. There is a tradition that says these seven angels are the seven archangels mentioned in Scripture and apocalyptic writings. We have already seen that Michael is mentioned in Daniel 10:13, 21; 12:1; and also Jude 1:9 (cf. Rev 12:7). Gabriel is mentioned in Luke 1:19, and Raphael in Tobit 12:15. All seven archangels are named in 1 Enoch 20:1–8. See Mounce, *Book of Revelation*, 180.

are punishments that are carried out on earth. On the other hand, we should not push this interpretation too far, as if it implies that God is in the habit of punishing people during their lives. This section of Revelation contains warnings for specific groups of people related to the persecutions that are in our past, and should not be used to justify the notion that human suffering in the contemporary age is in any way the result of God's punishment. Remember that John's point is to encourage the Christians of his own time to be strong in their faith and resist the demands to participate in pagan worship.

The first group of people to be warned of God's anger is the lapsed, those who submitted to the requirement of idolatrous worship and accepted the *libellus*, the mark of the beast. We have already seen the angel's warning that whoever accepts the mark of the beast will be judged for it (Rev 14:9–11). Now we are told that they will suffer a plague of sores. This has its parallel in the plague of boils brought on Egypt (Exodus 9:8–11). The effect of such sores in Jewish culture would have been to make one "unclean," that is, the person would have to be quarantined, but more importantly the person would be considered unfit to join the assembly in worship (Leviticus 13). In the church of the third and fourth centuries, the effect of having lapsed was excommunication from the table of the Eucharist and severe long-term penance, which included a time of separation from the assembly.

The second and third bowls are poured out on the seas and rivers, turning them to blood. This is parallel to the similar plague on Egypt (Exodus 7:14–24). Of course, just as in Egypt, the judgment is not on the water, but on those who would have to drink it. In this case, those who are warned of God's anger are the ones who persecute the Church (or who collaborate with the Roman persecution), "because they shed the blood of saints and prophets" (Rev 16:6). Those who spilled innocent blood will be given blood to drink, not literally, but in the sense that their actions will come back to them and judge them.

The fourth and fifth bowls are poured out causing extreme heat from the sun and then darkness (cf. Exodus 10:21–23). The fifth bowl seems specifically to be aimed at the emperors, "the throne of the beast" (Rev 16:10), and darkness here is certainly meant to be understood metaphorically as some kind of political decline. These opposite extremes of heat and the cold of darkness also cause people great pain. In each case, rather than turning to God in repentance, those who suffer these plagues curse God. It is interesting to note that the last of the persecuting emperors, Galerius, was afflicted with painful sores at the end of his life. His extreme suffering was thought by Christians to be a punishment from God for persecuting the Church. On his deathbed, he promised toleration for the Church, if only the Christians would pray to their God for him.[6] In spite of this, we should not interpret these plagues and afflictions literally. The point of the vision is to make a theological connection with God's deliverance at the time of Moses, and to proclaim the warning that those who deny Christ and those who persecute the Church (and, it is implied, who do so without repentance; Rev 16:9,11) will face God's anger, possibly during their lives, but certainly at the time of their deaths.

Just like the sixth trumpet, the sixth bowl concerns the Euphrates River.[7] The sixth bowl dries up the Euphrates, which opens a path for the kings from the east to invade the west. This "plague" is directed at Rome itself, as it sets the stage for its fall. The Euphrates was a historic boundary with Persia (the Parthian Empire), which was the Roman Empire's only real threat for centuries.[8] In the end, though, it would be other kings from the east, the barbarian kings and their nomadic tribes, who would invade the empire and cause the fall of the western Roman Empire. The fall of this western Babylon came in two phases. The first was the defeat of the self-deifying, persecuting emperors and the legalization of Christianity, which was the victory of Christ over the beast and the false prophet. The second phase was the disintegration of the Roman Empire itself.

THE MILLENNIUM BEGINS
(REVELATION 11:15–17; 19:11—20:6)

The beginning of the reign of Christ on earth is really the end of the reign of Satan. In the book of Revelation, the reign of the devil is most clearly manifested in the persecution of the Church. Therefore, the most significant aspect of the so-called "millennium" is that it begins with the binding of Satan. Put another way, the millennium begins when the per-

---

6. Eusebius of Caesarea, *Ecclesiastical History* 8.16–17.

7. Beasley-Murray, *Revelation*, 243–44.

8. The Euphrates River was also the eastern boundary of the Promised Land. Mounce, *Book of Revelation*, 298.

secution ends. In the sequence of the text of Revelation, the fall of Rome comes first, building to the fall of the evil force behind the empire, the devil. In terms of history, the reign of Christ began while the empire still stood, but the fall of Rome followed close behind.

In Revelation 19, John again sees a vision of heaven. The fact that heaven opens to reveal the vision shows that the warfare described is not warfare on earth but heavenly, spiritual warfare.[9] Christ appears, again riding the white horse of purity and victory. There is no doubt that the figure riding the white horse is Christ, since he is called "Faithful and True" (meaning that he is trustworthy and is worthy to be the object of our faith) and "The Word of God" (cf. John 1:1).[10] His clothing is dipped in blood, signifying that he is the forerunner of all the martyrs,[11] and he wears many crowns, not just the martyr's crown of victory over death, but the many crowns of the One who is King of kings and Lord of lords (cf. Deuteronomy 10:17). His flaming eyes see into human hearts, which foreshadows the coming judgment. However, this is not the second coming of Christ. Jesus does not yet come to claim the Church, but he comes to the aid of his Church by waging spiritual warfare in the heavenly realm. Christ on the white horse brings the end of persecution and the beginning of the millennial age of the Church, but this vision also represents the ongoing spiritual battle throughout the age of the Church, and the fact that Christ will continue to fight for his Church. This is not the battle of Armageddon, because it is not the final conflict between good and evil. On the other hand, this part of the vision does foreshadow the final judgment and the final defeat of evil that is to come at the end of the age of the Church.

The armies that follow the risen Christ into battle are the heavenly hosts.[12] Just as we have seen angels perform the function of priests (Rev 15:6), the heavenly soldiers are also angels dressed in the linen of the Old Testament priesthood. The sword that Christ wields is the sword of

---

9. Jewett, *Jesus against the Rapture*, 80.

10. Origen, *Commentary on the Gospel of John* 2.47–54.

11. Some interpreters argue that the blood is not his own but that of those who are to be judged, based on Isaiah 63:1–6. For this view, see Mounce, *Book of Revelation*, 345. This would be consistent with Revelation 14:19–20, but only as a foreshadowing of the final judgment to come.

12. Some medieval writers have interpreted the army as the Church, or as the saints in heaven, however there does not seem to be any evidence in the text to warrant this. For an example of this, see Bede, *Explanation of the Apocalypse* 19.14.

his word (Ephesians 6:17; Hebrews 4:12).[13] Though he is said to use it against the nations, this does not mean literal battle between countries of the earth. The word "nations" is used as it would be in the Old Testament to mean unbelievers, and here it means the enemies of God. The anger of God is directed toward his opponents, specifically those who have persecuted the Church. In this battle, the tables are turned and the oppressed Church is vindicated, as the persecuting empire becomes its servant. In other words, the Roman Empire will submit to the Church.

The image of birds eating the flesh of kings and their armies comes from Ezekiel 38–39. In that context it refers to the victory over Gog and Magog, the idolatrous enemies of God's people. The metaphoric Gog and Magog of John's situation is the same as Babylon—the Roman Empire. This vision promises for John's future that the persecutors of the Church will be defeated. Though the Romans may do all they can and use all the resources at their disposal, they will be defeated. In fact, there really is no war, per se, because as soon as the armies of God's enemies are assembled, the beast and the false prophet are captured and thrown into the lake of fire. This is a promise that the persecuting emperors (the beast) and the Roman religious system that supports them and encourages worship of them (the false prophet) are to be no more. The rest of those who support the current system of deifying emperors will be of no consequence because they will be destroyed by the words of Jesus, the gospel. In other words, just as God defeated Gog and Magog, God will destroy the persecutors and those who demand worship of themselves, and the gospel will do the rest.

In the early fourth century, the Great Persecution ended when Constantine legalized Christianity. Constantine became emperor in the western half of the empire in 312 CE, and in 313 he issued the Edict of Milan, which officially ended persecution and gave certain privileges to the Church. The point is not to glorify Constantine, since he was not what we might call an exemplary disciple of Christ. He was a soldier and an emperor first, sometimes murdering his political enemies (even when they were within his own household), and he postponed his baptism until he was on his deathbed, probably so that he would not be held to the ethical standards of the Church. But though he did not rule as a baptized Christian, he was what we might call a believer.[14] Constantine was first

13. See also Isaiah 11:4 and Psalm 2:9–11(12).

14. There is actually some debate over this, and not all historians agree that Constantine was a believer in Christianity. However, the fact that he postponed his baptism is

influenced by his mother, who was a Christian, and possibly also by his father, who does not seem to have enforced persecution in the areas under his charge. But the defining moment for Constantine was when, according to tradition, he experienced a vision from Christ that promised him victory in the decisive battle at the Milvian Bridge on the outskirts of Rome. This was the battle that would make Constantine the ruler of the western empire, and on the eve of battle he was directed by God to fight under the sign of Christ. On October 28, 312 CE, Constantine and his men marched into battle under the banner of Christ and were victorious.

In 324 CE, Constantine defeated his eastern rival and became sole ruler of the entire empire. He gave credit to the God of the Christians for placing him in that position. The next year he convened the first ecumenical council of the Church, the Council of Nicaea, and he sat among the bishops in debates over theological issues. Therefore, when we look at the message of Revelation in light of history, we see that Christ did come to the aid of his Church, not by fighting an earthly battle for Constantine, but by defeating the force of evil that was behind the persecuting emperors and their pagan priests, and by putting someone on the throne who identified himself with those who had been persecuted. The tables were turned, and the Church had conquered the Empire.

The millennium, a period of a thousand years according to John's vision, is the age of the Church, beginning with the end of persecution and continuing through the present day. From our perspective, we can see that it is not literally a thousand years, but in fact is approaching two thousand.[15] The length of time is approximate, simply meaning a

---

evidence that he understood the implications of baptism and did not want to be held accountable to God for the responsibilities that come with Church membership. Had he not been a believer, he probably would have been baptized simply for the leverage it would gain him with the Church, and the potential for using the Church to unify the empire. In addition, it is clear that Constantine's mother (known to the world as Saint Helen) was a Christian, and his father was at least sympathetic to the Church, since he did not enforce the persecution of Christians in the area over which he ruled.

15. The majority of early Church writers were in agreement that the millennium was not to be interpreted as literally lasting one thousand years. Augustine wrote that the one thousand years represented "the fullness of time," based on the observation that the number one thousand is the cube of ten, and while one hundred (percent) is the square of ten, it is still only two-dimensional, so therefore one thousand is something like one hundred percent made three-dimensional. Augustine, *City of God* 20.7. Also, Andrew of Caesarea said that one thousand years simply means many generations (cf. Deuteronomy 7:9). Andrew of Caesarea, *Commentary on the Apocalypse* 20.1–3.

very long time (2 Peter 3:8–9), and Christ's reign on earth is the time in which Christ influences human culture and society through the growth of the Church and the spread of the gospel.[16] During this time, it is said that Satan would be "bound," or limited in some way. In fact, there is an assumption that Satan is already bound in the New Testament era (2 Thessalonians 2:6–7; Jude 1:6; cf. Matthew 12:25–29). In one sense, Jesus bound the "strong man" with his death and resurrection, and so one could argue that the millennium is basically the age of the Church. However, in the context of Revelation, the persecution of the Church is clearly energized by the demonic, and so it makes sense to say that the millennium proper does not really begin until the Church is free of imperial threat.

With regard to the binding of Satan, it is clear that demonic activity has decreased since the time of Jesus and the apostles. The Gospels and the book of Acts are full of confrontations with the demonic, and even with the devil himself (Matthew 4:1–11), and while it is easy to dismiss these events as myths or as the product of a more primitive worldview, the general lack of such phenomenon today could also be explained by a limitation of demonic activity during the millennial age of the Church.[17] That is not to say there is no evil in the world. One only needs to browse the table of contents of any book on recent history to see that humanity has not created a perfect society. But most of the evil in the world today can be attributed to the misuse of human free will and does not require the justification that "the devil made me do it." The binding of Satan does not necessarily mean that evil should be non-existent. It simply means that during the millennial age of the Church, evil is restricted, either by direct divine control, or by the increasing spread of the gospel and the work of the Church. In fact, there is evidence that even today, when true

---

16. Augustine called the millennium "the Christian era," and "the span between Christ's first and second coming." Augustine, *City of God* 20.7, 9. Regarding the concept that Christ reigns through the Church, see Caesarius of Arles, *Exposition on the Apocalypse* 20.6. A fascinating study on the positive influence the Church has had on the world is Stark, *Victory of Reason*.

17. Though many would argue that the character of Satan is only a literary personification of evil, it is difficult to interpret the binding of Satan without reference to, at least, an evil force independent of human activity. If Satan is only a literary device, and evil is solely the product of humanity, then the binding of Satan would imply the restriction of free will.

demonic activity is rare, in those places where the Church is weakest such activity still exists.

In Revelation 20:4 we are told that the martyrs "came to life" to reign with Christ for the thousand years. The Greek actually says simply that "they lived," meaning that as John saw them they were not dead, but alive. This should be understood to mean that they came to their reward of eternal life, not that they came back to life as if they were resuscitated. They live to reign with Christ in heaven until the end of the age (cf. Matthew 19:28). This is clear when we remember that this is a vision in which heaven is opened to the seer, and the thrones that he sees are there in the heavenly court. The first resurrection, therefore, is the resurrection to eternal life that occurs when any Christian dies.[18] Working from this assumption, that would mean that an individual believer who dies in Christ at any time during the age of the Church goes to be with Christ in the spiritual realm that we call heaven (cf. Luke 23:42–43). However, those who die without Christ ("the rest of the dead") are not resurrected, and their spirits await the judgment at the end of the age in some other state of existence (Rev 20:5). They will be "raised" at the end of the age, but only for final judgment. This section of Revelation ends with a blessing for those who die in Christ and receive the first resurrection, for they will not experience the second death, which is eternal separation from God. Rather, they will reign with Christ in heaven during the millennial age of the Church (Rev 20:6; cf. Hebrews 12:1).

In chapter 11, trumpets introduced the spiritual warfare that began before John's time with the birth of Jesus. In verses 15–17, the seventh trumpet is finally sounded and becomes a herald of the outcome of that spiritual warfare, which is the defeat of the enemies of God and the victory of Christ and his Church over the empire. In a prophetic voice, the heavenly hosts proclaim that "the kingdom of the world has become the kingdom of our Lord and of His Christ, and he will reign forever and ever," words made famous by G. F. Handel's *Messiah*. The elders of the heavenly court fall down to prostrate themselves before the throne of God and thank and praise the Lord because he has "taken [his] great power" and "begun to reign." Of course, God has always been omnipotent and has always reigned from eternity past, but this taking up of power and beginning to reign refers to Christ and the beginning

---

18. Oecumenius, *Commentary on the Apocalypse* 20.4–8. Cf. Andrew of Caesarea, *Commentary on the Apocalypse* 20.5–6.

of the millennial age of the Church. Christ has taken back the power he voluntarily laid aside to become human (Philippians 2:6–8), and he has been exalted (Philippians 2:9–11). The fulfillment of Philippians 2 began at roughly the same time that the Church began—at the time of the resurrection and the ascension of Christ. But the fulfillment of this promise is progressive, and here at the beginning of the millennium the heavenly elders praise and thank God that the reign of Christ, which was at first known only to the Church, has now become manifest to the world— now he reigns over the earth through the Church. Yet, the progressive fulfillment continues, and we will wait until the final revelation of the Kingdom for every tongue to admit that Jesus Christ is Lord.

THE FALL OF ROME
(REVELATION 14:8; 16:17—19:5)

Of the three angels in chapter 14, the second announces the coming of the fall of Rome, promising that the persecuting empire will meet its deserved fate. The promise comes in the prophetic present, "fallen is Babylon" (cf. Isaiah 21:9), but this is a promise of a future reality that is meant to give comfort to the readers at John's present time. Not only has Rome persecuted God's people, it has also corrupted the known world with its immorality. For this the empire must fall. Therefore in the context of the herald angels of Revelation 14, Christians must hold fast to the faith and resist the temptation to give in to the idolatry and the immorality of Rome, because the empire is temporary, but the Kingdom of God is eternal.

The seventh bowl is God's anger poured out on the Roman Empire. This is the last of the plagues poured out against the enemies of God, and with the fall of Rome, "it is complete." The "great city" is Rome, not Jerusalem, which is clear from the reference to Babylon in verse 19. The fall of the city of Rome is announced by the apocalyptic earthquake, and the city is said to be split into three parts. The number three is symbolic and implies that God has dismantled Rome according to his perfect will and purpose. The city would be reduced to a fraction of its former self.[19] In fact, the emperor Constantine eventually moved the imperial court to Constantinople, effectively splitting the power base of the city by leaving the senate in Rome. If one wanted to push the prophecy more

19. Oecumenius, *Commentary on the Apocalypse* 17.15–18.

toward the literal, one could make the argument that there was a division of power that was split three ways after the beginning of Constantine's reign: Constantine brought the imperial court to Constantinople, leaving Rome in the hands of the senate and also the newest source of political power, the bishop of Rome.

The plagues that accompany the fall of Rome are, like the other plagues, symbolic warnings of coming divine intervention.[20] The hailstones are reminiscent of the plague of hail in Exodus 9:13–26,[21] and the fleeing mountains connect this event to the description of the coming Day of the Lord in Isaiah 40:4 (cf. Luke 3:3–6; Acts 2:19–20). The point of these plagues and apocalyptic scenes is not to imply that there will be actual hail, much less that mountains will disappear. The point is to emphasize the spiritual gravity of the events described. In the plagues of Revelation, we should not look for literal fulfillment on earth, but we should see in them connection to events in other parts of Scripture and the significance of those parallels. Each of the bowl plagues that are poured out are part of God's continuously unfolding plan, the same plan that included both the Exodus and the empty tomb.

Rome is described as the great whore who has prostituted herself with the nations, tempting them to her immorality. In her idolatry, the whore is the opposite of the faithful bride (Rev 21:9).[22] The fact that the whore sits on seven mountains (Rev 17:9) is an obvious sign that she represents the city of Rome, known around the world as the "City of Seven Hills."[23] She rides the "scarlet beast that is filled with blasphemous names." In other words, the cruelty and immorality of Rome is driven by the Roman emperors, with their claims to divine titles. She is wealthy and powerful and immoral. The name that marks her forehead says that she is the mother of atrocities, and she is drunk with the blood of the martyrs (cf. Jeremiah 51:7).

The seven heads of the beast represent the seven hills of Rome, but more importantly they represent seven emperors from Nero to

---

20. See Irenaeus of Lyons, *Against Heresies* 4.30.4. Also, Andrew of Caesarea, *Commentary on the Apocalypse* 8.7. Irenaeus and Andrew are examples of early Christian writers who interpreted these plagues as related to the fall of Rome.

21. See also Joshua 10:11 and Ezekiel 38:18–22. Mounce, *Book of Revelation*, 305.

22. Mounce, *Book of Revelation*, 307.

23. Cf. 1 Peter 5:13.

Domitian's successor, Nerva.[24] In John's time, five of the emperors had come and gone, and Domitian himself is the sixth, the one who is. The seventh is Nerva, who was yet to come in John's time, and who would reign only a short time. The one who was, and who is no longer, and who is about to come, is a reference to the quintessential beast, Nero, whose spirit was said to return in Domitian and the subsequent persecuting emperors.[25] The prophetic promise received by John is that this beast is headed for destruction.

The ten horns then represent ten emperors who are yet to come in John's time, who would each have their "hour." They will "wage war against the Lamb"—in other words, they will persecute the Church (cf. Matthew 25:40; Acts 9:4). However, the Lamb will prevail over them on behalf of his Church. These emperors in John's future made Rome desolate by depleting the economy and leaving the borders undefended to secure their power in Rome. The ten emperors who persecuted the Church from after John's time to the beginning of the millennial age of the Church were (with the years of their reigns): Trajan (98–117), Marcus Aurelius (161–80), Septimius Severus (193–211), Caracalla (211–17), Elagabalus (218–22), Maximinus Thrax (235–38), Decius, who ordered sacrifices across the Empire and required the *libellus* (249–51), Valerian (253–60), Diocletian (284–305), and Galerius (305–11).[26] Constantine came to power in the west in 312, and he became the sole emperor in 324.

Just as in chapter 14, chapter 18 begins with the announcement that "Babylon" has fallen. Once again the immorality of Rome is emphasized as the reason for her fall. Because Rome will fall, the people of God are called to "come out of her." They are warned not to participate in her immorality, or they risk also sharing in her plagues. To the degree that she has sinned, she will be punished. She will be paid back according to her works. In Revelation 18:7, Isaiah 47:7 is quoted in the context of the judgment of ancient Babylon. The city of Babylon, personified as a queen, says, "I will be queen forever." She cannot see the destruction

---

24. This numbering does not include Vitellius, whose reign was so short as to be overlooked by those in the provinces. Josephus does not consider Vitellius as ever having secured the throne. Josephus, *Wars of the Jews* 4.9.9. Eusebius of Caesarea also does not count Vitellius. See Eusebius of Caesarea, *Ecclesiastical History* 3.5.

25. Cf. Primasius, *Commentary on the Apocalypse* 17.1.

26. Cf. Oecumenius, *Commentary on the Apocalypse* 17.9–14.

that is coming, and in the same way, the Romans could not fathom the possibility that Rome could fall. The heavenly voice promises that all who participated in Rome's immorality will be shocked to see the great city burning. Kings, merchants, and sailors cry out, "Woe, woe!" for the destruction of the great city of Rome. The fall of Rome, then, is the third woe of the Apocalypse (Rev 11:14).

In fact, Rome did burn when it was sacked by the Goths in 410. This was the first time the imperial city was invaded, but not the last. This event, unthinkable as it was at the time, opened the door for the eventual fall of the western empire to the barbarians. The fall of the western Roman Empire was complete in 476 when the last of the western emperors was removed and Italy became the realm of the barbarian kings. Ironically, many non-Christians blamed the Church for the fall of Rome, which prompted St. Augustine to write his magnum opus, *The City of God*, in which he defended the Church and said that the only permanent city is the one not made by humans.

After the fifth century, the city of Rome would become a desolate place, almost a ghost town, and remain for centuries just a shadow of its former self. The heavenly voice of Revelation proclaims that while there will be no more rejoicing in Rome, heaven will rejoice over its fall, because Rome is guilty of the blood of the martyrs. God has judged the whore who had corrupted the world with her immorality and her idolatry, and God has avenged the murder of the saints. Rome, as a city and as an empire, tried to stamp out the Church, but in the end the Church was victorious, the empire fell, and the Church survives and flourishes throughout the millennium.

At this point, the following table may be helpful, to chart the major sections of the book of Revelation that are in our past, from the perspective of the twenty-first century:

First Woe	Generally depicted in the opening of SEALS	Refers to the Jewish-Roman war and the siege of Jerusalem
Second Woe	Generally depicted in the sounding of TRUMPETS	Refers to the fall of Jerusalem
Third Woe	Generally depicted in the pouring out of BOWLS	Refers to the fall of Rome

In the next chapter, we will turn at last to those warnings and promises of Revelation which are still yet to be fulfilled.

SUMMARY

- In John's vision, the "tribulation" is the increasing persecution of the early Church, especially the persecution under the emperor Decius in the third century and the Great Persecution of the early fourth century.

- The "mark of the beast" is the certificate required by Decius and other emperors as proof that one had made sacrifices to the Roman gods and to the emperor. In John's understanding, one can be marked either for God or for the beast (the emperors), but one cannot belong to both.

- The number 666 primarily refers to the emperor of John's time, Domitian, but as the "mark of the beast" it also refers to the stamp of approval of any of Domitian's successors who persecuted the Church.

- The bowl plagues are not the final judgment. They are punishments of God's anger poured out against the enemies of the Church. It is assumed that these enemies will also be judged by God's justice at the final judgment at the end of the Church age.

- Therefore, God's anger and God's judgment are two different things. Revelation warns of God's anger poured out on earth and in human history (though it may primarily only be realized at the time of death). God's judgment waits until the end of time and history.

- In the bowl plagues, God's anger is poured out against:

  □ Those who accepted the mark of the beast, who participated in idolatry.

  □ Those who persecuted the Church, or collaborated in the persecution.

- The "millennium" is the age of the Church, from the end of the persecution and the legalization of Christianity through the present day. In the millennial age, Christ rules on earth (influences human society and culture) through the universal Church. Strictly speaking, the millennium began when the persecution ended.

- During the millennial age of the Church, demonic activity is limited, either by direct divine control, or by the activity of the Church.

- The third woe is the fall of Rome.

- During the millennial age of the Church:

  - The first death is any person's physical death.

  - The first resurrection immediately follows the physical death of a Christian. Those who die in Christ are raised to eternal life, as Jesus said to the thief on the cross, "Today you will be with me in paradise" (Luke 23:43).

  - The second resurrection comes at the end of the age, at the time of the final judgment. All people will be raised to face God and answer for their lives.

  - The second death is eternal separation from God. Those who belong to the Lamb will not experience the second death (Rev 2:11; 20:6, 14).

9

Visions of John's Future (and Ours)

. . . after these things

INTRODUCTION

O UR PREMISE THROUGHOUT THIS study has been that most of the
book of Revelation refers to events that have already happened
before our time. Yet the apocalyptic nature of the book of Revelation
prevents us from interpreting everything as taking place within history.
Having presented as much as possible within the context of history, the
reader will probably be anxious to know what is left in our own future.
For all that John has seen and heard to this point, there remains to be
described the fulfillment of the revelation that he witnessed. What is
left for us to anticipate in our future is the realization of eschatological
promises, not least of which is the return, or "second coming," of Christ,
and the full and final revelation of the Kingdom of God.

In Jewish thought, the promise of the Messiah is tied to the promise
of the Day of the Lord, a time when God would intervene in human
history, vindicate the oppressed, and punish the oppressors. But as I have
indicated, the life and teaching of Jesus effectively split the Day of the
Lord in two. The first advent of Christ brought the *Reign* of God: it is the
Kingdom of God, but it is concealed within the hearts of believers and
within the Church (Matthew 13:31; Luke 17:20–21). The second coming of Christ will complete the Day of the Lord by revealing the *Realm*
of God, which is the future aspect of the Kingdom of God (Matthew
13:32–33). The entire book of Revelation leads up to this revealing (the
revelation) of God's Kingdom. In John's vision, the Realm of God is described as a new heaven and earth and a New Jerusalem, the heavenly
city of God (Rev 21:1–2).

In this chapter we will examine three main concepts referring to the time after the end of the millennium: the Wedding of the Lamb, the Final Judgment, and the Kingdom Revealed. However, these three concepts are not to be understood as three separate events. They are concurrent events that we often refer to collectively as "the end of the age." In fact, one could also say that since these events represent the end of time as we know it, with them we return to the realm of visions outside of time. Therefore, they should not be seen as happening in a chronological order, but as happening more or less simultaneously. But before we can look at the events surrounding the end of time, we turn to the last phase of human history envisioned in Revelation, the end of the millennial age of the Church.

THE END OF THE MILLENNIUM
(REVELATION 20:7–8)

In 20:7, the millennial age of the Church comes to an end, and Satan is released to deceive the world and to attempt to wage war against God. In the last chapter, we explored the possibility that the relative rarity of demonic activity in the world since the time of the apostles could be explained by the binding of Satan in the age of the Church. However, if we push this interpretation too far, it presents somewhat of a problem when we come to the release of Satan. If we attribute the release of Satan to God alone, that would arguably make God a collaborator in the deception of the world. In fact, while John does see an angel imprison the devil, the text does not say that God (or any of his angels) is the one who releases the evil one. Therefore, it is probably best to understand the meaning of the release of Satan primarily as an inverse relationship between the forces of evil and the activity of the Church. This is related to the authority of binding and releasing that was given to Peter (and the Church) by Jesus (Matthew 16:18–19). Where the Church is strongest, evil is weakest (Satan is bound), and there is less demonic activity. Where the Church is weak, evil is stronger (Satan is released to deceive the nations). In other words, Jesus gave to Peter and the Church the authority to bind Satan, and therefore, the Church has the power to suppress evil in the world.

Generally speaking, the millennial age of the Church is a time when the world is influenced by the spread of the gospel and the growth of the Church, which is to be contrasted with the way Rome influenced the world (Rev 17:1–6). To be sure, there are places where persecutions and exorcisms go on even today. Given the sense of ongoing spiritual warfare envisioned by John in Revelation, we may interpret the end of the millennium to mean that the Church's overall influence in the world will reach its peak and begin to wane. Jesus himself said that the end will be preceded by the gospel going into the whole world (Matthew 24:14). This does not imply that everyone in the world will become a believer in Christ, it simply means that there will come a time when the gospel has gone as far as it will go in the world. Just as the millennium began when the persecution ended and the Church was victorious over the Roman Empire, the millennium will end when "empire" once again becomes more influential than the Church.

It is also clear from the text that the end of the millennium is not one moment in time when the millennium ends abruptly, bringing an immediate end to history. The fact that John perceives a time at the end of the millennium for Satan to deceive the nations and to try to gather them against God implies that the end of the millennium is more of a gradual transition, or decline. Here "Gog and Magog" represent any nations or peoples hostile to God and to the gospel.[1] According to the vision, the enemies of God will be gathered together against the Church. In other words, the millennial age of the Church, in which Christ has been influencing the world through the Church, will come to an end when the world is no longer willing to be influenced by the Church.

What the text does not indicate is how long this decline goes on. The implication is that the duration will be less than that of the millennium, but this is not certain. At some point after the nations reject the influence of the Church in the world, God will intervene, and the "end of the age" will come (Matthew 28:20). However, based on Jesus' promise to Peter (Matthew 16:18), the Church will never completely die out. God will intervene before that happens because Jesus promised that evil would not win over the Church. Therefore the end will come at some point before the Church declines to the point of defeat.

THE WEDDING OF THE LAMB (REVELATION 19:6–10)

In Jesus' parable of the ten bridesmaids, the groom has been away, and his return for the wedding is delayed (Matthew 25:1–13). The bridesmaids

---

1. Mounce, *Book of Revelation*, 362.

(and, we can assume, the bride as well) wait for the groom's return. There is a strong thematic connection between this parable and the concept of the second coming in the book of Revelation.[2] The Church is the bride of Christ (2 Corinthians 11:2; Ephesians 5:25–27, 32) and has been waiting for his return since his ascension (Acts 1:11). In the book of Revelation, the second coming of Christ is not in the image of the warrior Christ riding into battle to defeat his enemies (as in 19:11–21), and it is only secondarily in the image of the harvester Christ coming at the time of judgment (as in 14:14). Primarily, the return of Jesus is depicted as the bridegroom Christ who comes to claim his bride, the Church.[3]

Weddings in the time of the New Testament had two parts. The first part was the engagement, in which a formal contract was made, and the bride and groom were considered married—the bride was called a "wife," and separation would require a divorce (cf. Matthew 1:19).[4] But the bride did not move into the groom's home until after the second part, the wedding ceremony. In the parable of the ten bridesmaids, Jesus used the familiar concept of the two-part wedding to describe the Kingdom of God. When Jesus brought the Kingdom in its concealed state at his first advent, he became engaged to his bride, the Church.[5] However, he is waiting to bring the full *revelation* of the Kingdom until his return (cf. Matthew 26:29). In the millennial age of the Church, we live in the time between the engagement and the wedding, between Christ's advent and his full and final revelation of the Kingdom. The Church waits for her Groom to return to take her to his home. In the analogy of the Kingdom

2. Several early Christian writers saw this connection, including Oecumenius, *Commentary on the Apocalypse* 19.6–9; and Bede, *Explanation of the Apocalypse* 19.7–8.

3. This is what Paul was talking about in 1 Thessalonians 4:17 when he writes that followers of Christ will "meet the Lord in the air." However, the popular sense of the rapture does not adequately comprehend Paul's concept or Revelation's vision. The concept of the rapture usually implies that after Christ claims his Church, the world will go on without them. According to Revelation, however, the second coming is the wedding of the Lamb, which takes place at the end of history. Note that the text alternates back and forth between our past and our future, and yet we must keep in mind that it was all in the future for John. We must also keep in mind the dream-like nature of apocalyptic vision, and we should not expect everything in the vision to be seen in the order in which it happens.

4. Mounce, *Book of Revelation*, 340.

5. Oecumenius, *Commentary on the Apocalypse* 19.6–9. Oecumenius spoke of the Holy Spirit as a pledge of engagement (cf. John 15:26; 1 John 5:7), like a kind of spiritual "engagement ring."

as a wedding, the marriage is now contractually complete and "legally" binding, yet not fully realized. That the Groom comes only to take the bride to his home (John 14:3) shows that the return of Christ is not a second coming in which Jesus remains on earth. The return, or *parousia*, of Christ is that intervention of God that was promised in the original prophecies of the Day of the Lord. It is his day, because it is his wedding day. He comes to claim his bride and to take her to his home in the Realm of God. Thus eternal life in the Kingdom of heaven is described as a celebration, something like a great wedding reception (Matthew 22:2; cf. 8:11).

Revelation 19:6–10 begins with, "And I heard . . . ," signaling a new scene.[6] John hears the heavenly court singing "Alleluia," which means, "Praise the Lord." The hosts of heaven rejoice because the wedding of the Lamb and his bride has finally come. In the vision, the bride is given a wedding dress of white linen, reminiscent of the priestly clothes we have already seen, but in this context we are told that the white wedding dress of the bride is the "righteous works of the holy ones" (cf. Matthew 22:11–13).[7] The bride of the Lamb is the Church, and she is adorned with the purity that the Groom imparts to her (Ephesians 5:25–27). Just as any loving groom would on his wedding day, the Lamb chooses not to see the faults of his bride, but to see only what is good and pure.

The angel instructs John to write a message from God: "Blessed are those who are called to the wedding banquet of the Lamb." This does not mean that there are some who are not invited (2 Peter 3:9; cf. Matthew 22:8–10). All are invited through God's grace, and all should realize that the invitation is a great blessing. To reject the invitation is to misunderstand the source of the invitation and the implications of such a rejection. Here in the midst of the vision God gives the reader a reality check, so that the point of the vision is not missed. The reader should hear, "*You* have been invited, and such an invitation is a great blessing . . . how will

---

6. Mounce, *Book of Revelation*, 339.

7. Righteousness and justice are synonymous in the biblical languages, so we should not read this as if it refers only to personal holiness and devotional practices and not acts of compassion. Both personal devotion and working for justice within community are assumed to be important, and are in fact two sides of the same coin. While there is a logical priority, in that Christians must seek Christ before they can serve him (Luke 10:38–42), one without the other is incomplete (James 2:14–20). I have translated "saints" as "holy ones" in this passage to emphasize that the reference is to all Christians, not just those who may be seen as exemplary.

you respond?" Both the blessing and the rejoicing in this context are related to Matthew 5:10–12, where Jesus told his disciples to "rejoice and be glad" (the same words used in Rev 19:7).[8] Jesus said that his followers are blessed when they are persecuted, and that they should rejoice for their reward in heaven will be great. No doubt John's original audience would be reminded of these words of Jesus and would take comfort in them as they lived through the persecution that Jesus had anticipated.

Once again John is confused and attempts to bow down to the angel, but he is told not to do so, because the one speaking to him is not Christ, but a messenger of the gospel just like John himself. The last line of verse 10 implies that the message comes from Jesus, through the Holy Spirit, the "Spirit of Prophecy."[9] Therefore, we are not to give undue honor to the messengers of the Revelation, since the word "angel" simply means a messenger. Whether the messenger is angelic or human, we worship only the Source of the message.

FINAL JUDGMENT
(REVELATION 11:18–19; 14:14–20; 20:9–15; 21:8)

The final judgment is foreshadowed in chapters 11 and 14 and realized in chapters 20–21 of Revelation. In chapter 11, verse 18 begins, "And the nations were enraged. . . ." The language comes from Psalm 2, which says that the Lord scoffs at the nations that presume to rail against him.[10]

The foreshadowed description of the final judgment is accompanied by the storms and the great earthquake, which signify divine intervention. Then the heavenly temple of God is opened, revealing the ark of the covenant. The ark of the covenant was the sacred container of the Hebrew people that held, among other holy objects, the tablets of the ten commandments. There was a messianic expectation within Judaism that the ark would return at the Day of the Lord.[11] For those whose names are in the Lamb's book of life, the ark of the covenant represents the presence of God among the people, implying eternal life in the Realm of God. Those who have died in Christ have already been raised to eternal life

---

8. Mounce, *Book of Revelation*, 339–40.

9. Beasley-Murray, *Revelation*, 276.

10. Mounce, *Book of Revelation*, 231.

11. Cf. 2 Maccabees 2:4–8. Mounce, *Book of Revelation*, 233.

and now officially receive their reward (Rev 11:18). Alternatively, John's vision of the ark may be understood to imply that the law will condemn those who are to be judged (Romans 7:7–12). Those who died without Christ are raised for judgment (Rev 20:5). They are said to be destroyed (Rev 11:18), but this need not be taken as meaning annihilated. It probably means that they have lost their reward and will be banished from the presence of God (Rev 22:15; cf. Matthew 22:13).

As for those who are alive when the judgment comes, the vision of Revelation employs the image of the harvest, as in Jesus' parable of the wheat and the weeds (Matthew 13:24–30). In Revelation 14, John sees "one like a son of man" sitting on a white cloud. Drawing from Daniel 7:13, and based on Jesus' own self-designation in the Gospels, it is clear that we are to understand this to be Jesus the Messiah. He wears a golden crown and holds a sickle. When an angel gives him the signal, "the hour to harvest has come," Jesus puts the sickle to the earth, symbolizing the gathering in of the people of the earth.[12]

Another angel joins in the harvesting, and when prompted by a third angel, also puts his sickle to the earth. This third angel is described as the one in charge of the fire, which means that this angel is calling forth judgment. What is implied here is that the harvest of the Son of Man is the gathering of those who are his own, those who will be exempt from judgment. The harvest of the angels is the gathering of those who will be judged (cf. Matthew 13:39–41).

---

12. It should not be surprising that in the vision Christ waits for a sign to begin the harvest. Jesus himself said that the Son does not know the day and the hour, but only the Father knows (Matthew 24:36). The imagery is meant to convey a consistency with Jesus' words in the gospels, as if to imply that the angel simply relays the message from the Father that the time has come. In reality, it is difficult to imagine that the glorified Christ would still be in the dark about the timing of the final judgment. It is assumed that the reason Jesus did not know these things during his lifetime was that such lack of knowledge was a function of his humanity, a product of his voluntary relinquishing of his own divine power (Philippians 2:6–7). In other words, Jesus could not experience full humanity and at the same time be omniscient or omnipotent, and he certainly could not be localized in time and space as a human being without also setting aside the divine attribute of omnipresence. These attributes rightfully belong to the Word (*Logos*) of God in his pre-existent state, but they are temporarily set aside for the incarnation. Therefore, any apparently miraculous power or knowledge that Jesus exhibited was not accomplished by his own divine power, but by the power of the Holy Spirit. On the other hand, it is equally assumed that at his resurrection (or possibly his ascension) his divine omniscience was reclaimed. Therefore, we can only speculate that the angel's cue to Jesus was more a matter of protocol than necessity.

The people who are "harvested" by the angels are compared to grapes, which are plucked and thrown into the wine press. Judgment is depicted as the crushing of grapes, which in this case yields, not juice, but blood. Blood represents life, and the draining of the blood means that those who are judged have lost their lives; more specifically, they have lost the reward of eternal life. The description of blood running up to the horses' bridles for 1,600 stadia (sometimes translated "two hundred miles") is clearly hyperbole. The number is probably meant to be the square of forty, as an intensification of the idea of divine punishment. In other words, in the account of the great flood, the earth was punished for forty days and nights, but the scope of this final judgment is measured as forty times forty—much more severe and vast.[13] The image of horses wading through the blood of sinners is also found in other apocalyptic works, and it is clear that this concept was commonly known as a feature of final judgment in Jewish apocalyptic thought.[14] The fact that the winepress is said to be "outside the city" may come from such passages as Joel 3:12–14,[15] but more importantly it is related to the idea that those who are condemned will spend eternity outside the heavenly city of God (Matthew 22:13).

At this time evil will be defeated once and for all, when the enemies of God are devoured by fire from heaven, and Satan is thrown into the lake of fire to join the beast and the false prophet there. The image of fire from heaven is one we have seen before, and comes from multiple Old Testament passages.[16] As we did with previous passages, we interpret both the fire from heaven and the lake of fire as symbolic of God's judgment, not as literal fire. We are told that the devil, the beast, and the false prophet "will be tormented day and night forever and ever" (Rev 20:10). Here is the image of fire as a never-ending process of purification. Those who persecuted the Church, along with Satan himself, are to be considered so evil that no amount of purification could make them clean. Therefore, the purification process goes on for eternity. This pro-

---

13. Beasley-Murray, *Revelation*, 230. Most commentators will also point out that 1,600 stadia is approximately the length of Palestine, which adds to the hyperbole, in that all of Palestine is depicted as flowing with blood. Mounce, *Book of Revelation*, 283.

14. Beale, *Book of Revelation*, 781–83. See also Josephus, *Wars of the Jews* 6.5.1.

15. Mounce, *Book of Revelation*, 282.

16. Cf. Genesis 19:24; 2 Kings 1:14; Ezekiel 38:22. See Mounce, *Book of Revelation*, 363; and Beasley-Murray, *Revelation*, 297.

cess is described as "torment," however the Greek word that is translated "tormented" originally meant "tested," just as in the context of the purification of gold. Gold that was purified by fire was said to be "tested" by fire. The process of testing first reveals the impurities, and then allows for their removal. Only later did this word evolve to have the connotation of "torture." The same Greek word is used to describe persecution in a letter by Clement of Rome, which was written about the same time as John's Revelation.[17] Therefore, the "torment" of the persecutors is their just payback for their torment of the followers of Jesus. But it is to be interpreted more as an ongoing purification process than as eternal torture. Since physical torture would have little meaning in the spiritual realm, the eternal punishment described here must be thought of more in terms of emotional and psychological torment, in other words, eternal regret.[18]

When we reach the actual moment of judgment in 20:11, God is revealed on his throne, and heaven and earth flee from his awesome presence, "and no place was found for them" (cf. Matthew 5:18; 24:35). This means that there is no place to hide from God's judgment (cf. Psalm 139:1–12). Then the underworld and the sea give up their dead.[19] "Hades" is not hell, as we might commonly think of it, but simply the underworld, the morally neutral place of the dead in Greco-Roman thought. "Death and Hades" (cf. Rev 6:8) is simply a Hebrew-style parallelism, a poetic way to refer to all those who have died, or to physical death itself. The point of mentioning the sea giving up its dead is to say that even those who did not receive a proper burial (because they died at sea) will be called forth to stand before God.[20]

Those who have been resurrected for judgment stand before the throne and are condemned. They are judged on two counts. John says, "Books were opened" (from Daniel 7:10), which presumably reveal the lives of those who are to be condemned, because they are judged

---

17. 1 Clement 6.1.

18. In the parable of the rich man and Lazarus (Luke 16:19–31), note that at least part of the rich man's torment was his regret, as well as the fact that he could see Lazarus in heaven and could see the vast difference between Lazarus' fate and his own.

19. This is further evidence that Revelation is not presented in chronological order. First the earth flees from God's presence, and *then* the sea gives up its dead! (Rev 20:11–13.) Note that the passing of the present earth is mentioned again in Revelation 21:1.

20. Mounce, *Book of Revelation*, 366.

"according to their works" (Rev 20:12; 1 Corinthians 3:13; 1 Peter 1:17).[21] Revelation 21:8 is a non-exhaustive list of those who are to be judged. The inclusion of the "cowards" is probably a reference to the lapsed, those who would forfeit their faith in the persecutions to save their lives.[22] But because all humans could be condemned by their behavior (Romans 3:23), the more important book to be opened is the other book, the book of life, which reveals that those who are to be condemned have rejected Christ, since their names do not appear in that book. All those whose names are not in the book of life join the persecutors in the lake of fire. Those who chose not to have a relationship with God in life will continue in that state in the afterlife. The lake of fire is called the "second death," which means spiritual death, or separation from the Source of life (Romans 6:23). This is eternal separation from God.

Finally, "death and Hades," or physical death itself, is thrown into the lake of fire (Isaiah 25:8; 1 Corinthians 15:26, 54–55). This means that physical death is destroyed and life becomes what it was always meant to be (Genesis 2:17; 3:19), but it also implies that life on earth as we know it has ended. No longer will people be born, live, and die on the earth. All ideas of death and Hades, heaven and hell, will be obsolete. Existence for humans is now either eternal life in the presence of God or separation from God.

THE KINGDOM REVEALED
(REVELATION 21:1–7; 21:9—22:5)

The eternal Kingdom of God is described as "a new heaven and a new earth" (from Isaiah 65:17). This is not to be understood as two separate places, as if the current distinction between heaven and earth will continue to exist. The fact that there is a new heaven and a new earth means two things. First, it means that the existing heaven and earth, with its perceived distinction between the spiritual and the material, is to be no more.[23] The earth that makes us work for a living will no longer have a

21. See also Psalm 62:12(13).

22. Beasley-Murray, *Revelation*, 314.

23. 2 Peter 3:7–13 describes the passing of the present heaven(s) and earth as a destruction by heat and fire, which some have interpreted as a prophetic description of the devastation that would come from nuclear war. However, the heat and fire are simply an image of purification. The destruction of the elements is not a reference to the splitting of the atom, but instead a reference to the purification of the earth by the

hold over us (Genesis 3:17–19), and the sea that gave up its dead will no longer be a threat.[24] This is not to imply that God will destroy creation, since it is his own handiwork, and it was created good. The present creation, which has been corrupted by human sin, will be renewed and re-created into a new reality; as God says, "Look, I am making all things new" (Rev 21:5). The new heaven and earth are really one, where the physical becomes spiritual (cf. 1 Corinthians 15:35–55) and the spiritual becomes "physical," in the sense that the new heaven and earth can be described as the *place* where God lives with his people. In fact, the phrase "he will *dwell* with them" (Rev 21:3) uses the same Greek word as the phrase "the Word became flesh and *dwelt* among us" (John 1:14). The new "heaven and earth" will be the Realm of God, the appropriate environment for the resurrection body.[25]

At this point in the text, the new heaven and earth come together in the image of the New Jerusalem (also mentioned in Galatians 4:26 and Hebrews 12:22). The fact that the heavenly city *descends* indicates that the revealing of the Kingdom is completed by divine intervention, not by the work of the Church.[26] The New Jerusalem is not built from the ground up, it descends as a gift from God, which shows that this is not an earthly city but a heavenly, spiritual one.[27]

In a way, the New Jerusalem is the glorified Church, though it is not to be equated with the Church on earth. It is not the institutional Church, but the people of God, who will be raised to eternal life, just as their Lord Jesus was raised. As such, it is related to the idea of "holy mount Zion" in Jewish apocalyptic thought (cf. Jeremiah 31:1–14; Zechariah 8:3). It is the fulfillment of the promise of the return of God to the people at the meeting place of the spiritualized Jerusalem. Therefore, the New Jerusalem is also the heavenly temple, since it represents the presence of God with and among the people. He will be their Father and they

---

removal of impure elements, just as gold is refined by melting so that the impurities float to the top and can be skimmed off.

24. In the ancient world, the sea was considered a fearful place, full of monsters. The beast of chapter 13 comes from the sea. Beasley-Murray, *Revelation*, 307.

25. Augustine, *City of God* 20.16.

26. Mounce, *Book of Revelation*, 378.

27. Just as the incarnation of Christ was a foreshadowing of God dwelling with his people in the revealed Kingdom, the Christology of descent (which emphasizes that Jesus is God who became human, not a human who became a god, cf. John 1:14 and Philippians 2:7–8) is a foreshadowing of the "descent" of the heavenly city.

will be his children for eternity. There will be no more death, no more mourning, no more sorrow, no more pain (Isaiah 25:8–9; 51:11; 65:19). Those who thirst will be satisfied from the spring of living water (Ezekiel 47:1–9; Daniel 7:10; Zechariah 14:8; John 4:14). The New Jerusalem descends, and heaven meets earth: the Groom comes to the bride, and they are united.

The New Jerusalem is described in terms that are reminiscent of the glory days of Solomon's temple. The fact that the building materials are precious gems highlights the divine nature of the structure. There are twelve angels who act as doorkeepers for the twelve gates of pearl (the "pearly gates"), which represent the twelve tribes of the people of Israel. The New Jerusalem is a perfect square (*four* sides = geometric wholeness) with three gates on each of the four sides (*three* gates = spiritual perfection; see Ezekiel 48:30–34).[28] The wall is built on twelve foundation stones, which represent the twelve apostles (Ephesians 2:19–22).[29] With its walls, the city is a perfect cube.[30] The city needs no actual temple structure, for the whole city itself is a temple, or more precisely, the temple is the presence of God the Father and Jesus Christ the Lamb.[31] The presence of God is also the light of the city, so the city needs no other

28. Many early Christian writers interpreted the three gates as a reference to the Trinity, the idea being that the divine can be accessed by any one of the three persons of the Trinity. Apringius of Beja said that the three gates on each of the four sides predicted that the whole world would accept the Trinity. Apringius of Beja, *Tractate on the Apocalypse* 21.13.

29. Andrew of Caesarea speculated on the representations of individual apostles in the twelve gemstones mentioned. In his interpretation, Jasper represents Peter, Sapphire represents Paul, Chalcedony represents Andrew, Emerald represents John, Sardonyx represents James, Sardius (Cornelian) represents Philip, Chrysolite represents Bartholomew, Beryl represents Thomas, Topaz represents Matthew, Chrysoprasus represents Thaddeus, Hyacinth represents Simon, and Amethyst represents Matthias (who replaced Judas). James, the son of Alphaeus, is missing from the list, having been replaced by Paul. Andrew of Caesarea, *Commentary on the Apocalypse* 21:19–20.

30. The inner sanctuary of Solomon's temple was also a perfect cube (1 Kings 6:20; see also Zechariah 2:1–6). Mounce points out that the measurements of the sides of the heavenly city are 12,000 stadia, and since a cube has twelve edges, the multiple of the length of the edges comes out to be 144,000 stadia. Mounce, *Book of Revelation*, 380. Note that the angelic cubit (the length of the forearm) is the same size as the human cubit (Rev 21:17), which implies that angels are the same size as humans, thus answering the old question of how many angels can dance on the head of a pin!

31. While Revelation 7:15 and 11:19 mention a heavenly temple, the image is metaphorical. It still represents the presence of God, though it relates to the heavenly court before the revelation of the New Jerusalem. Mounce, *Book of Revelation*, 383–84.

source of light. Just as the old earth will pass away, the old order of the universe, with its planets and stars, with light from the sun and moon, and with time measured by the rotation and orbit of the earth, will also pass away (Isaiah 60:19–20; cf. Zechariah 14:6–7).

All those whose names were found in the Lamb's book of life will live in the New Jerusalem. Though its gates are always open (Rev 21:25; Isaiah 60:11), no one who is not purified may enter (Rev 21:27; Isaiah 60:18). In the center of the city is the river of life and the tree of life. The river of life indicates that the source of eternal life is God the Creator and his Lamb, the agent of creation (Zechariah 14:8; John 1:3, 4:14). The tree of life represents a return to the paradise that was originally intended by God in the garden of Eden.[32] Its fruit is never out of season and its leaves "will be for the healing of the nations." This does not contradict the statement that there will be no pain or suffering there. On the contrary, the tree with its fruit always in season represents the fact that there will be no want or hunger in the heavenly city, and the healing leaves represent the fact that there will be no injury, in fact no need for healing.[33] The tree is said to be on both sides of the river, which is a confusing picture. It is reminiscent of Ezekiel 47:12, where there are multiple trees mentioned. In John's vision there is only one tree because of the connection with the tree of life in the garden of Eden, but the placement on both banks of the river probably symbolizes the inclusion of both Jews and Gentiles in the heavenly city. The addition of the healing of the *nations* here indicates that the New Jerusalem is not limited to any particular ethnic group(s), and that in the City of God there will finally be peace among all God's people.

That "there will no longer be any curse" is based on Zechariah 14:11, from a prophetic promise of the coming Day of the Lord. However, in the New Testament context, the "curse" probably refers to sin, and to death itself (cf. Galatians 3:13–14), which will not exist in the heavenly city, since all people there will be those who were marked for God. They will be his, and they will "serve" him, which means that they will worship him. Finally, they are said to "reign" forever and ever. It is not entirely clear what it would mean for everyone to reign. The very definition of reigning would seem to imply that there are some who are ruled over.

---

32. Some early Christian writers also saw in the tree a reference to the cross. Cf. Caesarius of Arles, *Exposition on the Apocalypse* 22.2; and *Homily* 19.

33. Mounce, *Book of Revelation*, 387.

However, since everyone in the New Jerusalem is presumably equal (cf. Matthew 20:12), the fact that the inhabitants of the heavenly city are said to "reign" cannot mean that they are all rulers, since there would be no one left to rule. It also cannot mean that they are equal to God, who reigns over all forever. The statement must mean that they are heirs together with Christ, and share in his inheritance, living forever in the "royal court" of God (Romans 8:14–17; Galatians 4:4–7; James 2:5).[34]

Thus the Kingdom of God is revealed. What Jesus promised in the gospels will become a reality at some time after the millennial age of the Church declines to the point where the Church can no longer influence the world for Christ. Then God will intervene, all of creation will be renewed, and God's people will live in his presence for eternity. We will know God as he has always known us (1 Corinthians 13:12).

SUMMARY

- The end of the millennial age of the Church is not synonymous with the end of the age, spoken of by Jesus in Matthew 28:20.

- After the end of the millennial age of the Church there will be a time of unknown duration when the Church's influence for Christ in the world will decline, and eventually the influence of evil will begin to overshadow that of the Church.

- God will intervene to bring about the end of the age at some time before the Church becomes completely ineffective in the world or dies out (Matthew 16:18).

- The end of the age is the final judgment, the revelation of the Kingdom of God, and the wedding of the Lamb, all happening more or less simultaneously.

- The second coming (*parousia*) of Christ is depicted in Revelation as the Bridegroom coming to claim his bride, the Church—not to remain on earth, but to take her to his eternal home (John 14:3).

- The fully revealed Kingdom of God is described in Revelation as a renewed heaven and earth, a re-created

---

34. This same idea is also expressed in Revelation 20:6, which says that the martyrs and saints of the Church will reign with Christ in heaven during the millennial age of the Church (cf. also Matthew 19:28; 2 Timothy 2:12).

creation, and as the New Jerusalem. It is a return to the originally intended state of paradise depicted in the biblical garden of Eden, and the realization of the promise of eternal life in the Realm of God.

- The revelation of the Kingdom, the New Jerusalem, will be completed by divine intervention, not by the work of the Church. The gospel will go as far as it can be taken, but then the decline of the mission and influence of the Church will precede the final intervention of God and the consummation of the age.

10

Jesus Saw It Coming—The Gospels and Revelation

INTRODUCTION

IN ADDITION TO PREDICTING his own death and resurrection (Matthew 20:18–19), Jesus warned his followers of what the Church would experience after his ascension. Any interpretation of the book of Revelation must be compatible with Jesus' apocalyptic teaching in the Gospels, not only for a consistent theology, but because John himself would not have understood his vision in a way that did not fit with the teachings of Jesus.[1] The purpose of this chapter is to take a look at Jesus' teaching on the events found in Revelation and to show that John's vision—and our interpretation of it—follows the words of Jesus in the Gospels. For our purposes, we will focus on the Gospel of Matthew, since the apocalyptic material in the other Gospels is mostly parallel to Matthew. We will look at passages from the other Gospels as needed, to highlight a point or to bring in some words of Jesus not found in Matthew.

---

1. There is some debate among scholars as to whether the apocalyptic material in the Gospels originated with Jesus or reflects more of the situation and agenda of the Gospel writers. It is the assumption of this interpretation that the apocalyptic discourses do convey authentic teachings of Jesus, and since we are dealing with the theological content in general (rather than a comparison of one gospel to another, for example), questions of source and redaction are outside the scope of the present book. Even if one does not accept that the apocalyptic sections of the Gospels are original to Jesus, the comparison of Gospel eschatology with Revelation is still relevant for two reasons. First, it is generally accepted that all three Synoptic Gospels were written before Revelation, and therefore the early Church's interpretation of John's vision (not to mention John's own interpretation) would be seen through the lens of the words of Jesus as presented in the Gospels. Second, those today who argue in favor of an interpretation that includes a "rapture" do so on the basis of a connection of certain gospel passages with Revelation, most importantly Matthew 24:40–41, and therefore we must deal with these passages.

The first thing that must be emphasized is that the concept of "tribulation" for Jesus is not a specific term, nor does it refer to one particular time, event, or series of events. The Greek word for "tribulation" can also be translated as "persecution," "oppression," "affliction," "suffering," or "distress." In Jesus' teaching (and, I would argue, in John's understanding), "tribulation" generally refers to two major concepts. The first is the suffering and distress that comes with war, specifically the war with the Romans that ended in the fall of Jerusalem and the destruction of the temple in 70 CE. The second is persecution, both at the hands of the religious establishment of first-century Palestine (cf. Acts 11:19) and at the hands of the Roman government. Therefore, one cannot speak of *THE* tribulation, per se, but only of tribulation in general, which encompasses both wartime suffering and religious persecution.[2]

JESUS PREDICTED THE DESTRUCTION OF THE TEMPLE (MATTHEW 24:1–8, 15–26)

Jesus said that there would come a time when "not even one stone will be left on another stone that will not be thrown down" (Matthew 24:2). He knew that war with Rome was coming, and he also knew that it would lead to the destruction of the temple in Jerusalem (cf. Luke 19:41–44; 21:20–24, where he described the siege of Jerusalem).[3] When he made this prediction, the disciples erroneously assumed that the destruction of the temple would be associated with his return at the end of the age (Matthew 24:3), to which Jesus responded, "See that no one misleads you. . . ." The war, he said, would not signal the end of the age, but would only be the beginning of the "labor pains." The labor pains represent tribulation, and the implication is that what was being brought forth in

2. Most of the popular understanding of a future tribulation lasting seven years comes from the book of Daniel, and is not found in Revelation. Because Daniel contains a prophetic vision of the Messiah, some interpreters assume that the events in Daniel's vision have to be folded into the vision of Revelation. This is not the case. Just as John looked ahead to some things that have already happened by our time, Daniel looked ahead to some things that had already happened by the time of Jesus and John. It is not necessary to make everything in Daniel fit into the book of Revelation, and in fact any interpretation that forces Daniel into Revelation obscures the meaning of Revelation (cf. Rev 22:18!). See Rossing, *Rapture Exposed*, 91–92.

3. Eusebius of Caesarea, writing in the fourth century, spoke for the majority of early Christian writers when he understood these words of Jesus to be a reference to the events of 70 CE. Eusebius of Caesarea, *Ecclesiastical History* 3.7.

birth after these labor pains was in part the millennial age of the Church, but primarily the eventual revelation of the Kingdom of God (Matthew 24:14). Jesus warned that there would be wars, and natural disasters (many of which are, as in Revelation, only symbolic of judgment and divine intervention), and even false messiahs, but all this "is not yet the end" (Matthew 24:6). Therefore, it is not necessary to connect specific natural disasters in the book of Revelation with those in Jesus' apocalyptic preaching, much less with actual events. The warnings of disaster are primarily images that bring to mind Old Testament events of divine activity, and we are not meant to see wars, famine, and earthquakes in history or in our own time as signs of the coming of the end (cf. Luke 17:20–21). They are symbolic of the "labor pains," the human suffering and even cosmic struggle (tribulation) that the world experiences leading up to, and throughout, the age of the Church.

In Matthew 24:15, the word "therefore" connects what follows with what comes before it. Jesus' point in the first half of chapter 24 is threefold: (1) wars, famine and earthquakes, and even the destruction of the temple, are not the end—all of this is only the beginning (verses 1–8); (2) before the end there will be a time of persecution and of the spread of the gospel, which is the Church age, including the millennial age of the Church (verses 9–14); and (3) therefore, when you see the destruction of the temple, do not assume that the end of the age has come and go looking for Jesus (verses 15–26), for the return of the Son of Man will not be confined to one place (i.e., Jerusalem; verse 27).

Jesus said to his disciples, "Therefore, when you see the sacrilege of desolation, which was spoken of through the prophet Daniel, standing in the holy place . . ." (Matthew 24:15). Jesus' reference to Daniel is not meant to imply that what the Old Testament prophet predicted had yet to take place in his own time or in the future. Jesus knew that the sacrilege Daniel spoke of had already taken place in the second century BCE (Daniel 9:27).[4] Instead, Jesus is saying that when you see the same desecration happening *again* in the temple, head for the hills, because then there will be tribulation. By "tribulation," he means both the suffering that will come with the siege and fall of Jerusalem as well as the persecution of the Church that is coming (cf. Matthew 24:9–13). This tribulation

---

4. In the middle of the second century BCE, Antiochus IV persecuted Jews and eventually put up a statue of Zeus in the temple. This is the sacrilege that Daniel predicted. See Beale, *Book of Revelation*, 434.

will be greater than ever was or ever will be thereafter. With regard to war and the destruction of the temple, Jesus' statement may be taken to imply that the temple will not be rebuilt as it was when it was destroyed in the past. With regard to persecution, we know that the persecution of the Church by the Roman government would come to a climax in the Great Persecution of the early fourth century, a persecution that would not be repeated in scope ever again. Though some interpret these passages as a prediction of a future persecution of even greater scope, the text does not require this. Jesus' prophecy has already come true.

Matthew 24:22 can apply to both these kinds of tribulation. The "elect" refers to the Church, those who would be looking to be saved from persecution by the return of Christ. But they are not to believe anyone who claims to know that Christ has returned to a certain place. In fact, false messiahs and false prophets will appear on the scene, some even performing signs and wonders to deceive the Church (cf. Rev 13:13–14; 19:20). Jesus says, "Look, I have told you about it before it happens." Christians are not to go out looking for the return of Christ when the temple falls, for when he does return, all will know it (Matthew 24:25–27).

JESUS SAW PERSECUTION COMING
(MATTHEW 5:11–12; 10:17–39; 24:9–14)

In Matthew 10, in the context of sending his disciples out to spread the good news, Jesus warned them that his followers would experience rejection and persecution at the hands of the leaders of the synagogues. The principle cited by Jesus, "A disciple is not above his teacher" (Matthew 10:24; cf. John 15:18–25), means that if Jesus is to be persecuted and put on trial, and even put to death, his followers should expect no less (cf. Matthew 10:38). Jesus' words on persecution in chapter 24, however, seem to be looking farther ahead to the persecution of the Church at the hands of the Roman Empire. In chapter 10, Jesus predicts that his followers will be brought to the synagogues and before governors and kings (Matthew 10:17–18; cf. Acts 24–26), but in chapter 24, Jesus says that they will be hated by all nations on account of his name (Matthew 24:9).

In both sections, Jesus predicts that allegiance to him will cause division, even among families. This is what he means when he said he did not come to bring peace, but a sword (Matthew 10:34–37). Here the sword symbolizes division and conflict. Not that Jesus advocated violence, but that he knew his very existence demanded a response, and that those who had opposing responses to him would be at odds. Also in both sections, Jesus tells his followers that people will hate them because of their identification with him (cf. John 16:1–4). But the good news is that God will not abandon them, and when they are called to answer for their faith, they will be filled with the Holy Spirit, who will give them the words to say to witness to their faith (Matthew 10:19–20, 28–33).[5] Jesus reassures his audience with the promise that everything that is concealed will be revealed (Matthew 10:26–27). Not only will their faith be revealed to their persecutors (putting them in danger), but someday the Kingdom will be revealed, and the works of the persecutors will be revealed to condemn them.

Though many will fall away (Matthew 24:10–12), the most important point is repeated verbatim in both sections: "The one who stands firm to the end will be saved" (Matthew 10:22; 24:13). Just as in the book of Revelation, Jesus' message here is an encouragement to persevere, and resist the temptation to abandon the faith, even to avoid execution. Whoever would deny Jesus to save his physical life will be denied by Jesus in the Kingdom and will lose the reward of eternal life (Matthew 10:33, 39). On the other hand, whoever admits an identification with Jesus will be admitted into the Kingdom (Matthew 10:32–33; cf. Rev 3:5).

JESUS PROMISED TO RETURN
(MATTHEW 24:14, 27–44; 25:1–13)

The assertion that Jesus promised to return begs the question, how do we know that he was not talking about his resurrection? Jesus did predict his own resurrection (Matthew 20:19), but while the resurrection would happen "on the third day," the return of Christ is associated with the end of the age (Matthew 24:27; cf. 24:3). Only when the disciples misunderstood Jesus did they associate the resurrection of Jesus with the revela-

---

5. During the persecutions of the third and fourth centuries, those who were arrested and had to answer for their faith before Roman magistrates, if they lived to return to the churches, were invested with great (but unofficial) spiritual authority because of these verses (cf. also Luke 12:4–12). In some cases, where the churches were left without bishops, these "confessors" (so called because they confessed their faith, even at the risk of their lives) became the spiritual guides of the laity, even though they were not clergy. In some places, Christians would go to the prisons to seek spiritual advice and even absolution from those awaiting martyrdom.

tion of the Kingdom (cf. Matthew 20:19–21). Note that twenty years *after* the resurrection, the apostle Paul knew that the return of Christ was still in the future (2 Thessalonians 2:1–3).

After the resurrection of Christ, and before his promised return, there is the age of the Church. The Church age would be characterized by persecution but also by the spread of the gospel (Matthew 24:14, Rev 14:6). In Matthew 10:23, Jesus said to his disciples, "you will not finish the cities of Israel before the Son of Man comes." The meaning of this verse has been interpreted different ways, but we must keep in mind that this was a message to the disciples whom Jesus was sending out, for their situation. Jesus said to them that they would not finish going through all the cities in Israel before the return of Son of Man. This is not a reference to the resurrection, nor does it imply that the return of Christ would happen in their generation. It simply means that they should not expect all of Israel to become followers of Christ. It does not imply that they *should* or even *could* finish going through all the cities of Israel. It means that if they are rejected or persecuted in a particular city, they should not waste time or risk their lives there. Instead, they should move on to the next town, because there are more than enough places to spread the good news, and they will not run out of places to go.

As we have discovered, the end of the millennial age of the Church is not identical with the ultimate "end of the age," the time at which Jesus promised to return. At the end of the millennium, the influence of the Church decreases to the point where the world has more influence on the Church than the other way around. In Jesus' parable of the fig tree (Matthew 24:32–33), the appearance of leaves on the tree means that summer is near. In the same way, the appearance of tribulation means that the coming of the Son of Man is near. But how near is "near"? The tribulations that followed the time of Jesus were the labor pains of the blossoms of spring, signs of the beginning of the summer that is the Church age. His return is related to the harvest, after the end of the millennial summer, or in the autumn (cf. James 5:7–8). The Church lives throughout the summer, but how soon will the harvest come? The end of the millennial age of the Church will be like the end of summer, and yet there will be a time of autumn before the harvest. During that time of autumn, evil will resurge as Satan is released to try to deceive the nations (cf. 2 Thessalonians 2:7–9).[6]

---

6. For Paul, writing to the Thessalonian Christians in the early 50s CE, the "man of lawlessness" may be a reference to the emperors who would demand worship (the

After the autumn of the Church, when the gospel has been preached as far as it will go (Matthew 24:14), and the world's influence on the Church is greater than the Church's influence on the world, the end of the age will come with the return of Christ. The so-called "second coming" of Jesus is known as the *parousia*, which literally means "coming," "appearing," "arrival," or "presence." As we have seen, the return of Christ will not be localized to one place, but will be the earth-shaking climax of human history (Matthew 24:27, 31). In Jesus' description of his return, he used some of the same apocalyptic imagery from the Old Testament prophets that John used to describe his vision. The sun will go dark and the trumpets will blow, signaling the arrival of the Day of the Lord (Matthew 24:29–31). The fact that Jesus said these things will happen "immediately" after the tribulation should not be taken literally, as if the return of Christ should happen at the end of a particular time of tribulation. As we have seen, Jesus considered the fall of Jerusalem and the destruction of the temple as part of the tribulation, yet they did not usher in the end of the age. The word "immediately" is really not much more than a transitional term in Matthew's Gospel. It should be understood more as an indication of cause and effect than an indication of a duration of time from one event to the next. After all, if a thousand years is like a day to God (2 Peter 3:8–9), what would "immediately" mean, anyway? Understood as a length of time, words like "immediately," "soon," and "near" are all relative. They cannot convey a particular length of time because "no one knows about that day and hour, neither the angels in heaven, nor the Son, but only the Father" (Matthew 24:36). It is important to remember that Jesus admitted even *he* did not know the day and hour, which shows that we cannot take words like "near" and "immediately," even when spoken by Jesus, as indicators of a short duration of time. What they do convey is the fact that the return of Christ is a certainty and logically follows from the historical fact of the tribulation. Just as sure as Christ's followers will suffer, so will he return for them.

Interestingly, Matthew 24:30 contains two distinct images of the coming of the Son of Man. In the first half of the verse, it is the *sign* of

---

"beast" of Revelation), but ultimately the "lawless one" (2 Thessalonians 2:8) is the devil himself, who is the evil force behind the emperors. Second Thessalonians 2:6–12 is Paul's version of the end of the millennium, with the release of evil and the deception of the nations. Note that Paul says the evil one is restrained *now*, during the age of the Church, which is consistent with our interpretation of Revelation on the millennium.

the Son of Man that appears in the sky. In the second half of the verse, after the tribes of the earth mourn, they see the Son of Man himself coming from the clouds—our familiar image from Daniel 7:13. This is not to be interpreted as a two-stage second coming, as if Christ comes once to "rapture" his people, and a second time to stay on the earth. In the first image, Christ does not actually return yet; only his sign is visible in the sky. The following interpretation may seem like a stretch, but bear with it for the moment.

As we have already noted, in 312 CE, the Roman general Constantine saw the sign of Christ in the heavens on the eve of the battle that made him emperor in the west and which gave him the power to end the persecution of the Church.[7] In a vision (or possibly a dream), Constantine saw a symbol in the sky, which he understood as representing Christ. It may have been a cross, but was more probably the "Chi Rho" monogram (it looks like an "X" overlaid with a "P," but is actually the Greek letters *chi* and *rho*, the first two letters in the Greek word for Christ). With this symbol in the sky, Constantine heard a heavenly voice say, "In this sign, you will conquer!" Constantine had the symbol placed on the standards of his soldiers and went into battle under the banner of Christ. He was, of course, victorious, and attributed his victory to the God and Father of the Lord Jesus Christ. Could it be that the first half of Matthew 24:30 predicts Christ's intervention in 312 CE, which marked the end of the tribulation and the beginning of the millennial age of the Church? If so, then the phrase, "and then all the tribes of the earth will mourn," could refer to the millennial age of the Church, during which the nations would be influenced by a Christian empire and the spread of the gospel (and mourning would mean repentance). If this connection between Christ and Constantine proves too much for the modern reader, then consider only that the sign of Christ that appears is the Church itself, signified by the cross. In any case, the point remains that Jesus' own predictions of his return leave room for the age of the Church, but do not leave room for a

---

7. Eusebius of Caesarea, *Life of Constantine* 1.27–32. Eusebius wrote that the sign Constantine saw was in fact a cross, though earlier versions of the story indicate that it was the *labarum*, or "Chi Rho" monogram. That the sign in the sky would be a cross seems unlikely, since it was Constantine himself who discontinued the use of crucifixion as a method of capital punishment. Therefore, at the time of his vision, the cross was still an image of shame. However, if Constantine did use the cross at this time, it would be an interesting turn-around: going into battle under a symbol of defeat, and turning it into a symbol of victory. See also Barnes, *Constantine and Eusebius*, 43, 48–50.

two-stage second coming that includes a "rapture." Finally, at the end of
verse 30, when the Church has done all it can do in the world, the trumpet will sound and the earth will be harvested, the followers of Christ to
be gathered into the presence of God, and the rest to judgment.

In Matthew 24:34, Jesus said, "Truly I tell you, this generation
will not pass away until all these things happen." First, this cannot be
interpreted to mean that Jesus would return within the lifetime of the
apostles, since he has admitted that he does not know when he will return.[8] We have also determined that this cannot be simply a reference
to the resurrection. The key to understanding this verse has to be in the
interpretation of the word "generation." On one hand, the word could
also be translated "race." Some have said that it refers to the human
race, but then what would the point be—that Jesus will return before
the human race becomes extinct? That hardly seems worth mentioning.
Others have said it refers to the people of Israel, the Hebrews. This is a
reasonable possibility, and it would be consistent with Matthew 10:23.
On the other hand, the word can also be translated "age" (cf. Ephesians
3:5). The meaning then would be that the age of the Church (indeed the
Church itself) would not pass away before the return of Christ. Though
the millennial influence of the Church on the world will decline, there
will not be a time when the Church becomes extinct, which is consistent
with Matthew 16:18. The deeper meaning, however, is to remember the
parables of the fig tree (Matthew 24:32–33), the watchful householder
(Matthew 24:42–44), and the ten bridesmaids (Matthew 25:1–13), in
which Jesus wants each generation to "know that he is near, he is at the
doors" (Matthew 24:33).[9] Christians of every generation should live as
though Jesus will return within their lifetime and they should conduct
their lives accordingly. The message is to be "ready" for Christ's return,

8. The apostle Paul seems to have held out the possibility that some of the apostolic
generation would be alive at the return of Christ. See 1 Thessalonians 4:15.

9. Matthew 16:28 is more difficult, since Jesus specifically says that there would be
some alive at that time who would not die before they saw him "coming in his kingdom."
In fact, this verse begs the question: If Jesus does not know the day or the hour, how
would he know whether some of his contemporaries would still be alive at that time?
Since Matthew 16:28 comes right before the transfiguration, it probably means that a
few who were there, namely Peter, James, and John, would see Jesus in the glory of the
kingdom at his transfiguration (Matthew 17:1–2). In any case, the interpretation of this
passage is not essential for our purposes, since virtually all interpretations of Revelation
require that Matthew 16:28 be taken as something other than a promise of the *parousia*
within the lifetime of the apostles.

because he will come without warning (cf. Rev 16:15; 1 Thessalonians 5:1–6). Each generation who hears or reads those words should behave as if Jesus is speaking directly to them.

Though Jesus did not know when the end of the age would come, he knows that his return will come as a surprise, just like the flood in the time of Noah (Matthew 24:36–41; cf. Luke 17:26–36). Though the people were warned that ignoring God would lead to destruction, they were not ready. Perhaps they thought there would be time for repentance later. Maybe they did not believe that they would ever have to answer to a higher power for their actions. Whatever the reason, they ignored the warnings and went about their lives, ignoring God as well. When the flood came, it "took them all away" (Matthew 24:39).

In Matthew 24:40–41, Jesus warns that "there will be two men in the field, one will be taken and one will be left. Two women grinding at the mill, one will be taken, and one will be left." Some have understood these words of Jesus as a reference to a "rapture," in which the followers of Christ will be "taken," (i.e., up to heaven) and the rest will be "left behind." But this is not Jesus' meaning.[10] When read in context with the previous verses about Noah, we can easily see that to be "taken away" is to be like those who were not in the ark and were swept away by the flood (*"They* did not understand until the flood came and took *them* all away"). In Genesis 7:23, it says that only Noah and his family were "left." Additionally, the Gospel text in the original Greek does not say that they were left *behind*, only that they were left (i.e., left alone). Therefore we conclude that verses 40 and 41 are a reference to tribulation that precedes the return of Christ (note the word "before" in verse 38), especially the wars or disasters in which some will perish (they will be "taken") and some will survive (they will be "left"). Understood in this way, our interpretation is consistent with sections of Revelation such as 6:8; 9:18; and 11:13, where a divinely appointed portion of people are said to be killed ("taken") and the rest are "left." To be "taken" is to perish, to be "left" is to be spared (see also Zechariah 13:8–9, where those who are "left" refer to a remnant spared by God). The point is that when the tribulations come, one should hope to be "left." This is unlike the interpretation that assumes a two-part *parousia*, in which Jesus returns twice—once to claim the Church and later to reveal the kingdom. As we have seen, there is

---

10. For a more detailed treatment of this passage in relation to the rapture interpretation, see Rossing, *Rapture Exposed*, 177–79.

no evidence in the text of Revelation, or the Gospels for that matter, to support the idea that the world will go on without the Church after Jesus' return, or that the gathering of God's people is at an earlier time than the full revelation of the Kingdom.

The other passage that is used to support the concept of a rapture is 1 Thessalonians 4:16–17. However, no such rapture is mentioned in the passage. In this passage, when Christ returns to claim the Church, it does not say that the rest of the world goes on without them. As Robert Jewett, Barbara Rossing, and others have pointed out, the point Paul is making in 1 Thessalonians 4 is precisely the opposite—at the second coming, no one is left behind![11] Christ's' return at the end of the age is not one more step in the process toward the revelation of the Kingdom. Christ's return *is* the revelation of the Kingdom, because he will return to claim his bride, the Church, and bring her to his home in the Realm of God. No time elapses between the return of Christ and the revealing of the Kingdom with the final judgment (cf. 1 Corinthians 15:22–24). When Jesus comes, he comes to take his people to his home—our new home in the New Jerusalem (John 14:1–3).

JESUS WARNED OF JUDGMENT (MATTHEW 25:31–46)

The famous passage of the "sheep and the goats" is usually the first to come to mind when one thinks of judgment in the gospels. In Matthew 25:31–32, Jesus says, "when the Son of Man comes in his glory . . . all the nations will be assembled in his presence, and he will separate them one from another, as the shepherd separates the sheep from the goats." There are two important things to notice in these verses. The first is that the judgment Jesus speaks of is associated with his return. The second is that this is the judgment of "the nations," which refers to Gentiles. This is the judgment of those who are not from the people of Israel.[12] It does not mean that all Jews will be exempt from judgment, but it does make the point (radical for its time) that some who are not Jews will be in the Kingdom. Therefore, when taken in context, we can see that this parable of judgment does not apply to Jews.

---

11. Jewett, *Jesus against the Rapture*, 139. See also Rossing, *Rapture Exposed*, 174–75. Note that the Greek word translated "caught up" in 1 Thessalonians 4:17 is the origin of the word "rapture."

12. Harrington, *Gospel of Matthew*, 356, 358.

Jesus is both judge and King, but ultimately he defers to his Father, since it is the Father's Kingdom into which the blessed go. The criterion for judgment seems to be whether individuals cared for "the least of these my brothers and sisters." To care for the brothers and sisters of Jesus means to feed them when they are hungry, welcome them when they need hospitality, clothe them when they are needy or homeless, visit them when they are sick, and visit them when they are in prison. But who are the brothers and sisters of Jesus? According to Jesus himself, they are the ones who do the will of the Father (Matthew 12:50; Mark 3:35; Luke 8:21). In other words, they are his followers, both Jews and Gentiles, and the judgment of the nations will depend on their treatment of them (cf. John 1:12).[13] We may see in the mention of prison Jesus' foresight of persecution, and therefore the overall condemnation for all who mistreat the people of God is quite consistent with John's Revelation.

Contrary to most sermons one hears on this passage, the point of Jesus' teaching in these verses is not an advocacy for works of charity, though he would certainly support them. On the contrary, the passage is less about good works than it is about the final judgment. In this light, the message to Jesus' Jewish audience would be that it is not only Jews who will be saved; Gentiles who follow Christ will also be welcomed into the Kingdom. They are the sheep who by faith in Christ become brothers and sisters of Jesus and adopted sons and daughters of God, and therefore heirs of the Kingdom (Matthew 25:34; John 1:11–13; Ephesians 1:4–5). On the other hand, to the Christian audience of Matthew's Gospel (quite possibly experiencing persecution themselves), the message would have been that those who mistreat the Church will be judged. They will be thrown "into the eternal fire, which has been prepared for the devil and his angels" (cf. Rev 20:15). These are the goats, and they will be judged by how they treated the sheep (and, we can assume, how they treated God's people the Jews). However they treated the followers of Christ is said to be the way they treated Christ. This is just what the risen Christ implies in his confrontation with the persecutor Saul (Acts 9:4; cf. also Matthew 10:40–42).

This does not imply a separate judgment for Jews and Gentiles, only different criteria. Jews will be judged by the law, Gentiles by their treatment of all of the people of God, both Jews and Christians. Ultimately, however, Christians will be exempt from judgment based on their faith

13. Ibid., 357–58. Cf. Matthew 18:6–7.

in Christ. The point of the passage for our purposes is that it is a picture of judgment, what the book of Revelation calls the second resurrection, though it only describes the critera by which Gentiles will be judged.

JESUS' PARABLES OF THE KINGDOM OF GOD

In one way or another, all of Jesus' parables are about the Kingdom. Of course, the parables of Jesus could be (and have been) the topic for a whole book, however we will devote the rest of this chapter to dealing with three major themes in the parables that are relevant to our study of Revelation. Taking advantage of a convenient and not-too-forced alliteration, the three themes are the *waiting*, the *weeding*, and the *wedding*.

The parables of waiting are the parable of the wise servant (Matthew 24:45–51), the parable of the ten bridesmaids (sometimes called the ten virgins, Matthew 25:1–13), and the parable of the talents (Matthew 25:14–30). The point of these parables is readiness. In all three parables, the authority figure (a homeowner, a groom, a master) is away (cf. the parable of the tenants, Matthew 21:33–43). While the authority figure is away, the others in the story await his return. The parables are a warning against spiritual weariness, just as we find in the book of Revelation. The one who will be blessed and rewarded is the one who is found to have remained faithful when the master returns.

Note that the return of the master will come at an unexpected time (Matthew 24:50; 25:13). At the end of the parables of the wise servant and the talents, the parables themselves shift from allegory based on everyday situations to apocalyptic scenes of judgment. The evil servant is cut to pieces and assigned a place with the hypocrites, where there is weeping and gnashing of teeth (Matthew 24:51). Likewise the worthless slave is cast into the outer darkness, presumably the same place since there is the same weeping and gnashing of teeth (Matthew 25:30). Just like the imagery in Revelation, this is not to be interpreted literally, since it would make no sense to be cut to pieces and *then* sent into a place of punishment. The point must be simply that the characters in these parables who were not prepared for their masters' return will share the same fate as the hypocrites (in the Gospels, these are primarily the Pharisees) and they will be left outside of the Kingdom (cf. Matthew 22:13). The parables of waiting, therefore, are about the age of the Church, in which we live, waiting for the return of Christ. The message is to keep the faith, especially in times of "tribulation," when it would be easy to abandon hope, either because suffering compels us to ask, "Where is God?," or because persecution pressures us to conform to the culture around us.

The parables of "weeding" are the harvest parables, the most familiar of which is the parable of the wheat and the weeds (Matthew 13:24–30, 36–43). The landowner (who clearly represents God) allows the weeds to grow up with the wheat until the final harvest, when the weeds will be pulled and separated and then burned. The concept of harvest is a common apocalyptic image of the final judgment when the saved are separated from the condemned. At the end of this parable, the weeds (those who were "stumbling blocks") are cast into the "furnace of fire," where they find the now familiar weeping and gnashing of teeth. It seems clear that the furnace of fire (cf. Revelation's "lake of fire") is equivalent to the place outside the Kingdom in the other parables. The "weeping and gnashing of teeth" need not be understood literally as physical pain (for what would physical pain mean in the spiritual realm?) or even as punishment, per se. More likely they represent sorrow and regret, the natural result of having chosen to reject God.

Finally, the most important image of the Kingdom in both the Gospels and the book of Revelation is the image of the wedding. The parable of the wedding banquet (Matthew 22:1–13; cf. 25:10) illustrates that what we as Christians wait for at the end of the age is a celebration— the final reunion of Christ and his bride, the Church. Here in this parable is a wonderful picture of the Kingdom, with its two aspects, which I call the Reign of God and the Realm of God.

The Reign of God is the present aspect of the Kingdom. The Kingdom is here (it is "at hand," Matthew 4:17; cf. Matthew 11:5 and Luke 4:16–21; and it is "among you," Luke 17:21), yet it is concealed, like a seed planted in the ground or like yeast folded into dough (Matthew 13:31, 33). In the parable of the wedding banquet, the present Reign of God is represented by the engagement period of the king's son. During the time between the engagement and the wedding, the king sent his servants out to extend the invitation to the wedding banquet. This time of invitation relates to the age of the Church, and specifically the spread of the gospel. But many whom the king invited decline his invitation. The fact that original invitees excused themselves opens up the guest list to those who were not initially invited to the wedding. The parable has multiple layers of meaning, but the most provocative message for its original audience would have been that the Kingdom of God would be opened up to the

Gentiles (cf. also the parable of the tenants, Matthew 21:33–43).[14] For our purposes, the important point is that the age of the Church is the engagement period, the time between the betrothal (Christ's first advent) and the wedding (Christ's return, cf. Matthew 25:10).

The Realm of God is the future aspect of the Kingdom. While Jesus' first advent brought the Kingdom in its concealed sense, his return will bring the fullness of the Kingdom in its revealed sense (Matthew 13:32–33; cf. Matthew 10:26–27). Certainly, the whole universe has always been God's realm. However, I refer to the fully revealed Kingdom as the Realm of God because of the promise that God's people will live for eternity in his presence. Just as the wedding ceremony would be the time when the groom took the bride to his home, the revelation of the Kingdom is the time when Christ takes his bride to his eternal home, to the "place" where God is, the Realm of God (John 14:1–3). In the present time, the Kingdom is the Reign of God, planted like a seed in the hearts of people and in the Church, and we wait while it grows.[15] But at the return of the Groom, the Kingdom will be revealed, like a full-grown plant. Now, the Kingdom is *in us*; then, we will be *in the Kingdom*, living eternally in God's presence. This is the Realm of God, or what we popularly call "heaven."

The parable of the wedding banquet ends with the curious account of the man without a wedding garment (Matthew 22:11–13). At the very least, these verses imply that not everyone will be in the Realm of God. Some will be banished from the presence of God, and left outside of the Kingdom in the darkness (away from God's light). Much has been made of a possible custom that the host of an ancient wedding banquet would provide the appropriate garment. This may or may not be true, but it is really not the point. Whether the wedding guest in the parable refused to

14. Note that Matthew 22:7 contains a possible allusion to the destruction of Jerusalem, potentially implying that God let Jerusalem fall because of the way the people had treated the prophets (cf. Luke 21:20–24). This could be related to Revelation 11:11–14, in which the fall of Jerusalem is somehow related to the death of the two witnesses, though it is the Romans who kill the two witnesses. In the spirit of the Old Testament, John seems to see Rome as God's instrument of punishment against Jerusalem, and yet Rome would also fall for its treatment of both Jews and Christians (Matthew 25:40, 45).

15. Note that it is God, not the Church, who causes the growth (1 Corinthians 3:6–7).

wear a garment offered to him or failed to bring his own, the garment is symbolic of something about the man himself (cf. Rev 3:4).

Just as we have interpreted the white garments in Revelation as images of purity of lifestyle, the underdressed wedding guest of Matthew 22 is lacking something in terms of moral conviction or sincerity of faith. He has not "put on the Lord Jesus Christ" (Romans 13:12–14). Even though the guest may have accepted the invitation to the wedding, his response to the invitation was incomplete, half-hearted or insincere. In other words, he didn't "walk the talk." In some way, his faith was not supported by his lifestyle (cf. Ephesians 2:10; James 2:14–17).

This interpretation assumes that the invitation in the parable represents God's grace, or God's offer of forgiveness and reconciliation that goes out to all people, which is based on God's love and mercy. The positive response to that invitation is what Jesus called repentance, what John called receiving Christ (John 1:12; 1 John 5:11–13), and what Paul called faith (Ephesians 2:8–10; cf. Romans 10:8–10). Jesus and the apostles agree that the natural and necessary result of accepting the invitation is participation in good works, motivated by gratitude and love. Jesus connected forgiveness and acts of compassion to judgment (Matthew 6:14–15; 18:34–35), Paul said spiritual gifts without love are worthless (1 Corinthians 13:1–3; cf. Galatians 5:22–23), James said faith without works is dead (James 2:17), and John said that we cannot claim to love God if we do not love our neighbor (1 John 4:7–8, 20). It may well have been that Jesus intended for self-righteous listeners, perhaps notably Pharisees with whom he was in conflict, to see themselves in the character of the underdressed guest. Though they went through the motions of their religion, he called them hypocrites because they excluded people for whom God cared, not to mention that they rejected God's Messiah.

The man in the parable without the wedding garment is thrown into the outer darkness (cf. Luke 13:25). Whatever else this may mean, it places him outside the Kingdom of God.[16] This is what we might call "hell." However, it is hell not so much because it is a place of punishment but because it is separation from God. It is the loss of the chance to live in the presence of God, where we will know God as he knows us (1 Corinthians 13:12), and that is the reason for the "weeping and

---

16. The opposite of the Realm of God in these parables is the place of outer darkness, or the image of the furnace of fire (which corresponds to the lake of fire in Revelation).

gnashing of teeth" described in Jesus' parables. To be banished from the Kingdom of God is to be consigned to an eternity of sorrow and regret. In Revelation, this is called the second death (Rev 2:11; 20:6, 14).

Interestingly, the prayer of Jesus, known as the "Lord's Prayer" or the "Our Father," contains both of these aspects of the Kingdom of God, God's Reign and God's Realm. When we pray, "Thy Kingdom come . . ." we are praying for the revelation of the Realm of God. And when we pray, "Thy will be done, on earth as it is in heaven . . ." we are praying for strength to do God's will in the world. We are praying for our lives here and now in the Reign of God. Therefore the prayer Jesus taught his disciples summarizes his teaching on the Kingdom in the parables. While we wait for the Realm of God, we live the Reign of God. Based on Jesus' parables, we are meant to understand the Realm of God as a celebration, to which all are invited (Matthew 22:9–10). The invitation itself is God's grace, embodied in Christ and the cross. Therefore, the cross stands as an open invitation to all people to accept the reconciliation that God offers. But just like in the parable, this invitation requires a response.

The summary below includes more references to Gospel passages and their parallels in Revelation.

SUMMARY

- The word "immediately" is only a transitional term in Matthew.

- Like John in Revelation, Jesus borrows his imagery from the Old Testament prophets.

- Jesus admitted he did not know when the Kingdom would be revealed.

- Just like Revelation, Jesus' message in Matthew 24–25 is to keep the faith.

- "Tribulation" in the Gospels does not refer to a specific time or event, but to general war and persecution, though Jesus did predict the war with the Romans and the destruction of the temple.

- The disciples erroneously thought the destruction of the temple would bring the revelation of the Kingdom.

- Wars and disasters are not signs of the revealing of the Kingdom, but of the beginning of the Church age.

- The Church age is a time of waiting for the return of Christ, like an engagement period, waiting for the wedding.

- The Church age is characterized by general tribulation and the spread of the gospel.

- The present (concealed) aspect of the Kingdom is what I call the Reign of God.

- Christ's return will not be confined to one place, but will be worldwide.

- The wedding banquet is the primary image of the revelation of the Kingdom, the New Jerusalem.

- Jesus did not teach of a "rapture" or two-part second coming.

- Jesus' return brings both judgment and the revelation of the Kingdom.

- The future (or revealed) aspect of the Kingdom is what I call the Realm of God.

- "Hell" is separation from God, banishment outside the Realm of God (i.e., from the presence of God).

- Matthew 10:1; 12:29 (cf. also 16:19) refer to the binding of Satan in the Church age (Rev 20:1–3).

- Matthew 10:32–33, 39 warns followers not to deny Christ (Rev 3:5).

- Matthew 13:39 speaks of the harvest of the earth by the angelic reaper (Rev 14:17–20).

- Matthew 22:7 is probably a reference to the destruction of Jerusalem (Rev 11:13–14).

- The wedding garment of Matthew 22:11–12 parallels the image of the white garment in Revelation (Rev 3:4, 18; 4:4).

- Matthew 24:23–27 warns of false prophets (Rev 13:13–14; 19:20).

- Matthew 24:28 speaks of scavenging birds (Rev 19:17–18).

- Matthew 24:30 is the mourning of the tribes of earth (Rev 1:7).

- Matthew 24:35 (cf. also 5:18) witnesses to the heavens and earth passing away (Rev 20:11; 21:1).

- Matthew 24:38–41 references the disasters that cause death (Rev 6:8; 9:18; 11:13).

- Matthew 24:50; 25:13 parallels the thief in the night (Rev 16:15).

- Matthew 25:31–46 is the second resurrection and final judgment of the Gentiles (Rev 20:11–15).

- Matthew 25:41 evokes the lake of fire (Rev 19:20; 20:15).

- Luke 19:41–44; 21:20–24 speaks of the siege and fall of Jerusalem (Rev 6:5–8; 9:1–12; 11:3–14).

- Christ and the cross embody the grace of God, the invitation that God extends through Christ to all people. This invitation requires a response.

11

So What? The Practical Implications
of This Interpretation of Revelation

INTRODUCTION

O UR INTERPRETATION HAS RULED out much of the popular understanding of what the book of Revelation is all about. As we have
seen, in the text of Revelation there is no rapture, there is no antichrist
per se, and there is no future expectation of a great tribulation. In fact,
to interpret the book of Revelation as a prophecy of a future persecution of the Church is a myopic Western viewpoint, since there are many
countries in the world where the Church is under persecution now and
has been for centuries.[1] On the one hand persecution has been almost
ongoing from the beginning of the Church in one place or another, and
yet on the other hand the worldwide persecution depicted in Revelation
is in our past, and there is no biblical reason to believe that it will be
repeated.

Our methodology has been to look at the images in John's vision and, whenever possible, connect them to events that have already
taken place. For example, if we see in the vision the destruction of the
Jerusalem temple, why would we interpret that as a future event (requiring the temple to be rebuilt so that it can be destroyed again), when we
know that the historical destruction of the temple was in John's past,
and probably burned into his memory as an unforgettable event? When
we see a world government persecuting the Church predicted in the
text, why would we assume it meant something in our future, when the
centuries immediately following the writing of Revelation were full of

1. For more information on the persecuted church, see the following websites:
http://www.opendoorsusa.org and http://www.persecution.com.

persecution by the Roman Empire? And why would we interpret the millennial reign of Christ as a political reign, when that is precisely the kind of temptation that Jesus rejected in his ministry (John 18:36; cf. Matthew 4:8–9)? As others have already noted, it simply does not make sense to have Jesus in his second coming be the kind of Messiah that he refused to be the first time.[2] Therefore, contrary to popular end-times fiction portrayals, we are not headed for a great earthly battle—the world against the Church—in which Christ comes to earth as a warrior, to defend or perhaps avenge the Church. The battle is a spiritual one, and it goes on in and throughout the age of the Church.

The plagues and disasters of Revelation are therefore simply symbolic warnings, calling to mind depictions of God's intervention in the Old Testament. They warn against mistreating God's people (Matthew 25:45–46), and they warn against apostasy and idolatry. As we noted in the case of Jonah, not all warnings need to come true for the prophecy to be of God. If these plagues and disasters are fulfilled, it is only metaphorically or in the spiritual realm (with a few possible exceptions), the point being that we have not found it necessary to try to connect each one with a specific event in time. In effect, we have freed ourselves from the obligation to read Revelation as a doomsday text. As a part of the Christian gospel (in the broadest sense), and as a *revelation* of the words of Christ, the book of Revelation is a book of good news, not bad news.

THE MESSAGE OF REVELATION FOR THE
TWENTY-FIRST CENTURY

If we are not using Revelation to look for the signs of the times, then what good is it to us? Even though most of the events symbolized in the book of Revelation are in our past, the underlying message of John's vision is the same for us as it was for its original audience. Above all else, Revelation is a book of hope for those who suffer for their faith. As Jesus himself warned, to be his follower will often mean persecution and suffering, and sometimes even death. But in the midst of the suffering, there is hope, the promise of a time when God "will wipe away every tear from their eyes, and there will be no more death; no more sorrow, or crying or pain . . ." (Rev 21:4). Of course, those who die in Christ before the revelation of the Kingdom will experience this as well. As the apostle

2. Rossing, *Rapture Exposed*, 135–36.

Paul pointed out, those who do not live to see the return of Christ are not at a disadvantage when it comes to resurrection (1 Thessalonians 4:13–15). Those who die during the age of the Church enter the Realm of God even before it is revealed to the rest of the world (Rev 6:11; cf. Luke 23:42–43). But for those who live and struggle in the age of the Church, the message of Revelation is the promise of an eternal life without suffering. Therefore, Christians are encouraged, and even warned, to keep the faith no matter what confronts them. To renounce one's faith in Christ, even to save one's life, might mean loss of eternal life. To keep the faith, even if it means losing one's life, means one can look forward to eternal life. In a way, the book of Revelation can be seen as an expanded commentary on Jesus' apocalyptic preaching in the Gospels. John's vision could be understood as a mystical sermon on these words of Jesus: "If anyone wants to follow me, he should him deny himself, and accept his cross, and follow me. For whoever wants to save his life will lose it, but whoever loses his life for my sake will find it. For what would be the benefit if a person should gain the whole world, but forfeit his soul?" (Matthew 16:24–26). ". . . but the one who stands firm to the end will be saved" (Matthew 10:22; 24:13).

The message of Revelation, therefore, is that those who follow Christ in suffering will surely follow Christ in resurrection. This should be a reassuring and hope-filled message for Christians of any time. In Revelation, we are not reading with the Bible in one hand and the newspaper in the other, looking for the signs of the times in the words of Scripture. We are living our lives in a world where human free will is consistently abused, and yet we anticipate a time of divine intervention when God will restore creation and reveal the Kingdom. In short, we look forward to the wedding of the Lamb and his bride, the Church.

THE WORLD COMES FULL CIRCLE

Before the return of Christ and the final revelation of the Kingdom, however, John's vision does alert us to a time when the millennial age of the Church winds down, and the nations are deceived toward idolatry. Some have said that we are heading into a post-Christian world, but that is not really the whole truth. It would be more accurate to say that we are coming full circle, back to a pre-Christian world. In other words, as the millennial age of the Church comes to an end, the world will revert back to what it was like before the millennium, and it will look more and more like the early Roman Empire, in terms of its religion, its values, and what is considered acceptable behavior. As the influence of the Church on the world tapers off, the world will enter a transitional time of unknown duration, in which the people of the world will increasingly turn away from God. And as the influence of the Church on the world tapers off, the influence of the world on the Church will increase.

So what will the world look like when the millennial reign of Christ comes to an end? It will probably look very much like the Roman Empire in the days of the early Church. Many people will find it inconvenient to be committed to a religion that includes standards of morality, especially when those standards conflict with business and career goals.[3] In fact, morality itself will become ridiculed as something old-fashioned that unenlightened people cling to. Religious and cultic options will multiply, with widespread suspicion of any religious system that demands exclusive loyalty. Relativism and syncretistic "salad bar" spirituality will become more accepted in the culture, as people try to hedge their bets by taking a surface acceptance of many religious systems, without going deep into any. Church attendance will decline as church membership becomes less and less culturally normative. Violence will be glorified, and gladiator-like games will offer up pain and blood as entertainment. Sexuality will also become a form of entertainment, not just the voyeuristic kind, but sex itself will become a sport, entered into purely for personal gratification without concern for one's partner (opponent?) or for the long-term psychological and emotional effects of the sexual union. Children will be seen as an obstacle in the pursuit of the aristocratic lifestyle, and population will decrease in developed countries as babies become unwanted, and even disposable.[4] The more people turn away from God, the more they will turn to other gods to fill the void. Most often they will simply make themselves their own god, as they demand the right to make them-

---

3. In the early days of the Church, even some Christians would postpone baptism until retirement so that the expectations of the faith would not hamper their careers. This was especially the case with men who held government jobs, which usually required participation in pagan cults.

4. Cf. Psalm 139:13–16. In the Roman Empire, it was legal to "expose" an unwanted infant. In other words, the father of a newborn had the option to leave it outdoors, exposed to the elements, where it would either die or be picked up by someone who would raise it as a slave. This was most often done with newborn girls, since girls were often seen as more of a liability than an asset in the family.

selves their own highest authority. And this idolatry is the deceit of the nations (Rev 20:7–8).

What I am describing here is the way life was in the early Roman Empire. If it sounds a lot like life in the twenty-first century, that may not be a coincidence. In those times and places where the Church was persecuted, being a Christian was inconvenient at best, and often dangerous, and therefore people joined the Church for one reason and one reason only—a deep conviction that it was the only real way to access the Divine. After the time of Constantine, when Christianity was legalized, it would become politically expedient and even fashionable to join the Church. This is the shadow side of the legalization of Christianity, and one of the results of a state-supported religion. People will join for all the wrong reasons. Rather than being a hindrance to the careers of the upwardly mobile, the Church came to be seen as a vehicle for networking. St. Augustine would eventually complain that his church was full of *ficti*, or fakes, what we would call nominal Christians.[5] But this is the paradox of Church membership, and the temptation of "church growth." When the Church is least accepted and most counter-cultural, its members tend to be the most committed, though there will be fewer of them. When the Church conforms to the culture, it attracts more members, but some of those members are there for reasons other than commitment to Christ or love of God and neighbor.

In the end, we cannot say whether we are living at the end of the millennium. If we did that, we would be guilty of exactly what I have criticized others for doing: looking for current events in the book of Revelation. Perhaps we are facing the end of the millennium, or perhaps this is just the next phase of the Church age, with Europe and North America becoming less Christian (as North Africa and Asia Minor did centuries ago), while in other places in the world the Church grows. Perhaps it is the case that the values of the Roman Empire have never really left us, and the observations above are in one way or another typical of all of human history. Even if we could say for sure that we are witnessing the decline of the Church, we do not know how long that decline will last, and we could therefore never say with any certainty what lies ahead for the Church.

We are probably not headed for another persecution of the Church on a worldwide scale, such as happened in the third and fourth centuries.

---

5. Augustine, *City of God* 1.35.

Interpretations that predict a worldwide government capable of reprising the Roman Empire's persecution of the Church are simply not supported by the text. The Great Persecution that John (and Jesus) foresaw has happened already, though this probably comes as little comfort to those who live in countries where even now governments persecute or discriminate against the Church. But while we are probably not headed for another worldwide persecution, we do seem to be headed into a time of increasing cultural persecution, when the values of society will be defined more by consumerism, the media, and even by entertainers than by the Church.

Unfortunately, as the Church becomes more and more countercultural (or the culture becomes less and less Christian), many will simply leave the Church (John 6:66–69; cf. Matthew 22:5, 24:12). Others will attempt to change the Church to make it follow the culture. But those who "stand firm to the end" will increasingly be made to feel like they are backward and unenlightened, and will be pressured to conform (but cf. Romans 12:1–2). Whenever the end of the millennium comes, the book of Revelation implies that it will be increasingly difficult to reconcile life in the everyday world with the expectations of the gospel. This is because life in the world will move farther and farther from the values of the Kingdom, and yet it will become even more important to live the values of the Kingdom in the world. But this will not be easy or convenient. It will take courage and sacrifice, and it may cause suffering. When Jesus said, "Whoever wants to save his life will lose it" (Matthew 16:25), he could just as well be saying to us, "Whoever wants to *preserve his lifestyle*, but does so at the expense of his soul, could risk losing eternal life." On the contrary, the follower of Christ is called to *deny himself*, not indulge himself. "For what would be the benefit if a person should gain the whole world, but forfeit his soul?" (Matthew 16:26). The book of Revelation calls the twenty-first-century reader to resist cultural conformity and consumerist idolatry. For "the one who stands firm to the end will be saved."

Though we cannot know if we are living at the end of the millennium, one thing is certain. It is as legitimate as ever to say that we are living in the "end times" (1 John 2:18), partly because Jesus expects all of his followers to be ready for his return, but also because faithful Church membership is becoming increasingly countercultural.

LIVING THE REIGN OF GOD

We know that the basic message of Revelation is one of faith and hope. This is consistent with what was stated at the beginning of this book: Revelation is not a book for the future, it is a book for the here and now. It was a book for the here and now in the first century, and it remains a book for here and now in the twenty-first century, as long as we interpret it correctly. Through John's vision, Christ tells his churches (and indirectly, he tells us) to keep the faith, and not to lose hope. Whether we are witnessing the end of the millennium or not, we undoubtedly live in the age of the Church, and until the return of Christ, we are called to live according to the Reign of God that is in us.

The concept of the binding of Satan has implied the principle that wherever the Church is weakest evil is strongest, and wherever the Church is strongest, evil is weakest. Therefore, even though we do not interpret Revelation as though the Kingdom will emerge through human effort, we can work at revealing the Kingdom that is within us a little at a time by living the values of the Kingdom in the world. In several of Jesus' parables, it is clear that the values of the world are backward compared to the values of the Kingdom (cf. Matthew 20:1–16). As people of the Kingdom, it is our mission to live the values of the Kingdom, in spite of the fact that by doing so we may be swimming upstream in the world. In this way we reveal a little of the Kingdom to those who need to see it. We may not be building the Kingdom, for it already exists, but we can participate with God in revealing it—to one person at a time—while we wait for God to intervene and reveal it to the whole world.

Twice in the Gospel of Matthew, Jesus quoted the prophet Hosea, saying, "Go and learn what this means: I desire mercy" (Matthew 9:10–13; 12:1–8). The complete verse of Hosea 6:6 is, "For I desire mercy, not sacrifice; the acknowledgement of God rather than burnt offerings." Jesus' opening phrase, "Go and learn what this means . . ." is his way of saying, "go and look it up." The verse that Jesus quoted is a Hebrew parallelism, in which *sacrifice* parallels *burnt offerings*, and *mercy* parallels *the acknowledgement of God*. In other words, to acknowledge God (the opposite of idolatry) is to show mercy to others. Said yet another way, true worship of God is acted out in works of compassion.[6]

---

6. For our purposes, "mercy" and "compassion" are synonymous.

Jesus himself connected mercy with the Kingdom of God in the parable of the unmerciful servant (Matthew 18:23–35). In this parable, the Kingdom of God is compared to the forgiveness of a merciful king. But in the parable, the servant who was forgiven a huge debt refused to forgive the much smaller debt of a fellow servant. When the king found out, he revoked his forgiveness. In this parable (and elsewhere), Jesus does two things. He makes a connection between salvation and forgiveness (cf. Matthew 6:12, 14–15), and he gives clear direction for the behavior of God's people as they await the revelation of the Kingdom. What is implied here is that living the Reign of God should be governed by three concepts: gratitude, forgiveness, and compassion. Jesus made it clear that the refusal to forgive is itself a sin (Matthew 5:23–24; 6:14–15). Also, Jesus places the expectation on all of his followers that they be motivated by gratitude toward God and compassion for others.[7] The unmerciful servant should have shown compassion toward his fellow servant, especially since God had shown compassion toward him. Living the Reign of God means living a life of forgiveness and compassion, motivated by the ever-present knowledge of what God has done for us in Jesus Christ, and by a desire to show our gratitude to God by loving others.[8]

Finally, as we do our works of love in the world, we must do them so that those who see us know that we do them in the name of Christ, and so that they might turn (or return) to God (Matthew 5:16).

CONCLUSION

So we have interpreted the book of Revelation. As I said at the start, this is not meant to be the last word on the subject, only a beginning to look at the text in a new way that adequately takes into account the history of the early Church in the Roman Empire. Hopefully, we have rescued the book of Revelation from an interpretation that requires us to fear the future, on one hand, or anticipate with perverse pleasure God's wrath against our enemies on the other (cf. James 5:7–9; 2 Peter 3:9). While we wait for the wedding of the Lamb, we have in our mind's eye a city set on a hill (Matthew 5:14), which cannot, and must not, be hidden. We can

---

7. Note how many times in the Gospels Jesus' actions are described as being driven by compassion, for example Matthew 9:36; 14:14; 15:32.

8. Note the comparison of parallel passages in Matthew 5:48 and Luke 6:36. What Jesus calls "perfection" in Matthew he calls "mercy" in Luke. In other words, a life that works toward perfection is a life that emulates and extends the mercy of God.

see it off in the distance, and we are called by our Savior to point it out to others. We are called to do all we can to show compassion toward others, and to participate in God's revelation of the Kingdom. In this way, we are doing what our God would do, and what God will do. We are passing on the message of faith, hope, and love found in the book of Revelation, and we are extending the invitation of the cross and the ministry of reconciliation (2 Corinthians 5:17–20).

SUMMARY

- The message of Revelation is to keep the faith and not to lose hope.
- The deceit of the nations is the idolatry of making oneself god (one's highest authority).
- We are called to avoid idolatry in all its forms (i.e., making anything more important than God).
- We are not building the Kingdom of God, but we can participate in revealing it.
- Life in the Reign of God should be motivated by gratitude, forgiveness, and compassion.
- During the Church age, we live the Reign of God by doing works of love.

Appendix A

The Book of Revelation in Plain English

INTRODUCTION

WHAT FOLLOWS IS NOT a translation of the text of Revelation. It is not even a paraphrase. Strictly speaking, it is only an interpretation. In the context of this book, it is also a summary of the interpretation I have outlined in the chapters. But the reader should understand, what follows is a recasting of the text of Revelation, without the mystery and beauty of the symbolism and apocalyptic imagery. I have replaced almost all the metaphorical language with the historical equivalents, and in the process I have reduced the symbolic connection with the Old Testament to narrative references. To make the interpretation even clearer, I have also rearranged the material from Revelation into something close to a chronological order. Therefore, this is not meant to replace the book of Revelation, and it should never find itself at the end of some edition of the New Testament. What I present here is for the purposes of study only, and in no way do I presume that my rendering counts as sacred Scripture.

To compare this rendering with the text of Revelation, use Chart 2: "Structure of the Book of Revelation." The section numbers below are listed in the chart under the column heading "Appendix A Section." Find the section in question in that column and read back along the same row to find the passage in Revelation. Note that in most cases, a section number is repeated and incorporates multiple passages. Alternately, use the chart named "Scripture Key to the Book of Revelation" to find the corresponding sections of Revelation for each section below. Text in parentheses is material that is implied but not expressly stated, or explains a historical fulfillment of what is stated in Revelation.

Finally, the reader should also keep in mind that, while this is my interpretation of Revelation, it is only my interpretation of *John's understanding* of his vision, so one should not confuse John's understanding within his first-century context with the opinions of the author of this book. For example, John's understanding of the vision does not allow that some responsibility for the war with the Romans might belong to the Jewish rebels who antagonized the legions. All the blame lies with the Romans, who are understood to be puppets of Satan, and unwitting agents of God's judgment. On the other hand, John's connection of the Roman attack on Jerusalem with that of Babylon in the sixth century BCE should not be read as anti-Semitic. John is merely positioning himself as an Old Testament prophet, critiquing his own people for their unfaithfulness, which in this case means that most did not accept Jesus as their Messiah. Therefore keep in mind that what you read here is still a first-century message, even though it is written in twenty-first-century language.

THE BOOK OF REVELATION IN PLAIN ENGLISH

1. To all the churches in the area for which I am overseer, and through them, to all the churches of the world.

From John, your brother and fellow servant of Christ, eyewitness of the ministry of Jesus Christ, and witness to the word of God—and because of that I am suffering this present persecution with you, persevering on hope in the coming of Jesus' Kingdom.

May grace and peace come to you from the eternal Father, the Holy Spirit, and Jesus Christ, who is the faithful witness—the first to die the martyr's death and the first to rise from the dead in resurrection. He has authority over all earthly rulers, yet he loved us so much that he was willing to give his life to release us from our sins. Not only has he freed us from our sins, but he has made us into a new people, united under his leadership, and he has made each of us ambassadors of his Father, who is God. Truly, all glory and power belong to him forever.

I have come to be in exile on the island of Patmos, which is my punishment for proclaiming the word of God, which Jesus Christ spoke to us. As I was in prayer on a Sunday, I heard an angel call to me. The angel told me to write down the vision that I was about to see, and send it to all of you. What I saw was a revelation of things to come from God through Christ, for all of his servants.

You who read or hear these words are blessed if you listen carefully and follow them, for the time for their fulfillment has already begun. And one day, Christ will return, and everyone on earth will have to acknowledge him, even those who killed him and those who persecute his followers. At that time, those who have rejected him will surely regret it. For God is omnipotent and eternal—the beginning and end of all things.

2. When I turned to see who was speaking to me, I saw Jesus Himself, truly present with you in your churches. He looked both priestly and royal, with an aura of purity about him that radiated with the glory of God, and I knew that he could see into my heart. He is the firm foundation of our faith, and he protects and cares for the churches and their leaders, for they are bringing the light of the gospel to the world. When he speaks, he speaks with all the authority and wisdom of the Creator, and his word is truth itself, separating right from wrong, good from evil, truth from falsehood.

When I saw him, I fell prostrate in fear and awe. But he touched me, and his touch was both strong and gentle, both powerful and protective. He reassured me, saying, "Don't be afraid. I started this world, and I will finish it. I died, but I am alive, and I am the one who lives for eternity, and I have authority over death itself. Therefore, write down the things that you have seen, the things that are now, and the things that will happen after these things."

The Things That You Have Seen . . .

3. Then I saw a vision of something that happened long ago—before the creation of the world. One angel refused to submit to God's authority, and convinced a portion of the other angels to reject God along with him. But the angels who were loyal to God opposed them, and the unfaithful angels were banished from the Realm of God. The leader of the rebellious angels would come to be known as Satan (which means "the antagonist") and the devil (which means "the accuser") because he and his banished angels would deceive the people of God's created world and try to draw them away from God.

Then I heard a voice that explained to me what I had seen. Even though this happened long ago, on that very day when the devil and his followers were banished from God's presence, the salvation of God was preordained. For even though Satan would accuse the people of the very sins he had enticed them to commit, God's plan for their salvation had already begun. This plan was for the Christ of God to come into the world with all the authority of God, and call God's people back to him. And the people would be able to have victory over the devil because the Christ of God became the Lamb of God and gave his life for them. What's more, many of Christ's followers would give their own lives for their witness, and for a testimony to him.

Therefore, those in the Realm of God are happy that Satan is gone from them, but the world suffers because of the presence of evil, and all the more because Satan knows his days are numbered, and his anger and frustration are taken out on the people as he struggles ever harder to draw them away from God.

4. Next I saw the pivotal moment in human history, when the Christ of God came into the world. I saw the young virgin Mary, daughter of Israel, full of the grace and glory of God. She was pregnant, and she gave birth to Jesus. This Jesus is the King of kings promised by the prophets, and the one whom we saw ascend to the Realm of God after his resurrection.

When Jesus was born, Satan tried to kill him (by using Herod, who murdered the babies of Bethlehem). But Mary and her family were led by God's providence into (Egypt), and remained there for a time of waiting and anticipation. The time of the holy family in exile reminds us that Jesus' family knew the fear of running for one's life, just as many of us experienced during the war with Rome a generation ago. God protected Mary and her Child from evil, just as he protected their ancestors, the people of Israel, when they were in exile, and just as he protects his people, the Church, in this time of persecution. For even if the devil should try to use the forces of nature itself against God's people, creation belongs to God, and it will bow to God's will, just as it did when the people of Israel walked through the Red Sea.

5. Then I saw a scene of great rejoicing and praise in the Realm of God. All the spiritual beings were celebrating the victory of Jesus over death and evil. For he had given his life like a sacrificial Lamb, but he has overcome death and was raised up again to reclaim his complete divine omnipotence. He lives in the Realm of God, yet he is omniscient and omnipresent in all the world through his Holy Spirit. In his resurrection

glory, he has all authority for judgment. He has conquered death and evil by his own death and resurrection, and he will conquer it finally and forever (when he returns to reveal the Kingdom of God).

I saw that God the Father had a plan for the revealing of the Kingdom and for the salvation of the people. But an angel questioned who was worthy to set that plan in motion and accomplish salvation. No answer to the angel's question was given, and it became clear to me that no mere mortal could do it, but also that no heavenly being could do it. In spite of my faith, I began to experience a feeling of despair. Then one of the ancestors who was in the Realm of God spoke to me and reassured me. He said that Jesus, who was the promised Messiah and the risen Lord, he is worthy to accomplish God's plan of salvation. (This is because he is neither a mere mortal nor only a spiritual being. He is both human and divine, a perfect representative of humanity and also God incarnate.)

Then all those in the Realm of God—what sounded like millions of voices—worshipped Jesus with music and presented to him the prayers of those still on earth. And they sang a new song that had not been sung before the time of Jesus, because it was about his victory over death. This was the song they sang to him:

> *You are worthy to reveal the will of God and enforce it*
> *Because you gave your life to save people of every race and nation for God*
> *And you have made them into a new people of ambassadors for God*
> *And they will share in your victory and in your Kingdom*
> *The Lamb of God who was crucified is now glorified*
> *He is worthy of all power and authority and lordship*
> *And all wisdom and honor and praise and blessing*

Then all creation joined in and the song continued:

> *Blessing and honor and glory and sovereignty*
> *Belong to God the Father and to the Lamb of God forever*

This song was acceptable to God, and the worship continued. At this point, I saw that the Lamb of God, Jesus, had set God's plan in motion. The salvation of God's people had begun.

6. However, the suffering of the world must increase before it decreases. In the vision I was given an understanding of the big picture of salvation history, a bird's eye view of what is to come, and I was told that there would be three great tragedies.

7. Since the devil could not kill Jesus as a child, (and since he could not prevent the resurrection), he has turned his attention and his anger toward Jesus' brothers and sisters—those who follow him in doing the will of the Father. The Church has become his target, and his weapon is persecution.

8. I saw in my vision that Satan had created an empire on the earth, whose emperors demand that they be worshipped. (This is the Roman Empire), and it encompasses all the land around the Mediterranean Sea. It is the most powerful empire the world has ever seen; strong, fierce, and swift to attack and kill its enemies. Few dare to resist its authority, and none can defeat it, because this empire's power and authority comes from Satan, who is the driving force behind it. The rulers of this empire are powerful and dangerous, and when their subjects worship them, they are really worshipping the devil. One of this empire's rulers (was the emperor Nero, who began the persecution of the Church just over thirty years ago, in 64 CE, when he set the precedent of executing Christians for crimes they did not commit). He was eventually assassinated, but his spirit lives on in his successors who have continued, and even increased, the demand for worship and the persecution of the Church.

9. Then I saw the Empire wage war against the people of God and their holy city (Jerusalem). For three and a half years, (from 66 to 70 CE), the Roman Empire turned this land into a war zone, and crushed the people of God, killing many of them. Just as the devil had pursued the Child Jesus, now he pursued God's chosen people, and set his sights on the holy temple of Jerusalem. Satan had given the Romans vast power and the arrogance that comes with it, and with evil on their side, they marched against the holy city and laid siege to it. In waging war against God's people, they had made themselves the enemies of God. Yet God allowed them to be victorious, and for the time being, to rule the world.

10. (In 70 CE), the legions marched on Jerusalem like locusts from hell. It was as if the devil himself was their general, bent on destruction, as the smoke of war filled the skies. Since the legions expected to take over the city and the surrounding land, they did not burn the fields or the vineyards. They surrounded the city and cut it off from help and supplies for about five months, during which the people of the city suffered

greatly.[1] Many followers of Christ were spared (because they had fled the city, heeding Jesus' warning to head for the hills).[2]

Inside the city walls the people starved as the rations gave out, and disease was rampant and domesticated animals went rabid and began attacking people. In all, the war took the lives of a significant portion of God's people. Those who were able to escape into the city and didn't die wished they would, as they waited in suffering for the inevitable. The siege of Jerusalem was the first of the three tragedies.

11. Then I saw into the Realm of God again, and I saw the martyrs who had been executed for their faith. Their willingness to die for Christ had purified them, and they had entered into eternal life. But they cried out to God for justice saying, "Oh Lord God, holy and true, how long will you wait to vindicate us? How long will you hold back your judgment against those who murdered us?" They were told to rest in peace, and that justice would have to wait, because more of their brothers and sisters were to be martyred before the end of the persecution. Then I could see that judgment was ready to be carried out on the earth, but it was being held back until all those who would be servants of God had a chance to make their commitment to him.[3]

12. During the time of the war, there were evangelists in the holy city, who testified to God and called the people to repent and turn back to him (by believing in Christ). They could not be silenced because they spoke with authority from God and their words destroyed the arguments of their adversaries. They were like Moses and Elijah, because they were able to perform signs to silence their enemies. These were the Lord's witnesses, anointed like Joshua and Zerubbabel in the time of Zechariah, but while Joshua and Zerubbabel were anointed to rebuild the temple, the testimony of these evangelists would precede the destruction of the temple.

---

1. The siege actually lasted four months and three weeks, from Passover (the fourteenth of Nisan) to the eighth of Elul in 70 CE. Josephus, *Wars of the Jews* 6.10.1. During the time of the siege, factions within the city were at war and destroyed the food supply, causing the famine. Josephus (writing to impress the Romans) blamed all of the suffering on the civil war that was going on before the siege and within the city walls during the siege. See Josephus, *Wars of the Jews* 5.1.4; 5.6.1; 5.13.6.

2. Matthew 24:15–22.

3. 2 Peter 3:8–9.

When the Roman legions entered Jerusalem, these evangelists were killed, and their bodies lay in the street, unburied.[4] The city that had harassed and killed the prophets, crucified the Lord, and persecuted the apostles, now also took the lives of these evangelists. Their bodies lay in the street in anticipation of their vindication, a silent testimony against both Jerusalem and Rome. When the sack of Jerusalem was finished, the legions celebrated their victory, and still the bodies of these Christians would lie in the street. Even some of the inhabitants of Jerusalem were secretly happy at the death of the evangelists, because they had been annoyed at their preaching and had rejected the gospel. But when their time of waiting was over, the evangelists were raised to life, in the very sight of those who had killed them. This caused great fear in the city, as Romans and Jews alike watched these evangelists ascend to the Realm of God, just as Jesus had ascended. (Be encouraged by this, because all who die for the gospel will also follow Jesus in resurrection).

13. When the inner walls of Jerusalem were finally breached after the five month siege, thousands of Roman soldiers, including mounted cavalry, poured into the city in a chaotic haze of fire, smoke and burning sulfur. There was great fear in the city, and the people cried out to God. It didn't take long for the city's defense army to be defeated, and then there was a moment in time, like the eye of a hurricane, when the inhabitants of Jerusalem looked to the temple, and prayed that God would spare it. But the order was given (by the general Titus, the son of the Emperor), and God allowed the soldiers to carry out the command, and the temple was burned to the ground, until only a few ruins of the outer courtyard remained. At that time, even many of the Romans knew that they had made a mistake and offended God, and they were afraid of what God might do to them.

The fall of Jerusalem, and especially the destruction of the temple, was an event of such devastation, that it had implications for the whole world, much like the destruction of Sodom and Gomorrah, the plagues of Egypt, or even the death of Christ.[5] In the destruction of Jerusalem and the temple, God used the Roman army to bring judgment on Jerusalem for its unfaithfulness. Ultimately, though, all this was the work of Satan,

---

4. According to Josephus, none of the dead were buried during the time of the siege. *Wars of the Jews* 5.1.5.

5. Matthew 27:51–53.

that angel who was once banished from the Realm of God. The fall of Jerusalem and the destruction of the temple was the second of the three tragedies.

A portion of the land and the people were destroyed,[6] many died of famine, and some died simply because they had no fresh water in the city. Most of the people were spared by God's mercy, however most of those who were spared did not turn to God or repent of their immorality or their idolatry or their treatment of Christ's apostles and evangelists—though a few who had heard the witness of the evangelists did turn to God. And though God used Rome to bring judgment to Jerusalem, God would punish Rome as well, just as he had done with Babylon in the days of the ancestors. For when the Roman general who ordered the destruction of the temple became the next emperor (in 79 CE), a great volcano by the sea (Mt. Vesuvius) erupted, (destroying two important Roman cities). At that time, Rome felt God's anger, for even the great Roman Empire cannot stand against God. But this was nothing compared to the third and final tragedy, which is still to come.

14. Then in my vision I saw our Lord Jesus, who came to me from God the Father, and reminded me that the time of Noah ended with the promise of the rainbow, and the time that the people of Israel wandered in the desert ended with the gift of a homeland. (In the same way, this time of persecution that we are in will someday end with the gift of God's peace.) Then Jesus told me something that I was not allowed to write down. But at the time when God's mysterious plan of judgment and salvation is accomplished, then this word from Christ will be known to all. Then Jesus promised me that (the destruction of the temple was a turning point, and that) God's plan would commence with no further delay. The martyrs who waited for their vindication would soon find their waiting at an end. All these words of Christ sounded sweet at first, like the anticipation of vengeance before it is taken, but I was told that

6. According to the text, one-tenth of the city's buildings were destroyed (Rev 11:13) and one-third of the people, or seven thousand people, died (Rev 9:15, 18; 11:13). The number seven is symbolic, though, so this does not suggest that the population of Jerusalem at the time was only 21,000. On the other hand, Josephus greatly overestimates the number when he says there were three million people in Jerusalem at the time of the siege. Josephus' description of the siege and fall of Jerusalem is important, even if it is a biased, pro-Roman account. For the complete narrative, see Josephus, *Wars of the Jews*, books 5–6. Regarding the famine, compare Revelation 6:6 with Josephus, *Wars of the Jews* 5.13.7.

it would be painful to bear, because our situation is going to get worse before it gets better.

The Things That Are . . .

15. Now we find ourselves part of an oppressive empire, the emperors of which demand that everyone worship them. (The current emperor, Domitian, requires that he be called *lord and god*.) Those who are not followers of Christ readily give in to his demands, and make sacrifices in his honor. Let me be clear, do not attempt to avoid the persecution by participating in unholy sacrifices to the emperor. You belong to Christ, the Lamb of God, and he has claimed you as his own from before creation. If it is your lot in life to be imprisoned, or even executed, accept this fate as from the Lord, because it is through the perseverance of your faith that you will be saved.

16. Just as Satan is the driving force behind the emperors of Rome, the devil is also the source of the evil in the Roman priesthood and its cults. The emperors and the priests work together to accomplish Satan's will in the world; the emperors give authority to the priests and the priests offer worship to the emperors. By leading the cult of the emperor, the priests encourage people to commit idolatry. They even perform signs by the power of Satan, just like the Pharaoh's priests did in the presence of Moses, in the hope that they can deceive the people, and they place statues of these false gods all over the empire so that they can be worshipped even in the remotest provinces. In this way, the priests become the voice of the emperors in the empire, not only demanding worship, but even enforcing the execution of those who refuse.

Make no mistake. Our current emperor is the spirit of Nero reborn, and he is even worse than his predecessor. But there is no need for me to mention his name to you, because it is written, in an abbreviated form, on the coins you have in your bag—the very coins you use to buy food for your family!

17. Now, the Holy Spirit has a message for the church at Ephesus—but all the churches should pay attention. Jesus Christ, the one who is with you and who protects you, says this:

I know your good works and your perseverance in the Christian faith. I know that you don't tolerate evil in your church, and that you are able to discern true Christians from those who are false. You do not accept heresy or immorality, and you have kept up your enthusiasm for the gospel.

But on the other hand, you have forgotten the devotion and the joy of worship that you had at the beginning. You cannot go out as evangelists if you do not first gather as a community and come to me in worship. Think back to how it used to be at the beginning, and regain that commitment to prayer and devotion. Otherwise, I will have to raise up new leaders among you who will follow me. But for those who remain faithful to the end, I will give the gift of eternal life in paradise.

18. The Holy Spirit has a message for the church at Smyrna—but all the churches should pay attention. The divine Jesus Christ, who died and was raised, (and who promises that if you follow him in death, you will also follow him in resurrection) says this:

I know that you are going through persecution right now, and that it has cost you much by the world's standards. But remember that when you are poor for my sake, you are spiritually rich. I know that some in the synagogue have betrayed you to the Romans. These people claim to be God's people, but they are not following God, they are following Satan. Do not be afraid of the suffering that is coming. (So far you have suffered only material loss, but soon you will suffer real human loss.) Some of you will be thrown into prison, so that you can witness to your captors. If your faith is tested through torture, it is the devil's doing (it is not from God). Just like Daniel and his friends, you will be forced to choose between your God and your emperor. Keep the faith, do not give in to their idolatry, and I will give you the victory of eternal life. The emperor may have authority over life and death, but I have authority over eternal life and over the ultimate death that is eternal separation from God. If you persevere to the end of your earthly life, then that kind of death can never touch you.

19. The Holy Spirit has a message for the church at Pergamum—but all the churches should pay attention. Jesus Christ, the Word of God, whose word divides what is true from what is false, says this:

I know that you live in a place where the power of evil is strong, and yet you hold on to the Christian faith. You did not give up the faith, even when one of your own, Antipas my faithful witness, was martyred.

But on the other hand, there are some in your church who advocate participating in unholy sacrifices to appease the authorities and to fit in with the society around you. Those who collaborate with the enemies of God in this way are hindering your faith and witness, and should not be tolerated in your church. You also have some among you who teach heresy and practice immorality. The word of God condemns these practices, and if you continue to tolerate them, I will have to do some house cleaning in your church.[7] But if you follow me and persevere to the end, I will call you my own, you will be my brothers and sisters, adopted by my Father, and his heirs with me. I will pronounce you acquitted of your sins, and I will give you eternal life.

20. The Holy Spirit has a message for the church at Thyatira—but all the churches should pay attention. Jesus Christ, the Son of God and the glory of God, the foundation of our faith, who sees into the hearts of all people and knows their deepest thoughts, says this:

I know your good works, and that you are people of service. I know that your love and faith are strong, and that you continue to persevere. In fact, your good works have increased since the beginning.

But on the other hand, you tolerate heresy among you. There is a woman in your church gathering a following and teaching something she calls "deep secrets," but which is really from Satan.[8] This woman, who calls herself a prophetess, encourages your people to participate in the celebrations of the unbelievers, with their immorality and idolatry. She teaches the innocent that such things will not affect their souls, but in doing so, she is leading my servants away from me. She has been confronted with her sin already, but she has not been willing to admit that she is wrong. If she and her followers do not stop teaching heresy, I will use the persecution to remove her from the church, and put an end to her movement. Then your church, and all the churches, will understand that I know the deepest secrets of every person. I know what's in your heart and in your mind. I know your works, but I also know your motivations. Everyone will have to answer for their works, but not only their works, also their thoughts and intentions. Nevertheless, those of you who have not participated in the teachings of this so-called prophetess, this warning is not for you—just keep up the good work until I return. And

---

7. 1 Peter 4:17.

8. Probably an early form of Gnosticism.

whoever perseveres and keeps doing my will until the end will be fellow heirs of God with me, and share with me eternal life in the Kingdom of God. And in the Realm of God, you will know my deep secrets, as I have always known yours.[9]

21. The Holy Spirit has a message for the church at Sardis—but all the churches should pay attention. Jesus Christ, the one who gives the Holy Spirit to the leaders of the churches, says this:

I know that you have done some good works, and that you have a good reputation among the churches, but you are spiritually dead, and so your works are incomplete in the eyes of God (like the temple that stands incomplete in your city—an embarrassment to the false god to whom it is dedicated). You have almost lost the gospel that was originally given to you. Remember it and turn back to it, so that you can rebuild on what little is left, before it's completely gone. If you do not, (you will be like the foolish bridesmaids, and) you will not be ready when I return at an unexpected time.[10]

But there are a few people in your church who have not corrupted themselves. They are holy to me, and therefore they are worthy to be called my followers. For whoever perseveres to the end will be considered pure, and they will not be excluded from the Kingdom, because I will acknowledge them as my own to my Father and his heavenly court.[11]

22. The Holy Spirit has a message for the church at Philadelphia—but all the churches should pay attention. Jesus Christ, who is holy and true, the heir to the throne of King David,[12] who does what no one else can undo, says this:

I know your good works, and though your church is small and humble, you have kept my word and you have refused to deny your faith in me. Therefore, I am giving you an opportunity that no one can take away. You will witness to those from the synagogue who are collaborating with the Romans to persecute you—they say they are God's people, but they are not because they are actually doing evil—and they will see that I love you and that you belong to me. Someday they will

---

9. 1 Corinthians 13:12.

10. Matthew 25:1–13.

11. Matthew 10:32–33.

12. Cf. 2 Samuel 7:12–14.

beg your forgiveness and join you, and worship under your authority. Then, when the persecution gets worse in the rest of the empire, and many people's faith will be tested, your church will be spared much of the suffering, (because those who wanted to persecute you will have reconciled with you).

I will certainly return, so hold on to your faith, for if you deny faith in me to save your life, you will lose your salvation. But whoever perseveres until I return will be claimed for God, and will have a place in the heavenly city. They will have eternal life in the New Jerusalem, the city of God.

23. The Holy Spirit has a message for the church at Laodicea—but all the churches should pay attention. Jesus Christ, the true and faithful witness, the source and the fulfillment of God's creation, says this:

I know your works, and I know that your faith has become lukewarm, (like the tepid water that flows into your city). Because your faith is lukewarm, you have become useless to me, and it makes me sick. You think you're rich, because of your great wealth, and so you think you are self-sufficient, (and you think you don't need to come together in worship). But spiritually, you are poor and blind and homeless. My advice to you is to forget about the gold, that you insist must be pure, and accept what I offer you—pure lives. (Purify your lives of immorality, and rely on your faith in me, rather than relying on your money.) Forget about your famous eye medicine that makes you so much money, and open your eyes to the truth, so that you may be acceptable in the eyes of God.

I am reprimanding you because I love you, like a parent disciplines a child. So turn back to me, and regain the enthusiasm for the faith that you once had. Look, I am waiting for you to come back to me. I am calling you back to worship—to the assembly, and to the table of the Eucharist. For whoever perseveres until the end will follow me in resurrection and eternal life, and will share in the Kingdom of God with me.

The Things That Will Happen ...

24. At this point, the angel who had first called to me now brought me into the heavenly realm, and I was allowed to see what will happen in the future. In the vision, I could see our all-knowing and ever-present God in all his glory. God, who is omnipotent, omnibenevolent, omniscient, and omnipresent, and whose very attributes proclaim his ultimate

holiness and his eternal nature. I could also see the ancestors and apostles of the faith in their eternal state, gathered in the presence of God. The whole Realm of God was alive with the presence of the Holy Spirit.

Everyone in the heavenly realm was worshipping our eternal God, giving thanks to him and acknowledging that he is the source of all glory and power and honor and blessing. I saw the ancestors and apostles of the faith give all the credit for their lives and their salvation to God, admitting that only God (and his Lamb) is worthy to receive praise and worship, for he is the creator of the universe. (Therefore, whatever is to come, remember that God is sovereign over all things, and he is always good.)

25. After the things we have seen take place, the gospel will continue to spread throughout the world. The good news of Jesus Christ will be proclaimed in every language, and people of every nation will worship the Creator. They will turn to him in reverence and give him praise and glory, and they will be called his own when the time for judgment comes.

26. In the persecution to come (in 250 CE), the emperor (Decius) will require everyone, regardless of social status, to carry the emperor's stamp of approval (in the form of a document, called a *libellus*, obtained by making a Roman sacrifice). This will amount to being "branded" as belonging to the emperor, something like the tradition of the phylactery, (except that those who belong to the emperor cannot belong to God). In order to buy or sell, everyone will have to have the emperor's stamp of approval.

27. But another angel assured me that the Roman Empire will fall, because it has corrupted the nations with its immorality and idolatry.

28. Then, a third angel said that whoever gives in to the requirement to worship the emperor and receives the emperor's stamp of approval (on a *libellus*), they will suffer God's anger. They will be judged, and the Lamb of God and the angels will see them excluded from eternal life in the Realm of God. Like Sodom and Gomorrah, they will be made an example for future generations.[13] Whoever denies their faith in Christ and worships the emperor will lose their salvation.

---

13. Those who made the required sacrifices were made an example in future generations, and even in their own generation. The debate over whether to allow them back

But those Christians who die for their faith will be blessed, and will have eternal life. To persevere as a holy person of God means to keep the faith in Jesus and to keep the commandments of God.

29. Then I saw Jesus, poised and ready to begin the final judgment, with all the authority to judge. (He is ready to judge the Romans who draw people away from God, and he is ready to judge those who commit idolatry.)

30. When the persecutors die and the Roman Empire falls, God's anger will be satisfied, as it was in the time of Moses in Egypt when he brought the plagues against the Egyptians. Then I saw angels who serve God in his presence, and they received from God the authority to carry out God's punishment against the persecutors and idolaters. For God is eternal and sovereign, and all of heaven waits for the time when God and his faithful people are vindicated. And the angels were given permission to begin.

31. When God's anger is poured out on the enemies of his people, it will be like the plagues of Egypt, for God alone is righteous and holy and eternal, and worthy to judge. God's anger will be poured out on those who worship the emperors, and on those who killed the apostles and other martyrs. But those who suffer God's anger will refuse to turn or submit to God, who has the power to end their suffering. Instead, they will curse God, and thus prove that God is justified in pouring out his anger against these people who have made themselves his enemies. God's anger will be poured out against Rome and its emperors, and the empire will suffer decline, and a time of great darkness, and there will be no peace. And still, the emperors will not turn to God, but they will continue to demand that they be worshipped.

32. For it has always been Satan who is the driving force behind the emperors. The first evil emperor (Nero) began the persecution of the church (in 64 CE), and then after him, there were four more. Then came the current emperor (Domitian), whom some unbelievers think is the

---

into the Church after the persecution subsided was the deciding factor in the election of the bishop of Rome in 251 CE. The tradition of penance became widely used as a way to make it possible for them to rejoin the Church. Later, in the Great Persecution, fewer Christians would commit apostasy because of what the lapsed of the Decian persecution went through.

reincarnation of Nero. But his reign will soon be over, and another will come after him (Nerva) who will reign for only a short time.

After this time, ten more emperors will persecute the church, (demanding that Christians choose between their emperor and their God). Each will have his time, in which he will call himself a god, but he will really be a puppet of the devil. But Jesus, the Word of God and the Lamb of God, will overcome them all. In fact he has already been victorious over evil in his death and resurrection, and he will vindicate his faithful followers, those whom he calls his own, because he has authority even over the kings and emperors of the earth. He is truth itself; in judgment he is righteous, and in conflict he is victorious.

Eventually, the emperors of Rome will turn on the empire itself, ruining its economy in a vain attempt to cling to their power, making the empire and the city vulnerable to attack and conquest. In this way, God will even use the emperors themselves to punish Rome, for nothing can prevent the word of God from being fulfilled.

The city of Rome will fall, (in 410 CE) to invaders from the east. More invaders will cross the eastern borders, and destroy the empire's stability and unity. And though the Roman Empire has followed Satan and tried to unite the world against God, the Lord will have his day of victory over the empire that has persecuted and murdered his servants. And Rome will become a desolate wasteland, burned and full of disease.[14] The city that thinks she is the queen of all cities, will become as destitute as a widow in mourning. God will judge the Romans for their idolatry and immorality, and for trying to use their power and wealth to convert the world to their ways. They are guilty of murdering many people, especially the apostles and other martyrs of the Church.

There is a war going on, but it is not an earthly one, for the warfare that I saw was taking place in the spiritual realm. It is a spiritual war between a satanic empire and God, in other words, a war between evil and good. And God will fight this battle for his people, just as in the time of Israel. God's army is made up of his loyal angels, (the same army that opposed Satan when he rebelled against God) and leading the angelic army is Jesus Christ himself. His word, which divides what is true from what is false, will defeat all who would join Rome in rebellion against God (just as all who joined Satan in his original rebellion were defeated and banished from the presence of God). In this way, Jesus Christ will

---

14. During the Dark Ages, the city of Rome was a virtual ghost town.

carry out God's justice. The enemies of God will fall, just as the enemies of God's people did in the great battles of our ancestors. They will fall, just as that idolatress Queen Jezebel fell. Rome will fall, and it will be an earth-shattering event that will have repercussions for the entire world.

No one would believe that Rome could fall, and yet it will. The city of Rome will become a fraction of its former self, it will never be the same again, and the empire will be divided. The allies of Rome and its provinces will be shocked to hear that Rome has been sacked and burned. The merchants and sailors and slave traders who made their money dealing with Rome will mourn, but for their profits, not for the people. The luxury and opulence of Rome will fade away, until it is only a memory. The city's shops and mills will become empty, and the joy of Rome's celebrations will turn to weeping. But the servants of God, in heaven and on earth, will rejoice because they will be vindicated when God claims his victory over the empire. All of heaven will shout praises to God, because he is right to judge Rome, and because only God can save his servants. With the fall of Rome, God's anger will be finished. (The fall of Rome is the third tragedy.)

All those who joined with Rome in its idolatry and persecution will die, and the emperors and the priests who supported their worship will be destroyed, (and the persecution will finally come to an end).

Therefore, the people of God are called to separate themselves from the immorality and idolatry of the empire and its emperors. For the sins of Rome are great in God's eyes, and whoever participates in the sins of Rome, will also share in God's devastating judgment against Rome. So Jesus reminds us always to keep ourselves pure and to be ready for his return, because he will come at an unexpected time.

33. When the time comes for the persecution to end (in 312 in the west, 324 in the east), God will intervene and give the Church victory over the empire.[15] Satan's activity will be limited, and he will no longer be allowed to control the empire so that it persecutes the Church. For many generations, Satan will be confined, and Christ will reign in the Realm of God

---

15. This is how John understood the events of 312–24 CE, in the context of his prophetic vision. In hindsight, we may understand the details of the political situation in a way that he could not, however we have to keep in mind that the message of Revelation is meant to be a message of hope for the people who are going through, or who will go through, the persecution. It is not necessary to critique John's understanding of events in his future from our perspective.

(and on earth through the Church).[16] At that time, all of heaven will worship God with great joy because the empire, and in fact the whole world, will belong to the Lord our God, and to his Son Jesus Christ, and he will reign over it for all eternity. Then the ancestors and the apostles who live in the presence of God will give thanks to our eternal and omnipotent Lord, because he exercised his power and put an end to the persecution of the Church.

Then I saw in my vision all those who had not given in to the pressure to make sacrifices to the emperors, and who had been executed because they refused to stop speaking of their faith in Jesus. They were resurrected, and had come to their reward of eternal life with Jesus in the Realm of God. All who die in Christ are holy and therefore they are blessed, because they will follow in his footsteps—after death comes resurrection, and they will not experience separation from God. On the contrary, they will share in Christ's reign and stand with him on the day of judgment. But those who had died, and who were not followers of Jesus, would have to wait to be raised until the day of judgment.

... After These Things

34. After many generations, (during which Christ will reign over the world through the influence of the Church), Satan will be released for a time, which means that evil will enjoy a resurgence and the influence of the Church in the world will decline. During the time of Satan's release, he will attempt to draw the people of the world away from God, and he will even hope to make them enemies of God. This will be the devil's last stand against God—his last attempt to rebel against the divine order and authority. But (at a time we do not know) God will tolerate it no more, and those who have chosen sides against God will be defeated, just like the enemies of God in the times of Elijah and Ezekiel.[17] And the devil will be banished from the presence of God, just as the emperors and priests of the empire were before him. He will remain in a crucible of regret for all eternity.

35. After the world has had its final time of rebellion against God, then comes the day of judgment. The end of the age will arrive with the inter-

16. Matthew 10:1, 18:18
17. 2 Kings 1:9–14; Ezekiel 38–39. Cf. also 1 Kings 18:38–40.

vention of God, just as God intervened in the time of the Exodus, and in the time of Jesus. In my vision I saw into the Realm of God, even into the holiest place of the glory of God. An angel emerged from the presence of God and called out to Jesus Christ, telling him that the hour had come.[18] The time to gather all the souls of the earth and to sort them out had arrived.[19] I saw Christ gather all those who are his own, and the angels gathered all those who do not belong to Christ and who are to be judged, and they were raised and assembled in the presence of God. At the same time I saw the earth and all earthly creation fade away as if fleeing in shame from the pure and holy sovereignty of God (for it had been corrupted by the evil of those who chose to follow Satan rather than God).

All the souls were there to be judged. Those who were the servants of God, the prophets and saints and all those who honor the name of Jesus Christ were to be rewarded; but those who rejected the Creator and worshipped created things were to be crushed like grapes in a winepress. They will be judged by their works, which God in his omniscience had seen them do, and their demise will be even worse than the fall of Jerusalem.[20] Those who gave up their faith out of fear for their lives, and those who participated in the idolatry and immorality of the Romans, and those who killed the martyrs, and in fact all those who are not called God's own, all will be cast out of the Realm of God, to be separated from God in the crucible of regret. Finally, death itself will be destroyed, and will exist no longer.

36. Since all of creation as we know it will have faded away, a new (or more precisely, restored) creation will be revealed. The Realm of God will be revealed and opened up to us, like a heavenly and glorious version of God's holy city Jerusalem. The heavenly city will be as if it's decorated for a celebration, because within the New Jerusalem is the glorified Church, the bride of Christ prepared for her wedding day. When Jesus Christ returns and the Kingdom of God is finally revealed, that will be the wedding day of the Lamb and his bride, the Church. Then all of the souls in the Realm of God will praise and glorify the Lord. For the Church has been purified by the faith of her holy ones and martyrs, and she is ready

---

18. Cf. Matthew 24:36.

19. Cf. Matthew 13:30.

20. Historical descriptions of the fall of Jerusalem sound similar to the bloody scene described in Revelation 14:20.

to begin her eternal life in the revealed Kingdom of Heaven. God wants you to know that those who are present at the wedding feast of the Lamb will be blessed—for though all have been invited, not all will recognize the blessing and accept the invitation.[21]

I must admit that at this point in my vision, I was overwhelmed, and fell down at the feet of the angel who brought this message to me. But the angel prevented me from showing him too much reverence, saying that he is a fellow servant of Jesus with me—and with you—for we all, Christians and angels, are messengers—coworkers in the gospel, sharing the testimony of Jesus Christ, which foreshadows all that I am telling you. Therefore, worship God alone.

At the revelation of the Realm of God, it will be like the days of our ancestors, when the presence of God was in his holy city. And the presence of God will be opened up to the people of God, and God will live among the people, and the people will live with God. There will be no need for a new temple in the Realm of God, because the people will live in the very presence of the omnipotent Lord God and his Lamb. God the Father and the Lamb (and the Holy Spirit) are the source of eternal life in the Realm of God. There will be no need for a new sun or moon, because the light of the glory of God and of the Lamb will be everywhere, and there will be no darkness. People of all nations will live in the light of God's glory, and the kings of the world will submit to God's authority. In the Realm of God there will be no more sorrow or suffering or sin or death, for God will purify and renew his creation (and make it like it was meant to be in the Garden of Eden). All who live there will have access to God, but no one who has participated in the idolatry and immorality of Rome, or who was unfaithful or untrue (to the faith), or who does not belong to Jesus Christ, the Lamb of God, will live there, for nothing that is not purified can come into the presence of God.

The New Jerusalem is not an imperfect city, made by humans, but it is the perfect and holy place of God's presence, given as God's gift to those who follow his Son, the Lamb, and the apostles. Though our earthly Jerusalem has fallen, it will be replaced with a more perfect, eternal Jerusalem, where the servants of God will worship in God's presence for all eternity, and they will all know God intimately, and he will love them and call them his own. God has spoken to me, and he told me that this is his true and trustworthy message to you. For he is the beginning and the

21. Cf. Matthew 22:1–14.

end of all things, and with the revelation of his Kingdom, his sovereign plan will be completed. Whoever looks to God for eternal life will find it. Whoever perseveres to the end will be an heir of God, and will share in the inheritance of God's Kingdom.

37. With the final revelation of the Kingdom of God, the enemies of God, including the emperors and their priests, will be defeated once and for all. And all those whose lives were lost in the persecution will be vindicated. As my vision came to an end, I saw all those who stood before God and the Lamb in the heavenly city, who were purified by the suffering of oppression or persecution or martyrdom. They had been brought through their ordeal to their reward, and they stood in the presence of God, ready to spend eternity worshipping God.

I saw descendants from every tribe of the people of Israel, who were the final remnant of God's chosen people. They belong to God the Father and to Jesus, the Lamb of God. They are followers of Christ, and they did not commit spiritual adultery by worshipping other gods. They kept themselves pure by holding on to the truth. They did not give in to the persecutors' demands to make an unholy sacrifice, but they kept the faith at the risk of their freedom, and their very lives. But now they are finally free, for the Lamb of God has freed them. Just as Moses freed the people of Israel from slavery in Egypt, the Lamb of God has freed them from sin and death. I heard them sing a new song to God and to the Lamb. This was a song that only descendants of Israel who had been saved by Christ could truly understand. This was the song they sang:

> Your works are great and wonderful
> Oh Lord, all-powerful God
> Your ways are true and righteous
> Oh King of all the nations
> Who would dare not glorify you, Oh Lord?
> For you alone are holy
> People of every nation will worship you in your presence
> Because your justice has been revealed

Then I saw a vast crowd of people, too many to count, from every nation and race on the earth. They too were standing in the presence of God and the Lamb, because they had been purified. Many of these had been martyred during the great persecutions. Their own blood was spilled, but it was the sacrificial death of Jesus Christ, the blood of the

Lamb of God, that has saved them. Ever since the time of their physical death on earth, they have been worshipping God, and the presence of God has embraced them.

All worshipped God in unison, chanting together (in gratitude):

Salvation comes from God and from the Lamb!

And all the angels and the ancestors and apostles in the Realm of God joined in the worship, saying, "Amen! All blessing and glory and wisdom and thanksgiving and honor and authority and power rightfully belong to our God, forever and ever. Amen!"

And they will never again experience hunger or thirst or the heat of the desert sun, for God and the Lamb are one, and he will care for them and give them eternal life, and make them happy forever.

Epilogue

38. Then the angel assured me that all that I had seen and heard was true and trustworthy, and that this message comes from the Lord—the same God who inspired the prophets—so that the servants of God in our own time would know that these things are already beginning to happen.

Once again, I was overwhelmed, and fell down at the feet of the angel who brought this message to me. But again the angel prevented me from showing him too much reverence, saying that he is a fellow servant of Christ with us, and that all who pay attention to the message of this book are one with the prophets and apostles of God. Therefore, worship only God. Then the angel said to me, "Do not keep this vision a secret, for these promises have already begun to be fulfilled, and the warnings must be taken seriously. If someone should choose to ignore the warnings of this vision, and continue doing injustice, then let him go ahead and risk the consequences. If someone still chooses to be immoral, let him go ahead and continue in immorality, but the ones who would be righteous, let them take care to continue in righteousness, and the ones who would be holy must keep themselves holy."

Finally, Jesus himself spoke to me, saying that he will surely return, and will bring with him the reward of eternal life. When he comes, all people will answer for their behavior, but everyone who pays attention to the message of this book will be blessed. Affirming that he is one with God, Jesus said to me, "I am the beginning and the end of all things."

Then he said, "I am the Messiah promised by the prophets of our ancestors, and I am the dawn of eternity. I have sent my angel to give you this message for the churches. Those who purify themselves and hold onto their faith in me will be blessed—they will enter the Realm of God and have eternal life. But those who participate in the immorality and idolatry of the Romans will find themselves outside of the Realm of God, along with the persecutors and the unholy priests and the traitors.[22] I, Jesus, endorse the message of this book, and say this to all who hear these words: if anyone distorts the meaning of this message by adding things that are not mentioned, or by removing things that are included, then the warnings of this vision will surely apply to that person and he will not receive the promised blessing of eternal life in the Realm of God. For I have seen the whole history of humanity, and truly I am coming back, and the events which lead up to my return have already begun."

Therefore let the Church, the bride of Christ, and the Holy Spirit that is within her, say "Yes! Come, Lord Jesus!" and let the Church pray for his return.[23] And let whoever seeks eternal life come to Jesus through his Church.

I can testify to this message, because I have seen and heard it firsthand, and I am John (the beloved disciple of Jesus). May the grace of the Lord Jesus be with you all. Amen.

SUMMARY

- Before time began—Satan rebelled against God and brought evil into the world.

- c. 6–5 BCE—The Messiah, Jesus Christ, was born into the world.

- c. 5–4 BCE—Herod tried to kill Jesus, but Mother and Child were protected by God.

- c. 32–33 CE—Jesus' death and resurrection, ascension and glorification, **the Church age began.**

  - During the Church age, Christians worship and pray to Jesus.

22. Cf. Matthew 22:11–13.
23. Cf. Luke 11:2.

- □ During the Church age, all who die in Christ will be raised to eternal life.
- □ During the Church age, the gospel will spread throughout the entire world.
- 64 CE—Persecution of Christians by the Roman state began.
- 66–70 CE—War between Rome and Judea culminated in the siege of Jerusalem.
- 70 CE—Jerusalem fell, and the temple was destroyed.
- 95 CE—John was exiled on the Island of Patmos, and had the vision.
- In the persecution, many were forced to choose between loyalty to God and the emperor.
- Don't forget to gather as a community in worship, because you will need the support.
- Hold on the gospel as it was originally given to you.
- Do not tolerate heresy or immorality in your churches.
- Do not give in to the persecutors' demands to sacrifice, or you will lose your salvation.
- 250 CE—Everyone will be required to make a sacrifice to the emperor, and carry proof.
- To persevere means to keep the faith in Jesus and keep the commandments of God.
- God's anger poured out: the persecutors will die and the empire will go into decline.
- 312 CE (the Milvian Bridge) – God will intervene and give the Church victory over the empire.
- 313 CE—The Edict of Milan will end persecution, **the millennial age of the Church will begin.**
  - □ In the millennial age of the Church, Satan's activity will be constrained.
  - □ In the millennial age of the Church, the Church will influence the world for Christ.

- 410 CE—The city of Rome will fall to barbarian invaders.

- 476 CE—The western empire will fall to barbarian kings, and the empire will be divided.

- After many generations, Satan will be released and **the millennial age of the Church will end.**

  - After the millennial age of the Church, the Church will no longer influence the world.

- After a time of the world's rebellion against God, **the "end of the age"** will come.[24]

- Corrupted creation will fade away to reveal a renewed creation, the New Jerusalem.

- The Kingdom of God will be fully revealed as the Realm of God is opened up to all God's people.

- Those who are to be condemned will be judged by their works.

- Those who persevered in Christian faith will be rewarded with eternal life.

- Jesus will "come again" to claim his bride, the Church, and take her to his home.

- The second coming of Christ is the wedding day of the Lamb, eternal life is the reception.

- In the Realm of God, there will be no sorrow or suffering or sin or death.

- In the Realm of God, the servants of God will worship in his presence for all eternity.

- In the Realm of God, we will know God as intimately as God knows us.

---

24. Cf. Matthew 28:18–20.

Appendix B

Revelation Timeline

Event	Date	Images in Revelation & Elsewhere	Season (Matthew 24:32–33)
The rebellion of Lucifer		Falling Stars	
The fall of Lucifer/Satan		The dragon	
The birth of Christ	c. 5 BCE	The Woman gives birth	Advent
Flight into Egypt	c. 4 BCE	The Woman escapes from the dragon and is protected	
Jesus' crucifixion	c. 33 CE	The Lamb who was slain	Winter
Jesus' resurrection	c. 33 CE	The risen Christ riding the white horse	Easter
Pentecost	c. 33 CE	The Church Age begins (the "age" referred to in Matthew 28:20)	Spring
The fire in Rome	July 18, 64 CE	The original beast, Nero, begins persecution	
The Jewish/Roman war	66–70 CE	Labor pains	
The siege of Jerusalem	70 CE	Locusts, famine and plague— the first "woe"	
The fall of Jerusalem	70 CE	Measuring the temple, the temple destroyed—the second "woe"	
Decius' persecution	250 CE	The mark of the beast, Decius requires sacrifices and the libellus	
The Great Persecution	303 CE	Labor pains	
Battle at Milvian Bridge	312 CE	The sign of Christ in the sky	
Edict of Milan	313 CE	Birth—The millennial age of the Church begins, Satan is bound	Summer
The fall of Rome	410 CE	Babylon is fallen, the harlot is judged—the third "woe"	

Event	Date	Images in Revelation & Elsewhere	Season (Matthew 24:32–33)
Decline of the Church		The millennial age of the Church ends, Satan is released	Autumn
The second coming of Christ		The wedding of the Lamb and his bride, the Church	Advent
Judgment		The harvest of the earth, the book of life	Harvest
The Kingdom is revealed		A new heaven and earth, the new Jerusalem	

Appendix C

The Emperors of Rome

Emperors of Rome	Dates	Major Events
Augustus (Octavian)	31 BCE—14 CE	Defeat of Marc Antony at the Battle of Actium—31 BCE
Tiberius	14–37	Pontius Pilate sent to Judea—26 CE, leaves in 36 CE
Caligula	37–41	Pontius Pilate returns to Rome in disgrace, exiled—37 CE
Claudius	41–54	All Jews temporarily expelled from Rome, 52 CE
Nero	54–68	Fire in Rome—64 CE, Peter & Paul martyred
Galba	68–69	
Otho	69	
Vitellius	69	Vitellius' reign not counted by Josephus, Eusebius and others
Vespasian	69–79	Jerusalem Temple destroyed by Titus' legions—70 CE
Titus	79–81	Vesuvius erupts—79 CE
Domitian	81–96	John exiled to the island of Patmos—95 CE
Nerva	96–98	Exiles released—96 CE
Trajan	98–117	Set procedure for persecution in provinces, Igniatius of Antioch martyred
Hadrian	117–138	Jews expelled from Jerusalem—135 CE
Antoninus Pius	138–161	Polycarp martyred
Marcus Aurelius	161–180	Issued edict ordering loyalty sacrifices in the legions, Justin martyred
Commodus	180–192	

Emperors of Rome	Dates	Major Events
Septimius Severus	193–211	Issued edict against Christianity, Perpetua and Felicitas martyred
Caracalla	211–217	All inhabitants of the empire made citizens—212 CE, all ordered to sacrifice
Elagabulus	218–222	Persecution Increased
Severus Alexander	222–235	Tolerated Christianity
Maximinus Thrax	235–238	Great earthquake occurred, Maximinus orders church leaders executed
Gordian	238–244	
Philip	244–249	Rumored to have been a Christian, or sympathetic to the Church
Decius	249–251	First empire-wide persecution—"libellus" required
Gallus	251–253	
Aemilianus	253	
Valerian	253–260	Tolerated Christianity briefly, then persecuted
Gallienus	260–268	Tolerated Christianity
Posthumus	268–269	
Claudius Gothicus	269–270	
Aurelian	270–275	
Probus	275–282	
Carus	282–284	
Diocletian	284–305	The Great Persecution begins 303 CE
Galerius	305–311	Stops persecution from his death bed, begs Christians to pray for him, Edict of Toleration—311 CE
Constantine	312–337	Battle at the Milvian Bridge—312 CE, Edict of Milan—313 CE

Chart 1

Scripture Key to The Book of Revelation
in Plain English

Appendix A Section	Passages in Revelation
1	1:1–11
2	1:12–20
3	8:10–11; 12:3–4a, 7–12
4	12:1–2, 4b–6, 13–16
5	5:1–14; 6:1–2
6	8:13
7	12:17
8	12:17—13:4
9	6:3–4; 11:1–2; 13:5–7
10	6:5–8; 9:1–12
11	6:9–11; 7:1–3
12	11:3–12
13	6:12–17; 8:1–12; 9:13–21; 11:1–14
14	10:1–11
15	13:8–10
16	13:11–18
17	2:1–7
18	2:8–11
19	2:12–17
20	2:18–29
21	3:1–6
22	3:7–13
23	3:14–22
24	4:1–11
25	14:6–7
26	13:16–17
27	14:8
28	14:9–13
29	14:14–20
30	15:1; 15:5—16:1

Appendix A Section	Passages in Revelation
31	16:2–11
32	14:8, 16:12—19:5, 19:11–21
33	11:15–17, 20:1–6
34	20:7–10
35	11:18–19, 14:9–20, 20:11–15, 21:8
36	19:6–10, 21:1–7, 21:9—22:5
37	7:4–17, 14:1–5, 15:2–4
38	22:6–21

Chart 2
Structure of the Book of Revelation

Section in Revelation	Passage	Outside of Time	John's Past	John's Present	John's Future (Our Past)	John's Future (and Ours)	Appendix A Section	Notes
Introduction	1:1–11			X			1	John on Patmos (95 CE)
Beginning of the vision	1:12–20	X					2	"One like a Son of Man" = Jesus Christ
To Ephesus	2:1–7			X			17	John's epistle to Ephesus
To Smyrna	2:8–11			X			18	John's epistle to Smyrna
To Pergamum	2:12–17			X			19	John's epistle to Pergamum
To Thyatira	2:18–29			X			20	John's epistle to Thyatira
To Sardis	3:1–6			X			21	John's epistle to Sardis
To Philadelphia	3:7–13			X			22	John's epistle to Philadelphia
To Laodicea	3:14–22			X			23	John's epistle to Laodicea
Vision of heaven	4:1–11	X				X	24	Back to the vision
Introduction to the seals	5:1–14		X				5	The Lamb who was slain = Jesus Christ
The first seal (white horse)	6:1–2		X				5	Christ rides the white horse

Section in Revelation	Passage	Outside of Time	John's Past	John's Present	John's Future (Our Past)	John's Future (and Ours)	Appendix A Section	Notes
The second seal (red horse)	6:3-4		X				9	The Jewish/Roman war (66-70 CE)
The third seal (black horse)	6:5-6		X				10	The siege of Jerusalem (famine)
The fourth seal (pale horse)	6:7-8		X				10	The siege of Jerusalem (plague)
The fifth seal	6:9-11		X				11	The Martyrs cry, "How long, oh Lord?"
The sixth seal	6:12-17		X				13	Egypt-style plagues
Holding back	7:1-3	X					11	The answer comes, "Not yet . . ."
The Jewish Church	7:4-8	X	X				37	The elect from among the 12 tribes
The Gentile Church	7:9-17	X					37	The elect from among the nations
The seventh seal	8:1-6	X					13	Reveals the seven trumpets
The first trumpet	8:7		X				13	Egypt-style plagues
The second trumpet	8:8-9		X				13	Egypt-style plagues (volcano?)
The third trumpet	8:10-11		X				3 & 13	Egypt-style plagues

Section in Revelation	Passage	Outside of Time	John's Past	John's Present	John's Future (Our Past)	John's Future (and Ours)	Appendix A Section	Notes
The fourth trumpet	8:12		X				13	Egypt-style plagues
The eagle	8:13	X					6	Announces the three woes
The fifth trumpet (locusts)	9:1–12		X				10	The siege of Jerusalem (Roman legions)
The sixth trumpet	9:13–21		X				13	Egypt-style plagues
The seven thunders	10:1–11	X					14	No more delay . . .
Measuring the temple	11:1–2		X				9 & 13	Foreshadows the temple's destruction
The two witnesses	11:3–12		X				12 & 13	The reason God allowed Jerusalem to fall
Fall of Jerusalem	11:13–14		X				13	The Temple destroyed (70 CE)
The seventh trumpet	11:15–17				X		33	Christ's millennial reign begins
Judgment foreshadowed	11:18–19					X	35	The enemies of God's people judged
The Woman gives birth	12:1–2, 5		X				4	The birth of Christ

Section in Revelation	Passage	Outside of Time	John's Past	John's Present	John's Future (Our Past)	John's Future (and Ours)	Appendix A Section	Notes
The dragon and the stars	12:3–4a		X				3	The fall of Lucifer/Satan
The woman escapes	12:4b, 6		X				4	The Holy Family's escape into Egypt
War in heaven	12:7–12	X					3	The rebellion of Lucifer/Satan
The woman escapes	12:13–16		X				4	The Holy Family protected
Persecution begins	12:17		X				7	"The rest of her offspring" = the Church
The beast	12:17–13:4		X				8	The Roman Empire and its emperors
The beast acts	13:5–7		X				9	The Jewish–Roman war (66–70 CE)
Persecution	13:8–10			X			15	The situation as it is in John's time
Revived beast (false prophet)	13:11–15, 18			X	X		16	Emperor worship
The mark of the beast	13:16–17				X		16 & 26	The libellus of Decius (250 CE)
The remnant	14:1–5	X					37	A new song
First angel—the nations	14:6–7			X	X	X	25	The spread of the Gospel to the nations

Section in Revelation	Passage	Outside of Time	John's Past	John's Present	John's Future (Our Past)	John's Future (and Ours)	Appendix A Section	Notes
Second angel—Babylon's fall	14:8				X		27 & 32	The fall of Rome foreshadowed
Third angel	14:9–13				X		28 & 35	Warning against apostasy
The harvest of the earth	14:14–20					X	29 & 35	Judgment foreshadowed
Introduction to the bowls	15:1				X		30	Bowls described as plagues
Victorious martyrs	15:2–4	X					37	Victory over the beast promised
Introduction to the bowls	15:5—16:1				X		30	Bowls poured out by seven angels
The first bowl	16:2				X		31	Judgment for those who accept the mark
The second bowl	16:3				X		31	Egypt-style plagues
The third bowl	16:4–7				X		31	Egypt-style plagues (martyrs' blood)
The fourth bowl	16:8–9				X		31	Egypt-style plagues
The fifth bowl	16:10–11				X		31	Egypt-style plagues
The sixth bowl	16:12				X		32	Euphrates dried up
Armageddon	16:13–16	X					32	Evil is defeated

Section in Revelation	Passage	Outside of Time	John's Past	John's Present	John's Future (Our Past)	John's Future (and Ours)	Appendix A Section	Notes
The seventh bowl	16:17–21				X		32	Egypt-style plagues (Rome falls)
The whore	17:1—18:24				X		32	The fall of Rome
The whore is judged	19:1–5				X		32	The Church is triumphant over Rome
The wedding of the Lamb	19:6–10					X	36	The second coming (*parousia*) of Christ
Spiritual warfare	19:11–21				X		32	Christ is triumphant over the beast
Satan bound	20:1–6				X		33	The reign of Christ through the Church
Satan released	20:7–8					X	34	The end of the millennial age
The final defeat of Satan	20:9–10					X	34	Fire from heaven
Judgment	20:11–15					X	35	The book of life
The Kingdom revealed	21:1–7					X	36	A new heaven and earth
Judgment recapitulated	21:8					X	35	The second death = separation from God
The Kingdom revealed	21:9—22:5					X	36	The people will dwell in God's presence
Epilogue	22:6–21			X			38	Come, Lord Jesus!

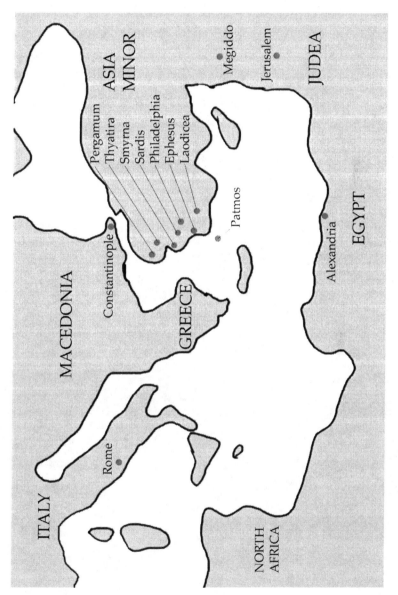

The Roman Empire with Places Mentioned in the Book of Revelation

Bibliography

Barnes, Timothy David. "Legislation against the Christians." *Journal of Roman Studies* 58 (1968) 32–33.

———. *Constantine and Eusebius.* Cambridge, MA: Harvard University Press, 1981.

Beale, G. K. *The Book of Revelation.* New International Greek Testament Commentary. Grand Rapids: Eerdmans, 1999.

Beasley-Murray, George Raymond. *Revelation.* New Century Bible Commentary. London: Oliphants, 1974.

Cary, M., and H. H. Scullard. *A History of Rome down to the Reign of Constantine.* 3rd ed. New York: Bedford/St. Martin's, 1975.

Court, John M. *Myth and History in the Book of Revelation.* London: SPCK, 1979.

Ellis, E. Earle. "Pseudonymity and Canonicity of New Testament Documents." In *Worship, Theology and Ministry in the Early Church: Essays in Honor of Ralph P. Martin,* edited by Michael J. Wilkins and Terence Paige, 212–24. Journal for the Study of the New Testament: Supplement Series, 87. Sheffield: Sheffield Academic, 1992.

Fekkes, Jan. *Isaiah and Prophetic Traditions in the Book of Revelation: Visionary Antecedents and Their Development.* Journal for the Study of the New Testament: Supplement Series, 93. Sheffield: Sheffield Academic, 1994.

Harrington, Daniel J. *The Gospel of Matthew.* Sacra Pagina 1. Collegeville, MN: Liturgical, 1991.

Hasel, Gerhard F. *Old Testament Theology: Basic Issues in the Current Debate.* 3rd ed. Grand Rapids: Eerdmans, 1972.

Hopper, Vincent F. *Medieval Number Symbolism: Its Sources, Meaning, and Influence on Thought and Expression.* Columbia University Studies in English and Comparative Literature 132. New York: Columbia University Press, 1938.

Jewett, Robert. *Jesus against the Rapture: Seven Unexpected Prophecies.* Philadelphia: Westminster, 1979.

Martin, Ralph P. *Worship in the Early Church.* Grand Rapids: Eerdmans, 1964.

Mounce, Robert H. *The Book of Revelation.* New International Commentary on the New Testament. Grand Rapids: Eerdmans, 1977.

Moyise, Steven. *The Old Testament in the Book of Revelation.* Journal for the Study of the New Testament: Supplement Series, 115. Sheffield: Sheffield Academic, 1995.

Papandrea, James Leonard. *The Trinitarian Theology of Novatian of Rome: A Study in Third-Century Orthodoxy.* New York: Edwin Mellen, 2008.

———. "Between Two Thieves: Novatian of Rome and Kenosis Christology." In *Studies on Patristic Texts and Archaeology: If These Stones Could Speak . . . : Essays in Honor of Dennis Edward Groh,* edited by George Kalantzis and Thomas F. Martin, 51–73. New York: Edwin Mellen, 2009.

Price, S. R. F. *Rituals and Power: The Roman Imperial Cult in Asia Minor.* Cambridge: Cambridge University Press, 1984.

Richardson, Alan. "Salvation." In *The Interpreter's Dictionary of the Bible*, edited by George Arthur Buttrick et al., 4:174. Nashville: Abingdon, 1962.

Rist, M. "Apocalypticism." In *The Interpreter's Dictionary of the Bible*, edited by George Arthur Buttrick et al., 1:158. Nashville: Abingdon, 1962.

Rossing, Barbara R. *The Rapture Exposed: The Message of Hope in the Book of Revelation.* Boulder, CO: Westview, 2004.

Sherwin-White, A. N. "Early Persecutions and Roman Law Again." *Journal of Theological Studies* 3 (1952) 211–12.

Stark, Rodney. *The Victory of Reason: How Christianity Led to Freedom, Capitalism, and Western Success.* New York: Random House, 2005.

Stevenson, J. *A New Eusebius of Caesarea: Documents Illustrating the History of the Church to AD 337.* Cambridge: SPCK, 1956.

Wright, N. T. *Jesus and the Victory of God.* Vol. 2 of *Christian Origins and the Question of God.* Minneapolis: Fortress, 1996.